58682

PN
1995
.M37
1977

Mast, Gerald, 1940-

Film/cinema/movie

DATE			

FILM/CINEMA/MOVIE

FILM/CINEMA/MOVIE

A Theory of Experience

Gerald Mast 1940-

HARPER & ROW, PUBLISHERS

New York, Hagerstown, San Francisco, London

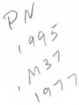

Grateful acknowledgment is made for permission to publish frame blow-ups from the following films:

Blazes courtesy of Robert Breer; *Citizen Kane* courtesy of Janus Films; *Dog Star Man* and *Mothlight* courtesy of Stan Brakhage; *The Drunkard's Reformation* and *Rescued from an Eagle's Nest* courtesy of the Museum of Modern Art; H_2O courtesy of Ralph Steiner; *Meshes of the Afternoon* courtesy of Grove Press Films, the sole distributor of the film; *A Movie* courtesy of Bruce Conner; *Permutations* courtesy of John Whitney; *Playtime* courtesy of Jacques Tati; *The Red Desert* courtesy of Michelangelo Antonioni; *Scenes from a Marriage* courtesy of Cinema 5; *The Wild Bunch* courtesy of Warner Brothers.

Library of Congress Cataloging in Publication Data

Mast Gerald, 1940–
    Film/cinema/movie: a theory of experience.
    Bibliography: p.
    Includes index.
    1. Moving-pictures—Aesthetics. I. Title.
PN1995.M37 1977   791.43'01   75–35679
IBSN 0–06–012822–4

77 78 79 80 10 9 8 7 6 5 4 3 2 1

Contents

Acknowledgments

I could never get a book like this together without the help, suggestions, criticism, and encouragement of my friends and colleagues. Although my simple thanks on this page cannot really repay the debt I owe them for their time and effort, I hope that the book which they have helped to be will convince them that their labors have produced something of use and value.

First, I must express my gratitude to those who read the manuscript, either in part or whole. To Rick Balkin, Cass Canfield, Jr., Marshall Cohen, Harry Dishon, Ron Gottesman, Bill Rothman, Bob Scholes, Win Sharples, and Burnell Y. Sitterly my thanks for their probing and prodding, their queries and quarrels. The distance this book has traveled from the manuscript they saw is, I hope, a sufficient indication of their immense contribution.

Next, I must thank those distributors of 16-mm films who graciously made prints available to me so I could check their details and my memory. Walter J. Dauler of Audio-Brandon Films, Peter J. Meyer of Janus Films, and Ruth Robbins of Cinema 5 have helped me immensely with this project, as they have with my others. As always I (and almost everyone else who studies film in America) owe the Museum of Modern Art my usual debt of gratitude, in particular its fine film study center presided over by Charles Silver and Emily Seegar.

The illustrations merit a special series of thanks, as well as a few words of explanation. Given my commitment to discussing in this book the ways we receive, perceive, understand, and feel the effects of cinema, I could not very well use production stills to illustrate my discussion. Such stills only approximate (and often not very closely) the lighting, composition, or action of a shot in the finished film. So the illustrations for this book are all frame blow-ups, which I made specifically to supplement, clarify, or expand my discussion in the text. I see these illustrations as neither decoration nor frosting, but as an intrinsic part of the text itself. I hope you will too.

For those who are interested, I made the blow-ups with a Honeywell Repronar, the most efficient, easiest, and best way I have yet found for making them. Whatever imperfections and inexpressiveness exist in the illustrations now should be attributed not to the machine but to the inevitable sacrifice of clarity and brilliance when using frame blow-ups (which were never meant to be published) instead of productions stills (which were) in a book, and to the inevitable fact that moving images are less brilliant and less clear when they are still and when they are not projected on a screen. My thanks to Robert DiMilia and Kalman Schissel of the Richmond College staff for their help in taking the pictures.

The first chapter of this book, "What Isn't Cinema?," originally appeared in *Critical Inquiry*. My thanks to them for allowing me to reprint it, as well as for the many encouraging reactions I received to the piece when it appeared there. Finally, I must mention that my research for this book was supported by a grant from the Research Foundation of the City University of New York.

Foreword

When I began this investigation, I wasn't sure exactly where it would take me. I knew I wanted to do a number of things: to sift through my thoughts about what I took the experience of cinema to be; to approach certain theoretical issues in ways that had not been attempted before; to refine certain false controversies and to define certain falsely stated problems that seem to have dominated previous theories of film or cinema; to account for the divergent tastes of different film critics and theorists in a way that would learn from such divergency; to clarify the carelessly stated relationships of cinema to the other arts.

In effect, I wanted to explore how I knew what I knew about the experiencing of cinema—how I felt things about a work of cinema, why I felt them, why I failed to respond to some kinds, works, or devices of cinema, what could be learned from both the communality and the divergency of responses to cinema. By exploring my own ways of understanding cinema and responding (or not responding) to it, I hoped to illuminate what cinema is, what it does, how it does it, and why it has done it so forcefully for so many of us in this century.

The result is a book that falls into two main sections. The first begins with a critical summary of current film thinking: of theories and critical attitudes that have dominated the writing and reasoning about cinema. It is, clearly, a "negative" section that questions and largely refutes extant views and principles. I restate the theories of others summarily, rather than in detail, assuming the reader's awareness of the major ideas about cinema that already exist. I keep the chapter much briefer than it might have been, for, after all, it is always easier to tear down someone else's construction than to build something yourself.

I then embark on a discussion of the most general and the most speculative questions about the experiencing and value of art—any art, not just cinema. I find, however, that I cannot speculate about the cinema as art without speculating about artistic pleasure in general. And I find I cannot speculate about artistic pleasure in general without speculating about the relationship of this activity to other human and natural processes. The section steadily moves toward a greater and greater specificity, beginning with speculation about the general relationships of all the arts to natural and human experience, concluding with the particular pleasures and effects of the cinema art.

The second section is much more specific, a detailed discussion of the immensely varied ways that cinema can affect and manipulate our responses. Many of these points may be familiar from "textbooks" on cinema rhetoric—the effects of lenses, film stocks, editing, color, and so forth. But my aim is not so much to prescribe laws that produce inevitable results, but to describe ways that the various cinema devices inform us or move us, either in isolation or in combination with other devices. My goal is not just to list such devices, but to classify and categorize them, creating a useful systematic classification into genus and species for treating the immense diversity, breadth, and integration of the cinema's rhetorical possibilities.

The book may seem dotted with deliberate paradoxes that challenge most of the classic notions of cinema theory. I maintain that the still picture is not the basis of moving pictures; that there is no cinematic "medium" at all; that there is no more nature in cinema than in any art; that synchronized dialogue is not a cinematic sin; that the commonly accepted terms of camera distance and angle (long shot, low angle, and so forth) have nothing to do with camera distance and angle; that the silent film was never really silent and that there was no truly silent film until there was a sound film. And there are many others. I come to these conclusions not out of a taste for outrageousness or paradox, but to demonstrate that there are other ways to approach these issues. I do not maintain that I have found *the* answers to these persistent problems, but I have found *some* answers, which, if nothing else, may provoke responses that are more precise, more careful, and more valid than many of the previous ones have been.

I especially enjoyed performing several kinds of detailed analyses that I have not had the opportunity to illustrate previously. I develop the specific moral contradictions in the ending of Fritz Lang's *You Only Live Once*, the surprisingly parallel structures of Orson Welles's *Citizen Kane* and Michael Snow's *Wavelength*, the relationship between content, composition, and pace in a single shot of Jacques Tati's *Playtime*, the principles of musical underscoring in George Cukor's *Camille*, the interrelation of imagery, cutting, and sound in two similes from Satyajit Ray's

Apu trilogy, the interrelation of action, composition, cutting, and sound in one shot from Ingmar Bergman's *Scenes from a Marriage,* the cumulative principles of rhythm and movement in Bruce Conner's *A Movie,* and many more.

As you can see from the range of films and types of analyses, my approach in this study is eclectic. I believe that eclecticism is now needed in film theorizing, for the evidence indicates that cinema is the most eclectic art in human experience.

I/Theories and Theorists, Art and Nature, Kinesis and Mimesis

1/What Isn't Cinema?

The Logician: You have got away from the problem which instigated the debate. In the first place, you were deliberating whether or not the rhinoceros which passed by just now was the same one that passed by earlier, or whether it was another. That is the question to decide. . . . Thus: you may have seen on two occasions a single rhinoceros bearing a single horn . . . or you may have seen on two occasions a single rhinoceros with two horns . . . or again, you may have seen one rhinoceros with one horn, and then another also with a single horn . . . or again, an initial rhinoceros with two horns, followed by a second with two horns. . . . Now if you had seen . . . if on the first occasion you had seen a rhinoceros with two horns . . . and on the second occasion, a rhinoceros with one horn . . . that wouldn't be conclusive either. . . . For it is possible that since its first appearance, the rhinoceros may have lost one of its horns, and that the first and second transit were still made by a single beast. . . . It may also be that two rhinoceroses both with two horns may each have lost a horn. . . . If you could prove that on the first occasion you saw a rhinoceros with one horn, either Asiatic or African . . . and on the second occasion a rhinoceros with two horns . . . no matter whether African or Asiatic . . . we could then conclude that we were dealing with two different rhinoceroses, for it is hardly likely that a second horn could grow sufficiently in a space of a few minutes to be visible on the nose of a rhinoceros. . . . That would imply one rhinoceros either Asiatic or African . . . and one rhinoceros either African or Asiatic. . . . For good logic cannot entertain the possibility that the same creature be born in two places at the same time . . . which was to be proved.

Berenger: That seems clear enough, but it doesn't answer the question.

The Logician: Obviously, my dear sir, but now the problem is correctly posed.

Eugène Ionesco, *Rhinoceros,* Act 1

When the most important theoretical essays of the French critic André Bazin were collected together in a single volume and titled *What Is Cinema?* they raised a question that Bazin never really answered. Nor did he intend to. Nor has it been answered by any of those other theorists who have risen to the question and who seem the most influential (and intellectually ambitious) spokesmen for the art. Rudolf Arnheim, Bazin, Stanley Cavell, S. M. Eisenstein, Siegfried Kracauer, Christian Metz, Hugo Münsterberg, Erwin Panofsky, Gene Youngblood, and others have failed to define what cinema essentially *is*. Unlike Ionesco's comically methodical Logician, they have been less than precise about posing the problem correctly. And so they have been less than successful with a deceptively difficult and complicated issue. True, they have defined some kinds of cinema; they have defined some of the qualities unique to those kinds of cinema; they have defined the characteristics and devices they find most valuable in some of those kinds of cinema; they have simply not defined cinema.

I can prove this failure so easily that it is almost embarrassing. My refutation requires one sentence for all nine of those theorists. Not one of them discusses animation as a relevant form of cinema. Nor do they develop terms, categories, and criteria that could even be applied to animated films. And if the animated cartoon, which could not possibly exist without the cinema, is not a unique cinematic form, what is?[1] Most theorists casually imply that animation is an exception—a special kind of cinema. To which implication I might casually reply, a special kind of *what?*

Of the two most important issues that have attracted the cinema theorists, the first assesses the relationship between the film art and nature. Since a film photographs nature (so the argument goes), what is its relationship to that which it photographs? Film "contains" nature in a way that no other art (except still photography) "contains" nature itself. The overwhelming weight of theoretical opinion (Bazin, Cavell, Kracauer, Metz) lies on the side of nature: since film photographs nature, its proper business is nature itself. Thus André Bazin:

> The guiding myth, then, inspiring the invention of cinema, is the accomplishment of . . . an integral realism, a recreation of the world in its own image. . . . The real primitives of the cinema . . . are in complete imitation of nature. [*What Is Cinema?* p. 21]

And thus Siegfried Kracauer:

> The basic properties [of film] are identical with the properties of photography. Film, in other words, is uniquely equipped to record and reveal physical reality and, hence, gravitates toward it. [*Theory of Film*, p. 28]

On the other side, the dissenters (Arnheim, Eisenstein) argue that celluloid and the cinematographic process are as artificial as the materials and methods of any other art. Rather than presenting some mere copy of nature, Arnheim argues in *Film as Art,* the cinema reduces three-dimensional life to a two-dimensional surface, removes any number of sensual stimuli from it, and thoroughly alters our perception of it with lenses (which see unlike the eye) and camera angles (which see what the artist allows). Although these antirealists are in theoretical disfavor today (if only because of their unbending opposition to sound, the wide screen, and color), their views seem surprisingly close to the new cinema styles of the last decade. Even Bazin's own disciples at the *Cahiers du Cinéma,* François Truffaut and Jean-Luc Godard, use bizarre, intrusive, and artificial cinematic tricks (freeze frames, accelerated and retarded motion, shockingly disruptive editing) that have more to do with the artifices of shooting and editing than with the mere recording of nature.

The unfortunate weakness of this nature-nurture controversy in the cinema is that a film does not necessarily photograph reality (for example, animated cartoons). In fact, you can make a film without photographying anything at all. Man Ray, Len Lye, and Norman McLaren have all drawn or designed directly on the celluloid itself and then printed their results. McLaren even has drawn his sound tracks. I have seen "scratch films" that have been made by scratching lines into the emulsion of black leader with a sharp pin and then coloring the scratches with a Magic Marker—a Technicolor scratch film, no less.

Even the historical argument can be refuted. Both Bazin and Kracauer argue that the moving picture descended from the still photograph. Although this argument seems to make perfectly good sense, I can just as convincingly demonstrate that the moving picture descended from the animated drawing—from the Zoetrope designs of 1832 and the von Uchatius drawings of 1853. The photographing of nature is an essential trait of some kinds of cinema (admittedly of most kinds and of most films), but it is not the essence of cinema itself.

The other central issue in the theory of film is the attempt to distinguish the uniqueness of the film art (or medium) from that of any other art (or medium). This kind of discussion gives rise to the term "cinematic," which vaguely means "that which pertains to the unique and best qualities of the cinema art." But this issue also drowns in a sea of non-definition and invalid assumption.

For one thing, so much attention has been paid to the conflicting claims of art and nature on the cinema that most enumerations of its "unique and best" qualities are merely deductions of its displaying a sufficient amount of one (Bazin, Kracauer) or the other (Arnheim, Eisenstein). For another, there is a potential conflict between the cinema's unique and best qualities—giving rise to a pragmatic and a puristic position.

The pragmatic theorist would define the cinema's "unique and best qualities" as those which the cinema does particularly well. A film is "cinematic" if it does something that film does well (or even best). For the purist, however, the cinema's "unique and best qualities" are those things which the cinema, and only the cinema, can do. The "cinematic" is that which is absolutely unique to the cinema. In this view, a novel should not include dialogue (for dramas do that), painting should not imply a narrative (for literature does that), and a film should not include plot, character, dialogue, still life, or any other ingredient of any other art.

The purist would win the Logician to his side; his notion of the "cinematic" certainly follows from a valid definition of "unique." Unfortunately, the traditions and practices of all the other arts are against him. Novels use conversation, plays use narration, operas and ballets tell stories about characters, sculptors have used color, paintings have implied stories. Indeed, a ballet of "pure" dance (Merce Cunningham, for example) is merely one kind (or use) of ballet, just as the film of "pure" cinema is only one kind or use of cinema.

On the contrary, the pragmatist certainly has pragma on his side. Unfortunately, in softening the definition of the "cinematic" from the unique to "that which the cinema does well" (or best), he has also slithered away from definition and toward his own personal preferences. (For example, Kracauer believes that dancing and the chase are cinematic because cinema does them well, but dialogue is not because it does not.) And so the terms "cinematic" and "uncinematic" frequently become mere synonyms for good and bad—what the writer likes or doesn't in the cinema. In the sloppiest and most familiar film criticism, when a critic calls a film uncinematic, you know he simply means he found it boring and didn't like it.

What happens to the word "cinematic" when critics attempt to apply it to the films of Charles Chaplin? Chaplin is, by consensus, one of the top dozen filmmakers in everyone's "pantheon," a genuine cinema author who exerted more creative control over his works than any other commercial filmmaker in history, and whose rich and long canon of films serves as the testament to both his conceptual genius and his superb execution. But in acknowledging Chaplin's brilliance, critical opinion is also quite unified in finding him "uncinematic"—not dependent on any of the cinema's unique visual devices, such as editing, costumes, décor, lighting, or anything to do with the visual image except his own hypnotic performances.

And those performances could (in fact, did) exist on the stage as well as on the screen. The critics "solve" this apparent contradiction by ducking the issue and making Chaplin another of those convenient theoretical exceptions—a genius of a performer who "just happened" to record those performances on film. His films are brilliant but uncinematic. So what value is the concept of the cinematic if it is irrelevant to the value of the cinema?

Perhaps no film has attracted so much theoretical abuse as *The Cabinet of Dr. Caligari*. Bazin, Kracauer, and Erwin Panofsky agree that it is merely painting made to move (but then so is animation; so are the magnificent ballet sequences of *An American in Paris* and *Singin' in the Rain*), that it is more a stylistic trick with the brush and canvas than with the camera and editing scissors, that it "prestylizes reality" rather than shooting reality in such a way that it has style.[2] Yet *The Cabinet of Dr. Caligari* continues to entertain, mystify, and captivate audiences over fifty years after it was made. Can an effective piece of cinema be an illegitimate piece of cinema? If illegitimate cinema can be good cinema, its legitimacy and all the reasons for it are themselves illegitimately irrelevant questions.

My basic conviction is that good films must be examples of good cinema, and good cinema must necessarily be "cinematic." As Francis Sparshott states in his thorough refutation of illegitimate cinema theories:

> The salient feature of film is the enormous range of its specific effects. . . . In view of this inexhaustible flexibility of the medium, it is ludicrous to lay down general principles as to what is a good film. Those critics who do so are in most cases obviously fixated on the kind of film that was around when they were first moved by movies. . . . take care of the facts and the values will take care of themselves.[3]

Let me try to take care of some of the facts. And let me play the Logician by posing the problem correctly.

MATERIAL, PROCESS, FORM

The familiar distinction between the terms "movie," "film," and "cinema" is merely connotative. We accept the terms as synonyms, reflecting the toyness, chicness, or pretentiousness of the critic. "Movie" is the most American of the three, the most "pop," the lowest-brow. The term itself is a healthy Americanism, a slangy contraction of "moving picture" that was already a popular usage in the Nickelodeon era of 1905–1910. Critics who use this term imply that a movie is fun, entertaining, enjoyable, easy, pleasant, trashy, silly, "camp," anything but "deep"—as in Judith Crist's classic description of Z as "a real movie movie." Perhaps America's outstanding movie critic—the critic who consciously thinks of film works as movies and insists that they be discussed solely as an enjoyable, fun, entertaining low-art form—is Pauline Kael. (The animus for her major piece on *Citizen Kane* was to demonstrate that this revered "art film" was really a great piece of low-art trash.) She appropriately called her first volume of collected reviews *I Lost It at the Movies.*

A "film," however, is more cultured, more intellectual, more genteel, a more distinguished work of "high seriousness." Perhaps America's outstanding film critic—the critic who consciously discusses film works in terms of other serious works of art, using the criteria and standards of those other arts—is John Simon. He appropriately called his most significant collection of reviews *Movies into Films.* When Pauline Kael became the film critic for *The New Republic,* she changed the title of the column to "Movies." But when Stanley Kauffmann succeeded her, he changed her slang back to the propriety of "Films," arguing that if films were movies, then books were printies. Kauffmann's argument, of course, overlooks the etymological legitimacy of "movie."

"Cinema," for the American at least, is also a far more genteel and "classy" term than "movie," perhaps even classier than "film." "Cinema," however, has a more generic meaning, inevitably appearing as a plural and standing for a whole class of works (a film, but a piece of cinema; a movie or a film, but the movies or the cinema). Perhaps America's outstanding cinema critic—the critic who consciously elevates popular American movies into a whole class of works with a unique set of criteria and categories of its own—is Andrew Sarris. He appropriately titled his most important work on the subject *The American Cinema.*

But there is a potential denotative difference in these three terms as well. This difference becomes clearer by examining the specific object to which the term originally referred, tracing the word back to its root. Film is the *material* on which a moving picture is recorded. Its literal synonym is "celluloid," not "movie," or "cinema," for which "film" is a more popular and less technical term. The film on which motion pictures can be recorded is distinguished by (1) its width (between 8 and 70 mm); (2) its length (number of feet or meters, number of reels); (3) its ability to record or reproduce colors (ortho- or panchromatic, the various two- and three-color processes); and (4) its speed (ranging from very fast—requiring little light—to very slow—requiring a lot of it).

Film is also the material of still photography, but that material differs significantly from the material of motion pictures. First, photographic film rarely comes in widths narrower than 35 mm. Since clarity and detail are the sole artistic and communicative sources for a still photograph's effect, it uses the larger gauges of film, which produce this sharper detail and texture. Conversely, the length of film is irrelevant to the effectiveness of a still photograph. The longest common length of film, thirty-six exposures, would run through a moving-picture projector in one and a half seconds.

Another difference is that the material of motion-picture recording is also the identical material of motion-picture viewing. The same kind of celluloid that runs through the camera runs through the projector. Originally the still photograph was reproduced from the same material from which it was made (when the original material was some form of glass or metal plate), and it can still be so reproduced today (when the photograph is mounted as a projectable slide). But it is extremely common for the final result of a still photograph to be reproduced on some material other than the original celluloid (an 8 × 10 "glossy"; a newspaper photo). The material of motion pictures has always been made of the identical celluloid in both the creating and the reproduction processes.[4] And the processes of recording on that material and viewing it are mirror images of one another: light through lens to film; light through film, through lens to screen.

To speak of a motion picture's *filmic* qualities, then, is to speak of its spatiality and its compositional values. This is precisely Siegfried Kracauer's subject in his *Theory of Film,* a book that begins with a lengthy section on the properties of still photography and then applies those properties to motion pictures. The essential characteristics of motion pictures for Kracauer are inevitably filmic (i.e., photographic) ones that also exist in still photographs—the accidental, the unstaged, the big, the small, the catastrophic, inanimate objects, and the like.

The strength of the filmic approach is its attention to space. Its inevitable weaknesses are the handling of time (hence Kracauer's failure to include any chapter on editing at all) and of sound. Although Kracauer includes a lengthy chapter on sound, his exhaustive analysis is exhausting without illuminating the potential problems of creating a still photograph (which is complete in itself) that makes noise. Neither time nor sound have anything to do with *film.*

Rudolf Arnheim's *Film as Art* is another aptly titled work, interested primarily in the filmic (spatial, photographic) elements. Arnheim's uniquely cinematic properties are actually filmic ones, equally applicable to still photography as to motion pictures—the conversion of three-dimensional life to a two-dimensional plane surface; the reduction of the appearance of depth; the use of tonal lighting and absence of sensual stimuli except visual ones; the use of lenses for altering relative distances.

Arnheim devotes one section to a uniquely cinematic property—the absence of the space-time continuum, by which he means the way that editing alters spatial and temporal continuity. He also worries more about the theoretical problem of combining sound with a photograph than Kracauer. Arnheim's answer was that you don't; the picture is complete in itself, and to add sound to what is complete is necessarily a redundancy. Although our Logician may have been delighted by this theoretical purity, over forty years' experience with sound films have proved it ludicrous. The conclusion follows, of course, from the filmic approach.

The term "cinema" derives from the influential machine that the Lumière brothers invented in 1895, the *Cinématographe*. This machine, amazingly enough, photographed, printed, and projected films, doing everything to a strip of celluloid that the cinema can do—except edit it. To speak of *cinema,* then, is to speak of the unique way that the cinematic *process* uses the film material. It adds the vector of time to the filmic dimension of space; it complicates the simple spatiality of the still photograph by adding elements of continuousness (of movement, of sound) and succession (of frames, of events). In the terms of G. E. Lessing's classic aesthetic work *Laocoon,* film (still photography) is a spatial art—its elements exist *simultaneously* in space—whereas cinema is a temporal art—its elements appear *sequentially* in time. The essential cinematic operation is this sequential linking of spatial images. In her essay comparing film and theater, Susan Sontag asserted that "there is no peculiarly cinematic way . . . of linking images."[5] She meant that no way was any more or less cinematic than any other since linking images was in itself cinematic.

Just one of the many indications of the complexity of the cinema as an art is that it is the only one that is a truly space-and-time art; it is certainly the only one in which space and time play a fully equal role. All theatrical arts are space-and-time arts, of course, but Rudolf Arnheim convincingly demonstrates that in drama, ballet, and opera the temporal element is clearly dominant.[6] For this very reason, he deplores the sound film as an artistic barbarity, lacking any such dominant element. Ironically, I could defend the infinite complexity of the cinema art on precisely the same grounds. (And I will.)

I see several central controversies in the *cinematic* approach. First, is space or time primary in the cinema? (Is the filmic or cinematic element dominant?) Second, is the essential cinematic operation the recording of an image or the projecting of film? Although it has never been perceived in these terms, the famous Eisenstein-Bazin "debate," certainly the most interesting and best-developed theoretical controversy in film aesthetics, revolves around precisely these two questions. On the surface, Eisenstein argues that the cinema communicates not by its recording of images but by the effects—both emotional and intellectual—of joining the images together. Bazin counters that Eisenstein's method breaks the wholeness of nature into tiny bits (both spatially and temporally). For Bazin, the cinema's guiding myth is man's drive to get nature into his power by recreating it whole, not by breaking it up. Beneath these arguments, however, Eisenstein sees time (succession) as primary in the cinema while for Bazin space is the dominant. And for Eisenstein the cinematic event lies in the projection process (after a film has been shot, edited and assembled), while for Bazin it lies in the recording process (the camera's capturing nature whole). They are both right (which means they are both half right).

Another theoretical issue springs from the uniquely cinematic way of using film. Because cinema is a sequential process, it demands comparison with that other sequential human process which serves the purpose of either communication or art—namely, language. Just as verbal (or linguistic) structures can produce communication between a speaker and a listener, as well as works of art (novels, poems, and plays), the cinema can both communicate information and create works of art. The "listener" (audience) can understand the statement of the "speaker" (the film's director, producer, writer, narrator, or whoever): "This is how Nanook catches fish." And it can be moved by the general experience of traveling through life with Nanook. The common assumption that there is a "grammar and rhetoric" of cinema indicates there is clearly some sense in which a sequence of visual images and sounds is analogous to a sequence of words. Because theorists wish to respect the unique claims of cinema and visual communication, they call their study one not of cinema language (which smells too much of verbal concepts), but of cinema semiology or semiotics.

The semiologist answers the question What is cinema? by calling it a sequential system of encoded signs. The signs can be spatial (for example, the way a particular lens and camera angle make a belligerent man in the foreground dwarf a trembling victim in the rearground) or temporal (for example, cutting from the attacker and victim to a slashing knife); they can be objects (the faces of attacker and victim, their clothes, voices, movements, habits) or inferences from additional narrative information (what we have seen these people do previously). But even the world's most influential semiotic theorist of the cinema, the French scholar Christian Metz, is extremely cautious about the analogies between the cinema and verbal languages. He is also extremely modest about how useful semiological concepts will prove in the study of cinema.

First, Metz admits that there is nothing comparable in cinema to the word (or morpheme—the smallest unit of meaning) in verbal languages. The science of linguistics depends upon breaking verbal communication into its smallest units of meaning. But in the cinema, unfortunately for science, the smallest unit of meaning is equivalent to one of the largest units of meaning in language. That unit in cinema is the shot, *not* the frame, for the frame has a *filmic* value but no cinematic meaning until joined with other frames that extend it in time. And a single shot (even in interesting movies like Hitchcock's *Rope,* Renoir's *Rules of the Game,* or Ophuls's *La Ronde*) can be three, five, even ten minutes long. Metz finds the shot at least as complex as a complete verbal statement or sentence— if not a paragraph. The least complicated and indivisible unit of cinematic meaning is not "cat," but "There is a cat," and, almost inevitably at the same time, "walking," "gray with black stripes," "slowly," "in the sunlight," "next to the red-brick wall," "where it scratches its back," "against the shiny garbage can," and so on and on.

Second, Metz points out that cinema is a "language" without a "code" (or with a very weak one). In verbal languages, the words (or mor- phemes) are "encoded." We know what the word "cat" always symbol- izes, and it is quite a different thing from "dog." We also "encode" the grammatical operations that can affect our notion of cat, so that we can say "the cat walks." To construct "dog cat walks" or "the cat dogs" would be either to create nonsense out of "cat," or to create our own private lan- guage (like Lewis Carroll's Cheshire Cat), or (just possibly) to create a sublime poetic trope. But even the poetic sublimity of "the cat dogs" would itself result from our awareness that encoded meanings and gram- matical operations had been violently violated.

Metz's point is that almost all effective cinema shots are complicated and original tropes. They can only be understood not by referring back to their encoded meanings, but in their own unique terms in that particular film, for the precise content of every cinema shot is infinitely variable. A few cinematic structures have indeed become codified. We understand that the protagonist of Hitchcock's *Strangers on a Train* is playing tennis *at the same time* that the villain is trying to plant a clue that will impli- cate him in a crime. On the other hand, we are aware that the climactic slaughter of the ox in Eisenstein's *Strike* does not necessarily take place at the same time as the slaughter of the workers in their tenements, but that the two actions bear a purely symbolic relationship, *unconnected in time and space.* However, many of the cinematic signs that have become most firmly codified (for example, the Western villain wears black and his virtuous counterpart white) are precisely those usages which the compe- tent cinema "speaker" avoids.

This feature of usage differs strikingly from that for linguistic structures. "The cat has four paws" is not a cliché but a simple (yet clearly codified) assertion. "It's raining cats and dogs" is a cliché, but it is so because it is a stale trope. So, too, are the black and white hats—a further support for the contention that the cinema "language" is composed exclusively of tropes. Despite these and other kinds of theoretical problems, it is clear that the very analogy between cinema and linguistics, no matter how tenuous, is a consequence of the unique cinematic process, deriving from the *Cinématographe*, which recorded and projected a sequential series of images.

Now, a movie is a specific kind of *Cinématographe* recording. "Movie" became the favored term for describing the new form of popular entertainment that the *Cinématographe* spawned, outlasting such clumsy rivals as "photo play," "motion picture play," "motion picture," and "moving picture," eventually eliminating them altogether from the vocabularies of the Faithful. A movie differs from the general process of *Cinématographe* recording in that it usually fulfills a conventionalized length (two hours, plus or minus twenty minutes); it uses elements borrowed from narrative forms (a plot with a beginning, middle, and end that is "an imitation of a human action"; character; cause-and-effect motivation; and so forth); it is manufactured and marketed within a commercial structure that has been specifically developed for producing it (the system of financing, distributing, and exhibiting movies); and it serves a specific audience function (entertainment—although "entertainment" in the broadest sense of perhaps provoking and stimulating rather than merely amusing or passing the time). Although "movie" is an Americanism, its implications apply to foreign "art films" as well, which, despite whatever intellectual and stylistic distinctiveness, share the same assumptions of length, narrative, commerce, and audience function as American movies. Of course, there are any other number of uses of cinematic recording: to provide information (newsreels, documentaries, travel films, how-to-do-things films), to experiment with abstract visual forms, to delight with animated cartoons. But most theoretical discussions of the cinematic process (or "language") have concerned themselves with how it has been applied to the movie form. The key distinction between cinema and movie, then, is that the former is a process and the latter a *form* that shapes the process.

If a theorist raises the question What is cinema? it is worthwhile knowing what question he is really asking. Very few theorists (Eisenstein and Metz come closest) have indeed asked, What is *cinema?* Many have asked, What is a movie? or How does a movie use cinema? or How ought a movie to use film? I find that André Bazin's real question is: How should a movie use space, given the fact that it contains filmed images?

> The realism of the cinema follows directly from its photographic nature. . . . The cinema is dedicated entirely to the representation if not of natural reality at least of a plausible reality of which the spectator admits the identity with which he knows it. . . . The cinema can be emptied of all reality save one—the reality of space. [*What Is Cinema?* p. 108]

Bazin is more concerned with synthesizing the two terms "movie" and "film" than he is with "cinema."

Stanley Cavell subtitles his study *The World Viewed*, "Reflections on the Ontology of Film," but he actually reflects on the ontology of movies. Like Bazin, Cavell links movie and film, arguing that the essence of film (photography) is to capture the world automatically, and the essence of movies is to project that world successively. "The material basis of the media of movies . . . is . . . *a succession of automatic world projections*" (*The World Viewed*, p. 72). That Cavell equates movie and cinema becomes clear in his covert attack on animated cartoons (which do not exist in his book and cannot exist in his system) and his overt attack on the kinds of cinema that manipulate the "pure" properties of the cinematic "language" (experimental, abstract modernist films). Neither cartoons nor abstract films contain "the world," but merely the film-maker's "narcissistic" references to his own fantasies or to the rhetorical devices of the cinema itself. Such films do not capture the world automatically; they create their own self-contained worlds.

For Cavell, the cinema is the movies. He even alters the concept of a cinematic medium by denying that the cinema is a single *medium* at all; rather, it uses many *media*. Cavell calls a medium simply a "way of making sense," and the cinema's ways of making sense are the familiar genres of Hollywood movies and the familiar types of Hollywood stars—gangster, Western; the Dandy, the Man, and the Woman. This kind of argument produces strikingly different conclusions from those which define the cinema in terms of its unique properties as a recording process, and it begins my lap dissolve into the next issue.

But first, let me recapitulate. Movies are a specific form of cinema. Others could be defined in lengths other than two hours ($\pm$), structural assumptions other than narrative, different commercial bases, and different audience relationships. Cinema is a specific kind of recording on film (others would be variations on still, or single-frame, photography). And film is the most general term that contains the other two. Although it may have seemed paradoxical to argue that there could be motion pictures without pictures (without photography), rest assured that there has never been a film without film.* The three terms reflect the fact that a motion picture is a material (film), process (cinema), and form (movie). My point in distinguishing among them is neither to perform calisthenics in word-splitting nor to force audiences into the alien exercise of differentiating among terms they are happy to accept as synonyms. Theoretical arguments, however, must be more discriminating, for using the terms synonymously has blurred the fact that the words do not refer to the same things.

FORM AND LANGUAGE

Is cinema a unique form or a unique language? There is obviously a sense in which a movie is analogous to a drama (or a novel, painting, poem, ballet, symphony, statue) in that it is a complete and self-contained artistic entity that uses its own medium (its unique processes, or materials, or both). But there is also a sense in which cinema is analogous to other semiotic systems of communication (linguistic systems; evocations of shapes, lines, and colors; symbolic physical gestures; evocations of successive pitches, timbres, and volumes). And, finally, there is a sense in which film is analogous to the materials of the other arts (canvas and paint, stone, sounds, print, and so forth).

The material of a literary art can either be sound (parallel to other forms of oral communication) or writing (parallel to all forms of written communication). The semiotic process (or "language") of literature is linguistic. And its forms can be such things as novel, story, drama, comedy, tragedy, narrative poem, lyric (depending on the criteria for categorizing the forms). To ask, What is oral communication? is obviously a very different question from asking, What is language? or What is a novel? When asking, What is cinema? these different kinds of questions have been less obvious. All books are not novels, but all novels are books (which is why novels need not be called printies, but some films can still be called movies).

The theorists have tended toward an exclusive concern for the film material and the cinematic process without a proper concern for the cinema's various forms, frequently dismissing such formal issues as impure borrowings from other (usually literary) arts. This tendency is both unwarranted and dangerous, for as Cavell develops, if the term

* And even this truism is not unequivocally true. Stan Brakhage's *Mothlight* (which will be discussed in due course) was not originally made of film and exists as film only in its final, projectable state.

"medium" is to mean anything at all, it can signify only the synthesis of an art's material and "language" with the structural forms by which those elements have been organized (or might be organized).

One danger is that the theorist can make an erroneous deduction based on a false definition of the art's material. My refutation of photography as the basis of the cinema art was an attempt to show that film and not the photograph is the material of cinema. But an even more dangerous error follows from an exclusive concentration on the cinematic language—primarily because the cinema has no language. It has, rather, many languages.

The cinema is the most hybrid artistic process in human experience, a truly American art in that it is the melting pot, the mongrel, of virtually all the other arts. The cinema obviously has much in common with music. First, most forms of cinema use music (and have always used music), underscoring the visual or narrative effects with tonal accompaniment. The use of music is as common to abstract films (like those of Oskar Fischinger or Len Lye), as it is to perceptual films (the *musique concrète* in some of the films of Bruce Baillie, Scott Bartlett, and Michael Snow), as it is to animated cartoons (Disney reached his artistic adulthood only when sound allowed him to synchronize his visual effects with music), as it is to movies (say, Gustav Mahler's unwitting contribution to *Death in Venice* or George Gershwin's to *An American in Paris,* or the intentional contributions of Duke Ellington to *Anatomy of a Murder* or Bernard Herrmann's to *Psycho* and *Citizen Kane*). Interestingly, few of the puristic theorists who wish to purge the cinema of its impure literary elements (i.e., narrative) are much bothered by its impure musical ones.

There is, however, another and much subtler sense in which music and cinema are analogous. If one can define music as a succession of related sounds producing kinetic (physical) and emotional effects but not necessarily conceptual ones, one can equally define the cinema as a succession of related images that can produce kinetic and emotional effects in addition to (or even rather than) conceptual ones. A stream of images, regardless of their content, can strike the eye just as a stream of notes strikes the ear. Eisenstein was perhaps film history's most sensitive cinema "musician," and if I read his montage theory correctly, I find he is as concerned with weaving a "musical" spell with his editing as he is in producing intellectual recognition and political results.

When I listen to music, I fear I am an inveterate head-bobber, unconsciously using my head to keep time with the physical and rhythmic sensations of the music. I suddenly became conscious during a screening of *Potemkin* that I was doing the same thing—bobbing my head in rhythm with Eisenstein's montage. Each of his individual strips of celluloid contains a visual tone, and splicing them together necessarily produces a rhythm, "volume," mood, and "melody." Eisenstein's detailed discussions of the dynamic visual potential of each shot reveal his concern for the purely physical sensations and energy the shot can generate, and little interest at all in its content (in the objects it photographs). Eisenstein sees the shot precisely as a composer hears a musical note or phrase—as an abstract physical-emotional impulse with a pitch, tone, volume, and rhythm. The languid tranquillity of the ships sliding through the fog in Odessa's harbor or the dissonant cacophony of the violent slaughter on the Odessa Steps of *Potemkin* have been composed of a succession of shots quite analogous to a succession of notes in a musical composition.

The films of Robert Breer also manipulate a visual "music," often developing a kind of assaultive, violent, smashing "melody" (perhaps by splicing twenty-four different frames together per second, or by rhythmically composing each second of film from six four-frame patterns). Like so many "experimental" films, Breer's make perfect test tubes for isolating cinematic elements. This fact does not necessarily make them better or even "purer" cinema, but it does make them good test tubes, since any useful experiment isolates the significant variables and eliminates the influence of any others.

Because the cinema has much in common with music, it not surprisingly shares many traits with dance. In its underscoring visual movement with music, the cinema parallels the familiar medium of ballet, especially in two kinds of films. In silent comedies, the clown performs feats of amazing physical dexterity, either supple, graceful, and lithe movements (as in Chaplin and Keaton) or frantic, hectic contortions (as in Lloyd, Turpin, or Larry Semon). The motion of these physical instruments contrasts with the static space that surrounds the dancer-clown and defines his movement. After seeing Chaplin in *The Great Dictator*, W. C. Fields caustically observed, "He's nothing but a damn ballet dancer." Fields was partly right (Chaplin was a few other things as well).

The balletic principle is equally strong in the animation or abstract films of Disney, Fischinger, Lye, and even the computer films of the Whitney brothers. The hypnotic movement of shapes, forms, lines, and colors on the screen is emphasized, punctuated, and underscored by the carefully coordinated music on the sound track. The silent comedies (especially Chaplin and Keaton) choreograph a ballet of physical bodies in space; the abstract or animation films choreograph a ballet of shapes and colors against a stable and defining matrix.

Clearly the cinema shares visual and compositional assumptions with painting. The screen is a two-dimensional surface; it can compose within that frame by using forms and colors; it is capable of using principles of perspective, depth, balance, and symmetry. The contrasts of its forms and colors can produce impressions of harmony or tension; the composition of its lines and shapes can produce both emotional resonances and intellectual inferences—perhaps felt unconsciously, perhaps perceived directly.

A movie also shares visual and spatial characteristics with its cousin in film, the still photograph. It can use lenses for distortion, perspective, and emphasis; it can use light for tone, texture, and depth of field; it selects, balances, emphasizes, and establishes the spatial relationships of those photographic objects which it captures permanently on film.

So, too, the cinema undeniably shares traits with the literary arts. A movie contains all six of Aristotle's elements of the drama—plot, character, thought, diction (in two senses: the diction of dialogue and the cinematic "diction" of the movie's visual style), melody, and spectacle. Yet a movie has as much in common with narrative fiction as with the drama. Like the novel it uses a focused narration (lens parallels narrator); like the novel it is freer in its manipulation of time and space than the post-Ibsen, realist drama.

Indeed, the cinema reveals its hybrid essence (or non-essence) in its perfect synthesis of Aristotle's dramatic and narrative "modes." We perceive the events in the dramatic "mode" directly; they play themselves out directly before our eyes. But we merely conceive the event from what we are told about it in the narrative "mode"; we get the events from some speaker's point of view. The cinema does both—alternately or simultaneously. Some scenes seem to take place before our eyes without comment; others (say, the familiar montage of an actress rising to stardom that uses speeding trains, newspaper headlines, glimpses of the curtain rising and falling, close-ups of applauding hands) are summarily told. But the cinema actually dramatizes and narrates at the same time, for even those scenes that seem to be played directly for a passive camera without comment can come to us only through the lens-eye of that camera. Its eye selects and arranges all the details and reactions that we are permitted to see.

Given the analogies with these six other arts, and given their undeniable contributions to the effects of some or all kinds of films, it seems reasonable to claim that the cinema communicates not only by manipulating its own "language" (whatever that is), but by manipulating the "languages" of all of them. How do we understand a moment in a movie (both comprehend its content and feel its effect)? Probably, the music gives us one clue; the dialogue actually tells us something more; the personalities and attitudes of the characters we have been following give us further information; the lighting imparts its tone and mood; the compositional balance guides our eye and interest to where they belong; the faces of the actors tell us something more; the sounds and tones of their voices add to that; the camera's positioning and activity give us literally its slant on the action; the function of the scene in the movie's plot conveys its importance and relevance; the colors (if the film uses color) saturate the action with their resonances; and probably then some. If one tried to eliminate all languages from cinema except the uniquely cinematic "language," one might well be left with a silent "scratch film" or one of Man Ray's collages.

Let me take a specific example. How do we know that Susan Alexander has attempted suicide in *Citizen Kane?* Two specific "signs," one visual and one sound, mark the precise moment of an action that is merely implied. First, we see a light bulb that suddenly snaps off. The electric power that has given the bulb life has suddenly been denied it, leaving the energyless filament to glow weakly and die slowly over a period of several seconds. Accompanying the "dying" lightbulb is the "dying fall" of Susan Alexander's reedy soprano voice, its nasal screech suddenly interrupted by some process which also implies that an electric current has been snapped off. The voice groans and falls to a stop, as if the stylus had remained on the phonographic disk after the power had been cut, precisely mirroring the slow death of the lightbulb's filament. The voice and bulb, no longer sustained by electric energy, become a metaphor for Susan's will to live and work, no longer sustained by human energy. The next shot merely reveals the huge glass, spoon, and bottle that dominate the foreground of the frame, with an inert, out-of-focus form breathing with difficulty on the rearground bed.

But the film has already established both the lightbulb and the voice as motifs in Susan's relationship with Kane, emblematic of her traumatic singing career. The lightbulb has repeatedly blinked on and off at the start of each of her disastrous operatic performances; it is a theater work light, whose blinking and extinguishing signifies the beginning of yet another humiliating performance. The rapidity and insistence of its blinking has increased steadily during the montage sequence that summarizes her disastrous singing career. That career and sequence reach their climax when the bulb blinks off and then dies, along with her dying voice, signifying the last time she will attempt to use that voice in a stage performance.

The film has just as carefully established the pathetically reedy and

Signs of suicide in *Citizen Kane:* the lightbulb, its dying filament, and the bedside table with spoon, glass, and bottle. *Courtesy Janus Films*

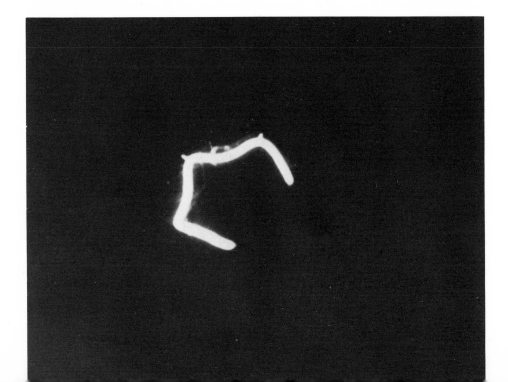

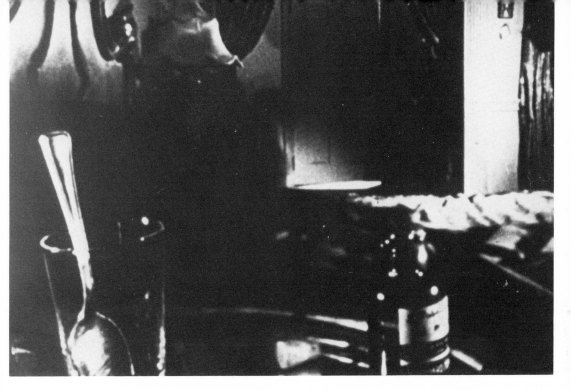

scratchy hopelessness of her singing voice. She first uses it to sing for Kane in her shabby parlor, on the night when she has a toothache and he is splattered with mud. During that first "performance," the set evaporates and is instantly transformed from the shabby parlor into the fancy one where Kane pays the rent, as well as for the singing lessons that he hopes can transform the squeaky voice. Finally, there is the tinny smallness of that voice, dwarfed by the immense opera houses it has been asked to fill, growing steadily louder and shriller during the montage sequence, seemingly battling with the increasing cacophony of the orchestra to be heard.

However, both the bulb and the voice have other clear relationships to the more general structural, psychological, and intellectual issues that the film has established. Kane decides to use Susan and her voice to vindicate himself with the "people" after they defeated him for governor—to remove the quotation marks from "singer." And he decides to make an opera singer out of her because her mother wanted her to sing opera; the sentimental Kane transfers his respect for his own mother to Susan's. His first marriage collapses after the public revelation of the "love nest" where the singing lessons take place. Susan must suffer the humiliating tour on which she meets jeer after jeer (except in the Kane papers), and she must endure the frantic and mounting pressure of performing in city after city, night after night (implied by the montage of newspapers, backstage preparations, that blinking light, curtains going up, and increasingly cacophonous sound).

The implication of the dying lightbulb and voice is not merely suicide, but the only way Susan can put an absolute end to an impossible and humiliating existence, for which she no longer has the will, energy, or strength, and in which she is simply a passive and manipulated object. It is the first time that this human being reduced to a mere object (in a film full of objects) refuses to be an object (mirrored by her walking out of his life and his castle at the end of their relationship). The only way to understand all that from the movie's semiology is to understand the whole movie.

The fact that a movie uses so many semiotic systems, so many "languages," convinces me that it is an inherently "impure" art. There are, of course, other arts that are similarly and necessarily "impure." As Arnheim develops in *Film as Art,* all the theatrical arts are inherently "impure": opera combines literary values (narrative), music, and visual stimuli; dance combines the same three, but in differing proportions with different emphases; drama combines narrative, "melody" (the sound both of speech and of other music), and the visual. Aristotle recognized this "impurity" in drama when he defined "spectacle" and "melody" (the physical sensations of sight and sound) as two elements of the drama that could not exist in the narrative "mode" (in which sights and sounds can only be imagined). And for this reason, Aristotle found drama the superior art, containing everything that narrative did and then some.

However, one consequence of a "pure" art that Aristotle may have overlooked is its infinitely greater complexity in manipulating the devices and effects of that single system. Both lyric poetry and, even more obviously in our century, the novel have been able to accomplish far more complicated manipulations of language than the drama. Samuel Beckett's plays use language much more simply and sparingly than his novels. He even seems to conceive the novel as something full of words (which it is), while the stage is an empty region where words are as spare as the landscape. Eugène Ionesco's streams of fairly simple puns, clichés, and spoonerisms seem more like delightful but playfully simple juggling alongside Proust's or Joyce's complex streams of consciousness. Painting and music (without a text or "program") are two other arts related to the cinema that can attain this complex purity, since they manipulate only a single kind of physical stimulus and a single semiotic system.

But in the cinema, purity is, first, questionably possible. Even if the cinema abandons narrative structure, it still must integrate three communicative systems and two physical stimuli—spatiality, visual temporality, and sound. And, second, purity in the cinema is questionably desirable. To eliminate any of these communicative systems might prove a revealing and pleasing individual experiment, but it is also a kind of emasculation.

This cinematic process of recording and projecting sequential images on film, juxtaposed with recorded sounds, does not have clear-cut categories of uses, effects, and devices but a *spectrum of shades of usage* that imperceptibly fade and melt into one another. An educational film does not differ from a movie (which, in turn, does not differ from an animated cartoon or abstract piece of cinema design) by being a fundamentally different thing, but in applying the same "languages" and devices in differing combinations and proportions. Is *Nanook of the North* more like *The March of Time* (because it is a nonfiction film and conveys information) or more like *Citizen Kane* (because it is beautiful and affecting)? Is Disney's *Song of the South* more like *Citizen Kane* (because it tells a story about living characters) or more like his own *Fantasia* (because it combines those living beings with animated drawings)? Is Robert Breer's *Blazes* more like *Fantasia* (because he shot it one frame at a time, as in animation) or more like Stan Brakhage's masturbatory mood piece, *Flesh of Morning* (because it is experimentally rebellious and rejects narrative structure)?

How can we draw useful distinctions between, say, an army training film for recruits on *How to Make Your Bed* (this film exists, I assure you) and a movie (say, *Citizen Kane*). *How to Make Your Bed* certainly does not dispense with camera angles, lighting, lenses, editing, human participants, narration, dialogue, structure, music, and so forth. It uses the same "languages" as the important work of art; it simply uses them differently to accomplish different ends. Ironically enough, *Citizen Kane* contains this identical point within itself: parts of it look like a shadowy and expressionistic "art film," parts of it look like a newsreel, and parts of it look like a Hollywood movie of 1941. *How to Make Your Bed* may be as competent technically as *Citizen Kane* at achieving its ends; it may even achieve them as well or better (a snappily made bed as opposed to yawning through the saga of Charles Foster Kane). One can find *Citizen Kane* the superior work only by discussing the superiority of its ends.

That discussion means formulating artistic values, not defining the medium and its language (and especially not defining them contrary to fact so that the desired answer is guaranteed by the false definition). The question What is cinema? differs from the question What is good cinema? The question What values are inherent in the art? differs from What values are best for the art? The questions that interest me are whether cinema can be defined in a way that does not exclude the legitimacy of any of its irrefutably legitimate forms and whether values can be deduced which will apply to all those legitimate forms.

2/Art and Nature

Suit the action to the word, the word to the action, with this special observance, that you o'erstep not the modesty of nature. For anything so overdone is from the purpose of playing, whose end, both at the first and now, was and is, to hold, as 'twere, the mirror up to nature. . . .

Hamlet, III, 2

Art is called art because it is not nature.

Johann Wolfgang von Goethe

According to a recent slogan of the French movie industry, "If you love life, you love the cinema." Although this advertising slogan may be more elegant and agreeable than its Hollywood counterparts, it is probably no more true. Tennessee Williams's Tom, in *The Glass Menagerie,* loved the cinema precisely because he loathed his life. And the familiar notion that movies are "escapist entertainment" certainly implies that something less pleasant exists outside the movie theater from which moviegoers come inside to escape. If people choose to spend some time with a movie rather than with their lives, it must be because the movie gives them something that their lives do not.

Precisely the same is true, of course, of any art/entertainment—painting, novel, play, symphony, ballet, photograph, even television. Using art and entertainment synonymously postpones consideration of a question that frequently obscures the discussion of cinema as an art. That question, of course, is whether cinema is an art (analogous to "serious" novels, paintings, and poems) or an entertainment (analogous to "unserious" dime novels, magazine-cover art, greeting-card poetry, television series, pop songs, and vaudeville). A more precise way of phrasing this question, however, is whether movies are a "high" or "low" art, and to answer it requires a definition of the values inherent in highness and lowness as well as a defense of the relevance and validity of such a dichotomy.

But that a movie is a work of art is a certainty, since it is very obviously not a piece of nature. A film is made of a highly artificial, man-made material (celluloid); people perform operations on that substance that are themselves highly artificial (such as exposing it to light, subjecting it to chemical processes, chopping it up and then pasting it together again, and projecting it with a machine). Despite some theorists' insistence on the large proportion of nature in this art, Susan Sontag ironically notes that to claim that "some arts [are] artificial but others are not" is a contradiction in terms.[1] Besides, is there really *more* nature in an unedited shot of leaves fluttering in the wind than there is in an ultranaturalistic piece of theater in which people eat, sleep, drink, belch, urinate, kiss, and even "have it off" (semisimulated perhaps) onstage?

Most theorists begin their definition of the cinema art with its unique relationship to nature (as we saw Bazin, Cavell, Kracauer, Panofsky, and Arnheim do). Because there was apparently "so much" nature in this art, many, applying Goethe's definition, have refused to call the cinema an art at all. But as Hamlet's advice to the players indicates, the tension between artifice and reality has existed in all aesthetic thinking, and for quite some time (indeed, the tension can be traced back to Aristotle, Plato, and Horace, who were among the first folks to occupy themselves with the issue). For thousands of years, a work of art in whatever medium has somehow paradoxically been both artificial and natural at the same time. Although the cinema may give this paradox a new twist, the new art obviously has much in common with those that have gone before it.

Any work of art is a self-contained little universe, a microcosm complete in itself. Our delight in such universes stems directly from the fact that they provide us with what the natural universe does not. The universe of the work of art is finite; it is ordered; its order is perceptible and comprehensible; it defines and then operates within a given set of laws; it is "logical"; it is permanent; and, ultimately, it is capable of perfection. For this reason, the "laws" of art have nothing whatever to do with the natural laws of gravity, relativity, or thermodynamics: economy (exactly as much as is needed—no more, no less), relevance (everything must function), balance, proportion, harmony, causality. Pirandello's six characters have gone in search of an author precisely because they seek someone who can shape the chaotic, disarranged, fluctuating fragments of their passion into the orderly, permanent *form* that is a work of art. True, the rebellion against artistic "logic" is one of the key motifs of twentieth-century art (surrealism and Dadaism, Jarry, Duchamp, Picasso, Artaud, Ionesco, Genêt, Robbe-Grillet, Beckett, Pinter). The practitioners of this brazen illogic, however, apply their "principles" as ruthlessly, consistently, and "logically" as any artist before them ever did.

To better understand this delight in the orderliness of art, as opposed to the antagonistic randomness of nature, let me depart briefly from the specific subject of cinema to examine an apparently universal human tendency that parallels our need for and delight in the experience of cinema and all the arts. That tendency is the general human desire to see the natural universe as both logical and comprehensible—in effect, the desire to convert the natural universe into a work of art.

NATURE AS ART

That art and religion are twins, born at the same time and of the same urge, is no secret; that the two were initially inextricable and identical is now accepted by students of history, culture, and the arts. There was no way for human beings to express their wonder at the natural universe—at its cyclical seasons, at its forces such as winds, water, storms, and sunlight, at its changes and yet orderly repetitions, at its violence and beauty, at its creators or controllers—except by telling stories, enacting playlets, performing dances, making music, or erecting statues. These concrete artifacts were originally symbols or metaphors for the abstract and intangible forces in the universe, which could not be depicted, much less understood, except by translating them into concrete and tangible human terms.

The gradual secularization of art over the centuries has led to our losing sight of the essentially "religious" function of art, as well as the underlying "artistic" implications of a religion. Motivation and causality, those two key features of fictional, narrative construction, were originally key features of religions, which attempted to account for the construction of the natural universe as well. If the earth is visited by terrible calamities—storms, plagues, bad harvests—it must be because the extraterrestrial forces are not pleased with the doings of the folks on earth. If the harvest is good and the earth at peace, it is because the extraterrestrial forces have decided to smile on those folks who walk and work the earth. The original function of the stories, playlets, songs, dances, and statues was not only to imitate this causal conception of the universe, but also to please and placate the forces that were thus imitated. The desire of primitive man to see the universe as rational, and therefore his own existence as rational, is as strong today as it ever was. The problem for each age has been the gratifying of this desire.

Why does the desire exist? Because the conviction that the universe is orderly is intimately connected with the belief that human life is significant. The geocentric universe of the pre-Galilean age provides a perfect metaphor, for it was also an egocentric universe. The earth was in the center of the universe, and the sun, the planets, the stars all twirled around it. At the center of the geocentric universe was the human being. This view of the universe was then translated into a work of art—a piece of wooden statuary with movable rings for each of the planets, all attached to the central earth by a stationary axis. We moderns have replaced this statuary with another—the globe of the earth. Despite its greater scientific accuracy, it is equally comforting. We are so much larger than it that we have it "under our power"; we can keep it inside our own homes. Chaplin's use of the globe as toy balloon in *The Great Dictator* was merely a magnification of our feeling of power over something we can regard as a toy.

Like the religions before it, the Christian Church supported its view of the universe's logic with public religious-artistic ceremonies that were intended as an imitation of the universe's order as well as a placation of the universe's orderer. It does not require the bizarre imagination of a Genêt to realize that the cathedral is a magnificent stage set, its priestly robes magnificently designed costumes, its liturgy a workable script, and the entire churchly experience (complete with music, props, and lighting) a kind of mammoth, "multimedia" theatrical extravaganza.

The discoveries of science poked holes in this fabric of perfect logic and weakened the universal conviction in these theatrical extravaganzas. The sun, stars, and planets did not revolve about the earth; the earth was not the center of anything and therefore man was not the center of anything. The age of science coincided with the decline in the catholicity of the church, which was firmly rooted in the age of logic. Despite this decline, the "watch-watchmaker" argument of the pantheistic and rational eighteenth century, which David Hume attacks in his *Dialogues Concerning Natural Religion,* also converted the universe quite literally into a work of art (or artifact): the universe is a vast and extremely complicated machine of interrelated parts, like a watch; for every watch there is a watchmaker; therefore . . . Q.E.D.

In the twentieth century, the attempt to convert the universe into art has been more subtle, shifting from the cosmic to the terrestrial plane, concentrating on the affairs of human beings—social, political, psychological, and moral. Nonetheless, human beings continue to attempt to make sense of human affairs by converting the potentially random workings of nature into the coherent order and form of art.

What else is psychology, the new religion of the twentieth century, except the application of fictional, narrative principles to the actual workings of human personality? The key terms for the psychologist are "motivation" and "causality," which are equally important to the critic of the novel or the drama. The psychologist (or psychoanalyst, or psychiatrist— I use the terms generically, hence interchangeably) sees the patient as a kind of literary character. Whatever the psychologist's bias (Freudian, Jungian, Ellisian, etc.), the assumption about the patient is that present problems are manifestations of past difficulties (as are Hamlet's, or James Stewart's in *Vertigo*) and can only be eliminated by discovering those original manifestations (in literary terms, by performing a detailed character analysis) and treating them. If the psychologist has become the confessor of the twentieth century, it is because, like the priest, he offers a justification for his client's circumstances—particularly his misery—as well as the hope of eventually eradicating that misery.

The very logic, the very artfulness of twentieth-century psychology is responsible for its being the foe of many twentieth-century artists. Pirandello's alienist in *Enrico IV* dispenses pat phrases and trite jargon as a means of summarizing the complex and confusing anguish of the play's central figure. Ionesco's *Victimes du devoir* converts the psychoanalyst into a brutal, B-movie detective and the psychoanalytic process into the fascistic desire to torture and dominate one's fellows. A similar view of psychology is either implicit or explicit in Camus, Genêt, Kafka, Pinter, and Beckett—many of the same artists who attacked the accepted logic of art for the same reason. For such writers, the difficulty of psychology is, first, that it views human beings as consistent, static, constant figures (exactly like characters in a play or novel) rather than as dynamic, inconsistent, and mysterious beings. And, second, that it is a closed system of terms and logic (exactly like the pre-Galilean universe), whose conclusions are inherent in the definitions and logical operations within it. If the psychological thriller is one of the favorite twentieth-century genres (Strindberg's *The Father*, Ibsen's *When We Dead Awaken*, Fitzgerald's *Tender Is the Night*, Hitchcock's *Spellbound*, *Psycho*, *Vertigo*, and several others, Shaffer's *Equus*, and many more), it is perhaps because there is something inherently dramatic in the psychoanalytic process itself.

What else is a courtroom trial except the attempt to assign guilt or innocence by converting a sequence of human events into a credible narrative that accounts for all the events in the "scenario"? The only way to account for such events is to account for the motivations (the literary term) or motives (the legal one) of the characters. There is a circular interdependence between events and personality in a courtroom, just as there is between plot and character in the work of art. The lawyer attempts to account for every event by fitting it into a consistent pattern of human behavior and attempts to show that the client is indeed a particular kind of personality by developing the consistent pattern of his actions. If certain events are inconsistent with that particular kind of personality (the client's "character"), the lawyer's scenario (not to mention his client) is in trouble.

Nowhere has the relationship between the rules of art and of law been so close and so apparent as in the fifteen months of Mr. Nixon's searching for a scenario that would "play" in the Watergate case—that would include all the events in the Watergate "plot" (the break-in, the money payments, the manipulation of government agencies), that would be consistent with his contention that he wanted to get at the truth, and that would also be consistent with our general notions of a law-abiding human being, much less a head of state. Mr. Nixon lost his public support because he could not satisfy the demands of art, in particular the laws of consistency, credibility, and probability (all of which are inseparable).

Indeed, what people wanted in the Watergate case (and perhaps want in any trial) was a final retelling of events that fixed them with the clarity, causality, and certainty of art: such and such people did this and that, for such and such a reason, which means that such and such are guilty. We wanted to discover the clear villain of the piece. The difficulty with life, however, in which the villain (unlike Richard III or Liberty Valance) neither wears clothes nor makes speeches that demonstrate his villainy, is finding our clear villains. Although we can all agree on the villainy of the banker in the black suit in a Western movie, we had much more disagreement about the bankers (and accountants) in Brooks Brothers suits on those televised hearings.

The conspirators in the Watergate case may never have sat down in a room one night and said, "Gentlemen, let us conspire together" (as did the conspirators that stormy night in the house of Brutus). A number of people apparently made a number of individual and separate decisions that seemed reasonable, justified, and necessary at the time. Those decisions were based on valid moral considerations: for example, loyalty to a set of ideals rather than to the letter of the law. That men are not absolutely subservient to the letter of all laws was the issue of the Nuremberg trials, in which those who were dutifully subservient to the letter of Nazi law were tried as war criminals. Out of this complicated tangle of conflicting memories, motivations, moralities, loyalties, and ambitions, we desired to deduce a simple, analytic conclusion: "conspiracy to cover up." We expect the conclusion in a real trial to be as convincing, as absolute, and as clear-cut as it is on the *Perry Mason* or *Petrocelli* television series, or in Preminger's *Anatomy of a Murder* or Wilder's *Witness for the Prosecu-*

tion. Perhaps courtroom dramas, like psychological thrillers, are popular because the process is inherently dramatic and the results satisfyingly conclusive.

This yearning to shape natural experience according to the rules of art also influences our view of history. "What will history say of the Nixon presidency?" asks some television commentator. Inherent in such a question is the implication that as an important person passes into the past, be it "honest" Abe Lincoln or evil Adolf Hitler, he becomes, like Shakespeare's Richards and Henrys, a fictional figure in the "World's Historical Pageant," about which opinion can become as certain as it is about the relative moral worth of Hamlet as opposed to Claudius or James Stewart (as Mister Smith) as opposed to Edward Arnold. History in this sense (and it is the most familiar sense) converts actual people and events into the characters and plot of historical drama, excluding all details of historical fact (for example, Hitler's reconstruction of the German economy) that do not fit the accepted probabilities of the story as aesthetically irrelevant.

These pervasive and seemingly universal attempts to convert nature into art are sincere and understandable. They are, above all, comforting. Human beings do not live well with the notion that they have been accidentally cast adrift on a meaninglessly infinite ocean, and that nothing they nor anyone else does is more significant than a tiny and irrelevant ripple in that vast sea. Human beings inherently suffer from what Parker Tyler called "cosmic paranoia." Nothing is so terrifying to some people as the fear that human life and experience make no sense at all and have no significance whatever. To impose form (art) on life is also to impose meaning and significance upon it. But it is nonetheless an imposition. The problem of reducing life to art is that it is a reduction. Life is more complex, more chaotic, more vast than the neatness and regularity of art, which insists on selecting "relevant" details and excluding the "irrelevant." If there is a sense in which art is superior to life (in its beauty, harmony, permanence, and logic), there is a sense in which life is superior to art: it is alive rather than dead; it is natural rather than artificial; it is vast rather than limited. There is a point at which the rules of art inevitably clash with the data of reality: as they did when the data destroyed the harmony of the Ptolemaic universe; as they do when the data call into doubt the processes of human justice or the terms, formulas, and phrases that psychology uses to anatomize human behavior.

The unique value, the advantage, of the work of art—of fiction, painting, cinema, music, sculpture, dance, drama—is that it does not reduce or impose on anything. There is no data to betray because its only data is itself. Because it is a complete, self-contained universe it is capable of satisfying our thirst for logic, order, form, and perfection without arousing any suspicion that reality has been betrayed. It is no accident that many of our greatest moviemakers—Chaplin, Renoir, Bergman, Fellini, Antonioni, Buñuel, Truffaut—either explicitly or implicitly develop the way that escape into the universe of art can help us (and themselves) evade the chaos and instability of nature.

In the twentieth century, with the erosion of belief in so many of the constructs that previously shaped human experience and the natural universe, the thirst for art is especially great. And certainly no previous era has slaked that thirst so much or so well. More people spend more time in the world of art in this era than ever before—especially since one need not leave one's home to enter that world.

CINEMA AS MICROCOSM

From this view of the work of art as a microcosm, tending toward perfection as its limit, several aesthetic values follow. First, the degree of internal perfection within that universe is one standard for measuring greater and lesser works. The various "laws" of art that have previously been mentioned—economy, relevance, balance, causality, and the rest—are merely suggestions for achieving this perfection, deduced from an observation of those works that seemed most perfect. Other familiar rules of fictional construction—for example, the prohibition against using a *deus ex machina* to resolve the action, or the prohibition against making a character perform an improbable or inconsistent action—are also specific consequences of the general premise: that the work of art be a completely self-contained and harmoniously logical universe.

In the same room of the Rijksmuseum that houses Rembrandt's famous *Night Watch* hang two paintings by lesser artists whose subjects are almost identical to Rembrandt's. Like the Rembrandt masterwork, these two paintings are large group portraits of the members of a company of civil guards. Unlike the Rembrandt work, however, the two seem strikingly horizontal and miscellaneous. The overwhelming effect is that the figures form a kind of chorus line of costumed gentlemen—many of the faces interesting, much of the clothing rendered with that wonderful silk-and-velvet texture that distinguishes Dutch portraiture, and the paintings containing many other fine touches and details that make the Dutch work so intensely alive and charming. Unlike a chorus line of Rockettes, however, there seems no reason for these chorus lines, these groups of people, to be standing there before us together, except for the accidents of time and place that made them members of the same company. The Rembrandt *Night Watch* is a masterpiece precisely because it organizes a disparate collection of individual people into a single group, mood, and entity. The painting is not horizontal but centripetal, with a clear center of attention (around that blazing torch), interest, and purpose. Whatever it is they are watching for, it seems intense, interesting, and important to them—and, hence, to us. The two lesser works lack the internal unity, harmony, and concentration of that successful universe of art that Rembrandt created.

Perhaps nothing is so disappointing as a generally fine movie that suddenly and shockingly breaks its spell by introducing some element that contradicts itself. As an example, let me refresh your memory of the ending of Fritz Lang's bitterly ironic *policier, You Only Live Once* (1936). Lang's movie tells the story of an ex-convict (Henry Fonda) who is both sensitive and intelligent (what else could the young Henry Fonda play?) and whose crimes have been of the petty and nonviolent variety (he was the driver of a getaway car). After leaving prison, his attempts to "go straight" with the woman he loves (Sylvia Sydney) are frustrated by society's view of him as a criminal (he is thrown out of a hotel on his wedding night; he loses his job). Circumstantial evidence implicates him in a brutal bank robbery in which several people die; a jury finds him guilty and sentences him to death.

The prisoner decides he can find no justice within the laws of society and attempts to escape from prison the night before his scheduled execution. However, at the very moment he is making his escape attempt, the police discover the real bank robber and murderer; they send a wire to the prison to stay Fonda's execution and release the unjustly condemned man. But when the warden tells the desperate and escaping Fonda this news, he naturally does not believe him: it must be another societal trick to get him back into prison and send him to his death. Nor does he believe the sympathetic priest (that inevitable figure of prison movies) who gives him the same news. Fonda continues his escape attempt and, in the process, shoots and kills the kindly priest. He is now a murderer indeed, and as he makes his escape toward the Canadian border with the woman he loves, the forces of the law gun them both down.

To this point in the movie, the work has been a consistently ironic treatment of the notion of justice (significantly, the movie's very first shot is of the "Hall of Justice"), intensified by the grim irony of Lang's title. Lang implies that there is no real justice in human society, that society itself turns men into criminals and murderers. And yet the last thirty seconds of the movie contradict the ninety minutes that precede it by introducing an irrelevant, unmotivated, and highly surprising "twist" (if that is the word for it). As Henry Fonda plods groggily toward "the border" (obviously this border is the one between life and death from the police bullets in his back), carrying the lifeless body of his wife in his arms, he hears the voice of the dead priest calling out to him. The echoing, heavenlyish voice tells Fonda that he now can find rest—and it is accompanied by an apparent choir of angels singing him to his eternal slumbers.

On a purely analytic level (that of simply trying to determine what precisely is happening), there are two ways to interpret the voices of the dead priest and the singing angels. Either they are the subjective projections of a groggy and crumbling brain at the border of death (as such, they would be related to the notion that a drowning man sees his entire life flash in front of his eyes before expiring); or they are to be taken as literal—the voice of heaven calling out its welcome to a battered human soul. The former interpretation would be the more attractive; it is human and psychological rather than mystical and metaphysical. But if Lang wants to end his movie with the psychological and subjective experience of death, why should it include the voice of a dead priest and a choir of angels? Why shouldn't Fonda see his whole ironic pilgrimage flash before his eyes in a flashback? Or why not a vision of the further ironies and impossibilities of earthly justice? Ultimately, the question of the appropriateness of the movie's ending cannot be satisfied by interpreting the event on a purely psychological level because you must explicate the voices of heaven in either case, as a product of either the convict's or the creator's imagination.

To satisfy the more complex and difficult evaluative question (Is the ending relevant, probable, and consistent?), one must speculate on why the movie ends with the voices of heaven. Here there also seem to be two possibilities. One answer might be that in order to get the film past the censors, or to please some sappy producer, or to reach its philistine audiences, Lang needed to end the film with some glorious affirmation after displaying such a grim and bitter sequence of human events. In effect, the apologist for the ending on these grounds would be saying that without the final thirty seconds of "Harps and Flowers" Lang could not have made the preceding ninety minutes of tough stuff. Would you rather the movie were not made at all? (No, I would rather have the movie than not have it.) Then you have to have it with this ending. Such a justification is completely plausible and convincing; it is also, however, an admission that the work is flawed and, as such, ends the investigation. The ending of *You Only Live Once* betrayed the universe of the work of art, but was necessary for "extra-artistic" reasons. A parallel justification is that the sappy ending is a deliberate burlesque, an intentional insult to the audience's "intelligence" since it assumes that the audience has none. Although such a justification makes the ending cleverer, it does not make it more organic.

There is, however, a more organic way of justifying the movie's ending—a justification that would attempt to show that Lang's ending does not betray the terms of the work itself. Since Lang's movie chronicles the impossiblity of earthly justice, it follows logically that the only place where justice is possible is in heaven. Although this argument is undeniably logical, I have no conviction in it, nor do I feel that it has anything to do with the movie. I would wonder if the maker of such an argument did so because it was possible to do so or because he or she actually believed it. It fails to convince me because, first, the movie has nothing to do with heaven but with earth (as the title brutally reminds us). Second, you must believe in heaven to believe in the ending; the movie does not contain its own development and definition of heaven (as it does of earth). And, third, you must believe in this particular, very literary, nineteenth-century, angels-with-harps-and-wings conception of heaven.

Are all references to such ridiculous sorts of heavens necessarily bad in movies (for example, *The Horn Blows at Midnight, Here Comes Mr. Jordan,* or *It's a Wonderful Life*)? Obviously not. (These movies have other problems, but heaven is not among them.) Why are heavenly references more acceptable in these movies? First, these movies are comedies (and comedy-fantasies at that); the probabilities of both comedy and fantasy differ from those of "serious drama."[2] Second, these heavenly beings are inherent in the premises—the *données*—of these three movies and do not suddenly drop into them for their conclusions. Another of the familiar "laws" of art is that the author can take many more liberties with probability at the beginning of his work, as he starts his universe in motion, than at its end, after it has been functioning by itself and according to its own laws for two hours. The heavenly ending of *You Only Life Once* introduces a "priestus ex machina," perhaps for solid commercial reasons. The information on the sound track in its final moments contradicts the previous information of the entire movie's grim events and disturbingly dark visual imagery. In this internal contradiction, the ending parallels the heavenly pageants that conclude D. W. Griffith's *The Birth of a Nation* and *Intolerance* (except for the fact that Griffith's irrelevant pageants had nothing to do with commerce and were so bizarrely imaginative and semisurreal that they are a lot more interesting).

This view of the work of art as a microcosm, complete in itself, necessarily excludes another view of art, which would attack this art-as-microcosm position as "formalistic." A Marxist critic might find the ending of *You Only Live Once* objectionable on grounds that differ completely from those above. For the Marxist, the ending might be unacceptable not because it violates the terms of the rest of the work, but because it implies that human beings are helpless to alter injustice and that heaven is man's only and ultimate recourse. The movie fails to teach man how to attack the pervasive system of injustice that it so forcefully develops. The assumption of such a view is that the work of art is not an independent universe which is to be enjoyed as a more satisfying alternative to our own, but that the work is valuable only insofar as it helps human beings change their own world. Between these two views of art as essentially didactic or as essentially experiential the only possible reconciliation might be that didactic art usually best succeeds in teaching the more important matters (such as political and moral attitudes) by first creating an "experientially" successful work of art, one that is a powerful and effective universe, complete in itself. For art to move human beings to action, it must first be moving.

The degree of internal perfection within the universe of the work of art is not the only standard for assessing its value. A second consequence of viewing the work of art as microcosm is that in works with an equal degree of internal perfection, the more complex and complicated is the superior manifestation of the human spirit than the less complex and complicated. The universe that is perfect and complex is more interesting than the universe that is perfect and simple. This is, of course, the major premise that underlies the distinction between art and entertainment, between high and low art. On the basis of this distinction, a painting such as Picasso's *Guernica* is generally considered more significant than one of Jan Steen's delightful caricatures of drunken middle-class dinners; the Mozart Requiem more sublime than Cole Porter's witty "You're the Top"; the vastness of Shakespeare's *King Lear* more awesome than Feydeau's delightful farce *La Puce à l'oreille;* and the morally complex and ambiguous *Citizen Kane* or *Rules of the Game* more "pantheonic" than the delightful musical *Singin' in the Rain.* Such value judgments assume that the artists have made their universes with equally masterful skill, that their means successfully accomplish their ends. The question becomes instead to assess the relative value of conflicting artistic purposes, of differing artistic ends.

This is, of course, an exceedingly difficult and delicate operation. There are many who would question the desirability or the possibility of comparing works of art in this way. For some the relative evaluation of admittedly "good" or successful works is not only irrelevant, but immoral. Good is good—and there an end. To find Mozart superior to Cole Porter is like finding *steak au poivre* superior to chocolate torte. Ironically, many of the very people who argue against distinguishing between good and better art are those who instinctively and automatically accept the familiar distinction between art and entertainment, a restatement of the same issue. Although Susan Sontag is "against interpretation," she concludes her marvelous essay on the science-fiction film with this evaluation:

> What I am suggesting is that the imagery of disaster in science fiction is above all the emblem of an *inadequate response*. I don't mean to bear down on the films for this. They themselves are only a sampling, stripped of sophistication, of the inadequacy of most people's response to the unassimilable terrors that infect their consciousness. The interest of the films, aside from their considerable amount of cinematic charm, consists in this intersection between a naïve and largely debased commercial art product and the most profound dilemmas of the contemporary situation. . . .[3]

What she means is that the sci-fi movie is a less complex, less honest, and more facile way of depicting our society's fears of machines, weapons, and annihilation than a more complex, modernist work—like *Hiroshima Mon Amour* or *Dr. Strangelove*—would be. The sci-fi movie, despite its imaginative and entertaining devices, is a less significant response (morally and socially, but not psychologically) to the modern condition than certain modernist films.

For others, the standards of complexity are themselves conflicting and potentially contradictory—especially in so complicated an art as cinema. For example, is Peter Yates's *Bullitt* more or less complex than Chaplin's *City Lights?* It is clearly more complex in its manipulation of the stylistic devices of cinema—cutting, color, sound, the use of lenses, composition in the wide screen. It is just as clearly less complex in its range of emotional effects, in its observation of social roles and structures, and in its probing of psychological patterns and needs. Is cinema more significant in its complexity of style or of content? Is it more remarkable for its kinetic (visual, physical) or mimetic (imitative, narrative) elements?

Those who argue for the latter are precisely those that some cinema critics dismiss as "literary." To concentrate on the mimetic elements of cinema is necessarily to examine those elements that the cinema shares with the novel and the drama. But those who argue for the former often fall into the trap of worshiping machines and mechanical processes as ends in themselves. They are precisely those who develop theories of cinema that are erroneously based on purely mechanical processes and that cut the cinema off from the experience of the other arts with which it has so much in common.

The universe of the work of cinema art is obviously the product of some kind of mixture of the mimetic and kinetic, and it is to these two terms—and their interrelationship—that I now turn.

3/Kinesis and Mimesis

When primitive peoples first began to make those little universes of art which mirrored and praised that great one, they might have taken one of several divergent paths. On the one hand, they could fashion works—paintings, plays, poems—that imitated nature with personages, actions, and conversations such as one might meet in natural experience. On the other, they might have fashioned musical works, which did not specifically imitate anything at all but were purely sensual experiences that obliquely stimulated human passions and reflection. A middle path, however, was the dance, which combined both the imitative and the sensual, the mimetic and the kinetic, the drama and music. By combining a dramatic presentation—its depiction of humans and human events—with music—its sensuous succession of tones and rhythms—primitive peoples created a truly kinetic-mimetic art whose imitative elements were more metaphorical and allusive, controlled by rhythm and physical movement, and whose sensual elements were more comprehensible and concrete, controlled by the demands of the action and the passion of the personages.

Perhaps the dance is the most basic human art, if one is to judge by its almost universal presence in every tribe studied by anthropologists. Its two components tend in two opposite and ideal directions. According to some theorists (Erwin Panofsky is among them), all arts aspire toward literature. This view implies that "poetry" (novel, drama, lyric, narrative) is the most complexly mimetic art, and that mimetic complexity is the highest value in art. According to others (Rudolf Arnheim is among them), all arts aspire toward music. This view implies that music is the purest kinetic art and that the pure abstraction of the kinetic universe, with no specific relationship to any other except itself, is the most sublime kind of art. These two pure tendencies were combined in the earliest tribal dances, but they have since been refined, separated, or remixed in the course of civilization. The cinema constitutes another of these unique and novel mixtures of the mimetic and the kinetic.

MIMESIS

What is the pleasure of mimesis? Why have humans found and taken pleasure in imitating other humans and other human events for thousands of years? Aristotle claimed that we delight in recognition—delight to see things in a work of art (fixed permanently in the form of art) that are also familiar to us from our experience in nature. This position is not far distant from André Bazin's claim that humans seek to get control over nature by fixing it permanently in the form of art. Although I would agree that we must recognize before we can delight, the source of our delight is not the recognition itself; recognition is the means to our delight. The delight itself is a result of our psychological relationship to the mimetic universe, and to develop this psychological relationship I find many of the cinema theorists quite useful. Although they believed that they were addressing themselves to the specific appeal of the cinema, their views have a much broader application.

Siegfried Kracauer, for example, contends that one of the unique pleasures of cinema is its ability to show us devastating catastrophes that either could not be experienced in life at all (without killing the participants) or could not be experienced without revulsion, horror, and pain.

> Elemental catastrophes, the atrocities of war, acts of violence and terror, sexual debauchery, and death are events which tend to overwhelm consciousness. In any case, they call forth excitements and agonies bound to thwart detached observation. . . . The medium has always shown a predilection for events of this type. . . . [*Theory of Film*, p. 57]

Susan Sontag's article on "The Imagination of Disaster" makes a similar point.

> Science fiction films are not about science. They are about disaster, which is one of the oldest subjects of art. . . . The science fiction film . . . is concerned with the aesthetics of destruction, with the peculiar beauties to be found in wreaking havoc, making a mess. ["The Imagination of Disaster," p. 425]

Certainly the "New Wave" of disaster pictures (*The Poseidon Adventure*,

Juggernaut, Airport, Airport 1975, Earthquake, The Towering Inferno, Jaws) supports the Kracauer-Sontag observations.

But haven't the mimetic arts always been interested in disaster? Kracauer certainly concurs: "Since time immemorial, people have craved spectacles permitting them vicariously to experience the fury of conflagrations, the excesses of cruelty and suffering, and unspeakable lusts . . ." (*Theory of Film,* p. 58). Oedipus puts out his own eyes after his wife-mother hangs herself—not to mention all the other cheery events in that grim saga of the House of Atreus, including serving a father a pot roast composed of the carcasses of his own sons. Agamemnon returns home after ten years of warring (and after murdering his own daughter as a sacrifice), only to be murdered by his wife and her lover on arrival; and then Agamemnon's son returns home to murder the wife (also his mother) and lover in their turn. Gloucester gets his eyes squashed to jelly as we look on in horror, Milton's angels fight a cosmic civil war which rips the entire universe asunder, Goya's rebels stand in terror as they face the rifles of the firing squad on May 3, 1808, and Madame Lafarge sits quietly knitting while the heads keep plopping in the basket. The way we experience the disaster (and the degree of the experience's intensity) indeed differs from art to art. And the differing proportions of mimetic and kinetic elements in different arts are precisely what control this different degree of experience. But disaster, catastrophe, and other events too horrible to endure in reality have been one of the constant delights of the mimetic arts.

How can we delight in witnessing something so painful? The classic answer to this question (ranging from Aristotle to Santayana to Sontag) is that the painful experience produces some positive, healthful result—a "catharsis" or purgation. This answer seems questionable, however. First, it speaks to our psychological state *after* the experience, and as a result of it, not during the painful experience itself. Second, it equates a painful experience in the universe of art with a painful experience in nature. It does not consider the possibility that our emotional relationship to the universe of art does not allow us to feel the pain that we would experience in reality. Can a painful artistic experience be considered *painful* in any way at all?

Much more to the point, I think, is Stanley Cavell's description of our psychological relationship to the world as projected on a screen. Cavell sees the movies as inherently voyeuristic. The pleasure they give is that of wrapping the spectator in a cloak of invisibility, allowing us to be present and not present at the same time—a viewer with no responsibility except to view, a participant whose only participation is emotional.

I have spoken of film as satisfying the wish for the magical reproduction of the world by enabling us to view it unseen. . . . [*The World Viewed,* p. 101]

But isn't precisely the same true of our relationship to any mimetic work? We voyeuristically live through the fortunes of Lear or Blanche DuBois or Emma Woodhouse or Hazel Motes. Whether they "live" on page, stage, or screen, we are present and not present to them at the same time, participating only with our eyes, ears, and feelings. Although, as with our experiencing of disasters, the kind and degree of voyeuristic experience differs from art to art (again, the product of the particular mimetic-kinetic compound of each medium and work), voyeurism is a constant of the audience-reader's relationship to any mimetic work of time-art. This voyeuristic experience is unique to what Lessing called the "time-arts," for it requires a period of time to "live through" an experience.

Voyeurism allows us to experience all the excitement of disaster, catastrophe, and pain, to witness the most horrible human events, without any danger of feeling real pain. The catastrophe is very real (for there it is before us) and absolutely unreal (for we know it has already occurred or is only a fiction) at the same time. Disaster is exciting because it is extraordinary and bizarre (it is certainly the economic life-blood of the tabloid newspapers). The mimetic work of art allows us to experience this extraordinary excitement; it even heightens its exciting extraordinariness. D. W. Griffith found a real World War I battle less interesting than one of his staged battle sequences, and look how clumsily "staged" was Jack Ruby's shooting of Lee Harvey Oswald.

The imitation of catastrophe gives us the experience as real as it can possibly be, but not real at all—so we get only the pleasure of the surrogate experience with none of the pain of the actual one. Not only is this delight in disaster a constant in the history of the mimetic arts, but there is absolutely no evidence that there is anything unhealthy or harmful in it (an answer to those who deplore the violence in today's films and television programs). It may even be quite healthy, for Aristotle's "catharsis" would be a potential result of our previous voyeuristic delight.

In this sense, the mimetic work of catastrophe is very much like a nightmare—real and unreal at the same time, emotional participation in a horrible sequence of events but no physical danger (unless you fall out of bed). That films have been frequently compared with dreams is well known.[1] But our experience with all the mimetic arts shares this same quality. Works of art have certain advantages over nightmares, of course. They are safer; not only need we not fear falling out of bed, but we are also very conscious of our safety rather than unconsciously floating in the frightening sea of our own imagination. They are carefully constructed to produce the most exciting effects, whereas nightmares often wander, drift, repeat themselves, and dissipate without reaching climaxes. The mimetic universe of art imposes form on the natural experience of nightmares. These catastrophic works of art are controlled nightmares, controlled by both the artistic consciousness of the creator and the consciousness of the spectator (who knows he is experiencing a nightmare and can therefore luxuriate in it).

A catastrophe movie is a kind of idealized nightmare. We can thrill to the possibility of a man turning into a wolf when the moon is full; to sitting in an airplane whose flight crew has been killed or whose engines cease to function, one by one; to having our spines gripped by a lobsterlike "tingler" (indeed, in William Castle's *The Tingler* they connected electrical wires to the seats to shock the audience quite literally with extra tingles for that tingler). Perhaps no current filmmaker better understands the nightmare possibilities of the screen than Roman Polanski. His *Rosemary's Baby* is familiar nightmarish material, complete with the mixture of baloney physics and baloney metaphysics that makes us feel so comfortable with Wolf Men, Frankensteins, and Tinglers. But his nightmares like *Knife in the Water* and *Chinatown* are far more subtle, for they turn our ordinary and familiar reality into the stuff of nightmares.

How else can one understand the pleasure of audiences with *Chinatown*, one of the most subtly nasty and ugly popular films ever made? *Chinatown* is a film in which a tyrannical rich old man swindles all the citizens of Los Angeles, murders his former partner (who is also his friend and son-in-law), rapes his own daughter, and is responsible for her brutal murder. His punishment for these peccadilloes is that he not only escapes the law, but even gets the chance to rape his granddaughter, who is also his daughter by the first rape. The film opens with a salacious series of pornographic photographs. Among its other appetizing details are the fat and sweaty walrus who is the city coroner (surrounded by the naked and grotesque stiffs of his trade), the slimy police inspector (who in this film is not slimy?), and the whitehead-flecked face of the "weasel" in the department of records.

Like J. J. Gittes himself, whose spiffily natty and fashionable clothing covers the vulgarity that can be seen in his occupation, his jokes, and his metaphors, the film is one of beautiful surfaces and corrupt interiors. Even worse (or better) is that Polanski is nasty and salacious enough to find this ugliness grotesquely funny at the same time. The ultimate uglinesses of the film, of course, are the sliced nose of the protagonist (which Polanski thrusts in our face for an hour and a half, emphasized by the blotch of bandages or the prickly stitches, sticking up and staring at us) and the bloody aureole that is the empty eye socket of the leading lady, blown out by a stupid policeman's bullet (an eye hole which falls out of an automobile and into a close-up with sudden and sickening swiftness).

Polanski's world in *Chinatown* is a perfect universe of essential ugliness and injustice. Its ending contrasts markedly (and perhaps intentionally) with the ending of *You Only Live Once,* in which the police also kill a woman, with a bullet in the back. But she dies softly and sweetly, like Juliet, not falling violently out of a car, but lifted from it gently by the arms of her also dying Romeo, accompanied by those voices from heaven. The ending also contrasts markedly (and certainly intentionally) with *Bonnie and Clyde's,* in which Faye Dunaway's body previously fell out of an automobile—but only after an epiphany of violence-as-beauty in a slow-motion ballet. For Polanski, violence is not beautiful, but a horrifying, irrational nightmare (so irrational that it is ironically funny as well as terrifying), and he sustains this nightmare world to the end of *Chinatown* without awaking the audience and returning us to safety (as *You Only Live Once* and most catastrophe films do). When the lights come on in the theater, neither the light, nor the people, nor the walls feel the same as they did before the lights went out. In *Chinatown* Polanski makes us experience vicariously the irrational nightmare reality that he experienced literally after Charles Manson's Family visited his family.

In her lengthy and ambivalent piece on *Chinatown,* Pauline Kael denied neither the audience's attraction to the movie (which she observed) nor the frightening power of the movie (which she felt). She, however, attacked the movie as symptomatic of the "new" nihilism, perversity, and emptiness of the movie business and audience that could produce and accept such moral nastiness and emptiness in a work of art.[2] To deplore the morality of liking such a movie, however, is to miss the point that the work is not interested in commenting on moral choices, nor in spinning a good but empty yarn (like *The Big Sleep,* to which the film has been often compared but with which it has merely surface affinities). Polanski's aim is the creation of a perfectly nightmarish fantasy of human existence as malevolent and perverse as can be imagined.

Martin Scorsese's *Taxi Driver* is another immensely successful commercial movie that carefully converts reality into a controlled nightmare fantasy. For two hours we live life as Travis Bickle, sealed inside his taxicab, cut off from human beings by glass windshields, windows, rear-view mirrors, and television screens. We participate vicariously in Bickle's mental demise, dragged hypnotically, inevitably, and irreversibly into the orgasmic act of violence that is his only way of making contact with another, his only way of turning masturbatory fantasy into concrete action, as well as the only way he can commit a spectacular suicide. As if in recognition of the movie's nightmarish descent into the underworld, its makers end it with a coda which did not exist in the original script, returning us to the safety of conventional reality and society (as *Chinatown* did not).

But the very audience that can enjoy these idealized fantasies of perfect ugliness, injustice, and frustration can (and indeed does) enjoy the idealized dream of perfect justice in a film like *Mr. Deeds Goes to Town.* I am as gladdened, as warmed, as moved to something close to joyful tears by the just and joyful ending of *Mr. Deeds* as I am shaken by the grim and brutal injustice of the ending of *Chinatown.* Those same student audiences that Ms. Kael found nasty enough to respond to the nastiness of *Chinatown* also respond to *Mr. Deeds* with laughs and sniffles precisely where Capra wanted them—precisely where they came for the audiences of forty years ago.

Why am I (and many others) affected, moved, convinced by the ending of *Mr. Deeds?* Since I don't consider myself especially sentimental, sappy, or stupid, that question is no less puzzling than why I (and many others) are affected by movies as perverted as *Chinatown* or as maniacal as *Taxi Driver.* For we know that the perfect justice and benevolence that ultimately triumph in Frank Capra's universe has nothing to do with the realities of the natural universe, just as the perfect injustice and malevolence that rule Polanski's universe have nothing to do with the realities of the natural universe either. Both universes are too logical for nature (because, of course, they are universes of art). They are false. Or rather, they are idealizations—idealized malevolence, idealized benevolence.

If idealized catastrophe in the work of art resembles the experience of nightmares, idealized benevolence and justice in the work of art are its opposite, resembling the experience of much sweeter dreams. The same voyeurism and vicariousness that allow us to experience painful catastrophes with pleasure also allow us to experience idealized goodness with pleasure. For I know that Frank Capra's *Mr. Deeds* is morally silly, politically simplistic, and intellectually banal. Who doesn't? But I also find the movie extremely satisfying emotionally. And so do most of us who see it. The saccarine, sentimental populism of Capra's politics is quite as revolting (when considered rationally) as the nastiness of *China-*

town, the salacious enjoyment of disaster in *The Towering Inferno,* or getting our thrills from demonism, vampirism, and lycanthropy in *The Exorcist, Dracula,* or *The Wolf Man.* One does not need to believe in the devil to be frightened by *Rosemary's Baby* or *The Exorcist.* We can enjoy vicariously the sensations and experience of what it might feel like *if* one believed in the devil and *if* the devil existed. Similarly, with *Mr. Deeds* we can enjoy vicariously the sensations and experience of what it might feel like *if* there were absolute innocence and goodness in the universe and *if* the ultimate wisdom in the universe ultimately rewarded that innocence and goodness. Those *ifs* represent the conventional agreement, the Aesthetic Compact, we make with the artist. They are his *données,* his "givens" (that which we give to him and he gives to us without question).

People have nightmares; they also have more pleasant dreams. And in this polarity one can see the basis of our experience with the mimetic arts, which are concrete, controlled, and "logical" dreams and nightmares. If it has not yet become apparent, to this polarity literary tradition has assigned the two idealized and archetypal labels comedy and tragedy, which we might define as the idealized dream of goodness, justice, and things working out well as opposed to the idealized nightmare of catastrophe, horror, and things working out ill. The possibility that neither of these archetypal idealizations might ever exist in a pure form in a work of art is irrelevant. The very fact that terms like tragicomedy, melodrama, comic drama (or Polonius's tragical-comical-historical-pastoral) exist reveals that the pure archetypes are capable of different kinds of blending. But then so are our dreams—which may not be purely pleasant or horrifying either.

Mimetic art allows us to experience both a world much better, pleasanter, and more harmonious than our own and a world much harsher, uglier, and more painful than our own. The work of art pushes the ordinariness of everyday life, its fluctuating moments of joy and sorrow (and most that are neither), to limits of extraordinary purity and consistency. Mimetic arts allow us to undergo the extraordinary experiences that everyday life does not, and to experience as much of the extraordinary and as many kinds of extraordinariness as possible. They take us not only out of our lives but out of our skins, allowing us to see and feel life vicariously within as many other kinds of skins as possible. The mimetic arts free us from the hard shells of our own bodies, cultures, thoughts, and experiences to enable us to live the life of Proteus. To those who would counter that the goal of realism (perhaps the dominant mimetic movement of the last hundred years) was to allow us to experience the ordinary, indeed, the ordinariness of our own lives, I would argue that the goal of realism was to make the ordinary extraordinary. To experience an idealization of the mundane problems of daily life became another of the guises that our protean and vicarious experience of art could adopt.

But in order to experience this surrogate, vicarious existence with a mimetic work, in order actually to "live through" this concrete dream or nightmare, you must be convinced that you are living through it (at the same time that you know very well you are not!). You must have *conviction* in the experience. You cannot feel the terror of being trapped in a towering inferno unless you have conviction that you are actually undergoing that terrible experience. And those who laughed at and during that film simply demonstrated their lack of conviction. This notion of conviction can best be defined by reference to the two kinds of knowing.

There are at least two senses in which we know things. On the one hand, we understand things rationally, cognitively, intellectually: for example, two plus two are four; all men are mortal. On the other, we can know things experientially, personally, internally ("in our guts," to use the vernacular). For this reason, children learn that two plus two equals four by adding apples or oranges, so they can see and touch their twoness, plusness, and fourness. For this reason, we do not really *know* what mortality means until someone close to us dies. Though we know all men are mortal, we tend to live our lives as if we did not—until some personal experience really makes us *know* what we know. In the same way, the successful work of mimetic art makes us *know* we are undergoing an experience at the same time that we know we are sitting in a theater or in our homes. These two forms of knowing are what Benedetto Croce labeled logical and intuitive knowledge, and the distinction between them marks the starting point of his entire *Theory of Aesthetic*.[3] My notion of conviction (and Croce's of intuition) also parallels Tzvetan Todorov's concept of "verisimilitude": that which *feels* real to the viewer despite the fact that it is obviously not.[4]

Indeed, this "conviction" parallels several more familiar and traditional narrative concepts. Like "the willing suspension of disbelief," "conviction" implies an internal, emotional response on the part of the viewer, who gladly and willingly accepts a fiction as a kind of truth. Like "empathy" or "character identification," "conviction" implies the sympathetic response of the viewer to a person or persons in the mimetic work, who serve as his surrogates. Like Robert Scholes's notion of "narrativity," "conviction" implies that we participate in a mimetic work not solely because of what is in the work, but because of the way we personalize, internalize, and, in effect, recreate the work imaginatively within us.[5] The only reason I suggest using this new term, "conviction," when we seem to have so many functional ones already is that it emphasizes the reciprocal relationship between viewer and work. We will only suspend disbelief to participate in the fiction as "real" if the work *convinces* us to do so. And once we have been convinced, we accept the "realness" of the fiction until the work does something to unconvince us.

It is easier to show how works fail to convince us of their verisimilitude than to demonstrate the means by which they necessarily succeed. The actor who forgets a line or stumbles over a speech in a play instantly reminds us that he is an actor doing an impersonation, shattering, perhaps only for an instant, our conviction that he is Hamlet. Although the multiple takes of movies allow us to avoid this kind of shattering, the film actor can destroy our conviction if the line sounds hollow, faked, forced, or somehow out of keeping with the personality of the actor, the character, the situation, or ordinary human intelligence. I feel a parallel lack of conviction in many Italian films—particularly those in English like *The Damned* and *Death in Venice*—that dub the dialogue after shooting rather than recording picture and talk at the same time ("post-synching" is the standard Italian practice). Although this post-synching method saves time and money, it never convinces me that the speakers are really speaking. Not only are there slight variations between sounds and lip movements, but also the timbres of the human voices differ from those that would be produced in the course of action or agitation in that specific audial environment. As for foreign-language films dubbed into English—I don't know whether they are more painful and less convincing to watch or to hear.

Films can destroy our conviction in their verisimilitude in other ways. Many of the early one-reelers of the pre-Griffith era (for example, Edwin S. Porter's *Rescued from an Eagle's Nest* of 1907, in which Griffith starred) contain obvious mismatchings of shots that we are supposed to accept as a matching, continuous sequence. Porter shot part of his film outdoors, amid genuine hills, trees, and rocks, and part of it inside the studio, amid cardboard renderings of the same. Griffith was lowered down a tortuous cliff (which Porter shot in a real location) to do battle with a vicious eagle (which Porter shot inside the studio). Nothing looks quite so ludicrous as the flat lighting and flatly painted rocks and trees masquerading as the identical natural objects from the preceding shot—except perhaps for the puppet-stringed eagle masquerading as a dangerous bird. This "terrifying" clash between man and bird usually gets the bird

Rescued from an Eagle's Nest: two consecutive shots. Artifice masquerades as nature when the father (played by D. W. Griffith) is lowered by rope along an obviously natural hillside, only to land in an obviously painted eagle's lair.

(and assorted other hoots) from audiences today, who have great conviction in it as terrible rather than terrifying. Forty years later there is a similarly unfortunate bit of fakery in Chaplin's *Monsieur Verdoux* (the night-into-day, moonlight-into-sunlight dissolve that implies the movie's first murder), in which a painted backdrop of a city masquerades as a real one.

A familiar bit of movie fakery that "reads" instantly as fake is day-for-night filming, shooting during the day but using filters and laboratory processes so that the hour looks vaguely and bluely nightish. The world turns a bluish color such as has never been seen in nature, and the actors cast shadows that could never be thrown in the fullest and brightest moonlight. Indeed, the coming of color and the wide screen deprived filmmakers of more and more of these tricks they could get away with in the small screen and black-and-white. The point of Truffaut's *Day for Night,* a lovingly ironic examination of cinema artifice, is that the artifice must never seem to be artificial.

From this kind of evidence one could deduce (as did Bazin) that the untampered rendering of nature is one of the chief sources of conviction in a movie. But the same evidence yields another conclusion, which does not deny the verisimilitude and the legitimacy of films like *The Cabinet of Dr. Caligari* and the ballet sequences of *Singin' in the Rain* and *An American in Paris,* which clearly tamper with nature. If the scenery is supposed to look natural, it had better look like nature. If the scenery is not supposed to look natural (as in *Caligari* and cartoons), it need not. We will not have conviction in an obvious lie—that a flat piece of painted muslin is a tree—unless the artist admits it is a lie and is using that lie for some artistic purpose (for example, to develop the distorted point of view of the narrator in *Caligari*). In such a film, we are not asked to have conviction in painted muslin as a tree, but in a world in which painted muslin impersonates a tree. Only when the artist tells us that the obvious muslin is a tree and he sees it as exactly that do we suspect that he is either blind, stupid, lying, or some combination of the three. Things in a mimetic art had better seem to be what they are supposed to be—especially in cinema, in which we can see so clearly what they seem to be.

Of course, I expect an objection here about scenery in the theater: "*King Lear* can be played on a bare stage, but we are supposed to believe he is on a heath." And so forth. My answer is that we are not supposed to have conviction in a heath but in Lear on a heath; and if he says he is on a heath, that is all the heath we need. But should the designer choose to give us an absolutely real-looking heath, he is pretty much committed to giving us an absolutely real-looking everything else. If the scenery on a

stage does not ask us to believe in it as literal (as in Shakespeare, Sopho-
cles, and Brecht), we need not. Conversely, I have heard an audience in
the theater titter at a seemingly realistic stage set (one of those perfect,
post-Ibsen renderings of a drawing room, study, or kitchen) that shook
seismically when a character exited with the angry bang of a door.

The difference between theater and film décor is that the theater can
choose its proportions of realness and stylization in its imitation of nature.
But when the cinema purports to imitate nature, its possibilities for stylization are severely limited. This is the reason (as Bazin noted) that film
décor gravitates more toward nature and the real than that of the theater.
But the general principles of conviction and stylization apply equally to
both. I take this fact as further evidence that our impression of reality in
a mimetic work (be it novel, play, or movie) has nothing to do with the
"amount of reality" that literally exists in it (as Kracauer and Bazin
maintain). Instead, our accepting the mimetic world as real comes from
our internal belief, our conviction, that the artistic universe is consistently
"real" in its own terms.

It is possible, of course, to feel a limited conviction in a mimetic
experience, both to feel some conviction of "actually" undergoing a real
experience and to be aware of trickery and fakery at the same time. Our
pleasure in the classic horror films (*Frankenstein, Dracula*) or in *King
Kong* or in the Busby Berkeley musicals is of this kind, both convinced
about the experience and not convinced, but admiring the imaginative
devices for depicting it. This pleasure is well known as "camp." If there
were no conviction in the experience at all—no interest in the fable of
Frankenstein or *Kong* or the physical movement in a *Gold Diggers*—the
result would be not "camp" but a few minutes of cynical amusement
followed by ninety minutes of boredom.

So many of the critical objections to some mimetic work are merely
statements of the way the work violated the particular critic's conviction
in its verisimilitude. In *A Short History of the Movies,* I make the
following critical remark about the film of *West Side Story:* "But how to
make a film audience believe that a group of juvenile delinquents would
pirouette down a real New York street with real graffiti on the walls and
real garbage in the gutter?" (p. 335). What I meant was that I had great
conviction that I was actually experiencing life in New York City. Given
the magnificent helicopter shots of Manhattan Island which swoop down
into the city from aloft to open the movie, it would be difficult to lack
that conviction. What I could not believe, after that swooping down, was
that any human beings (especially allegedly tough ones) would comport
themselves on a convincingly real street in the manner of the balletic Jets

and Sharks. (My difficulty was analogous to that presented by *Rescued from an Eagle's Nest,* in which fake studio shots followed immediately upon the real location shooting.) Ballet dancers comport themselves in that manner on a stage. Only one musical sequence seemed to solve this problem of the conflicting demands of reality and stylization in the movie —which is the central problem for any musical film. The number was "Cool," performed in absolute blackness (a dark garage), punctuated and highlighted by automobile headlights (which served the same stylizing function as theatrical spotlights, but without "violating the realism of the cinema").[6]

To give one further example, I summarize my displeasure with Jerry Lewis in *The Comic Mind* as follows: "Lewis's characterization is a deliberate contrivance imposed from outside the essential personality. . . . [He] seems to say over and over again, look at me, I'm funny; look at that, that's funny" (p. 299). I meant that I had no conviction in the character that Lewis was impersonating, no conviction in the comic process he was undergoing, and no conviction in the gags that thereby spun off from both the character and the situations. I felt I was watching a manipulator of comic devices (sometimes a pretty good one), but I was in no way caught up in a complete comic world (as I am with Chaplin or Keaton) in which character, situation, and gag are all one and all inseparable from that whole.

Now, I am not alone in these opinions of both *West Side Story* and Jerry Lewis. Both would probably pass for prevailing critical opinion. On the other hand, there are others who love *West Side Story* and who love Jerry Lewis. For those who do, it is not simply that their taste differs from mine. Their senses of conviction are different. They have conviction in the balletic movement of *West Side Story* or in the character and situations that Jerry Lewis develops. How is it possible for different people to have different senses, standards, and thresholds of conviction? This can perhaps be answered by returning to that 1907 one-reeler.

Did the audiences of 1907 find the mismatching of shots as obvious and as ridiculous as we do today? As obvious? Perhaps. It is not clear today how early audiences perceived films, or how aware or tolerant they were of mismatching in an assembled succession of shots. As ridiculous? Almost certainly not. If so, why would thousands of such (and even cruder) films be made every year and why would thousands go to see them every day?* If they noticed the mismatching, they probably ac-

---

* The intellectual snobs in the 1907 audience saw the ridiculousness, but they found "the flickers" a continual subject of ridicule and went to the nickelodeon only to snicker. Or perhaps they had already discovered the pleasure of "camp."

cepted it as conventional, as one of the inevitable *données* of a work that does not require conviction. Those who like *West Side Story* may well accept the dancing in the streets as conventional ("That's what they do in movie musicals"); those who like Jerry Lewis may well accept his over-statement and exaggeration as conventional ("That's what they do in comedy"). Of course, that isn't what they all do in musicals or in com-edies. And if the 1907 audience accepted the mismatched cliffs in *Eagle's Nest*, it may well have been because that's what they all did then. But they don't all do it now, and we know more now than they did then.

Our senses of conviction (and therefore of taste) are the products of our experience and knowledge and views of both life and art. I remember as a child I had great conviction in *Abbott and Costello Meet Franken-stein*. No, I did not find Abbott and Costello particularly funny (even as a child I had *some* sense); but I screamed with terror at Frankenstein, Dracula and the Wolf Man, all three of whom Universal had teamed (for the first and last time) to scare Lou Costello and me. When I saw the movie a few years ago on television, I found it terrifying in a very differ-ent way. Could I ever have responded so violently to *that?*

More experience with mimetic works, more knowledge (both of life and of art) necessarily refines, develops, and changes our senses of con-viction. It does not necessarily improve them. Many modernist thinkers and artists—Jarry, Apollinaire, Artaud—believed that refinement meant constriction (which it does) and therefore corruption. But those of us with that (or any) refinement can no more cast it out of ourselves than the innocent can suddenly acquire it. We can no more eliminate the years of cinema that followed 1907 than we can remove the telescoping of those years of movie experience within ourselves.

Our sense of conviction is perhaps the most individual and personal response we make to a mimetic work and it differs considerably even among those of equal experience, knowledge, and refinement. An actor friend of mine has no conviction in Joseph Cotten's portrayal of the aged Jed Leland, especially his senile Southern drawl; I, however, hear the drawl as a sloppy and slovenly distortion of his crisp, young Yankee speech, which has collapsed and dissipated with a lifetime of waste and booze. Our sense of conviction is a function of our experience in life (for example, a psychiatrist might not "buy" *Spellbound*), of our experience in art (for example, I don't "buy" Jerry Lewis, Abbott and Costello, and the Three Stooges partially because I have seen Keaton, Chaplin, Fields, and the Marx Brothers), of our political and moral beliefs (for example, a political conservative might not "buy" *State of Siege* and a taxi driver might not "buy" *Taxi Driver*), or any combination of these. What we will "buy" in a work determines if that work works for us, and what we "buy" is a consequence of what we are.

The surprising thing about the most successful works of mimetic art is their ability to produce a considerable unanimity of response from our absolutely unique senses of conviction. And one of the ways that movies achieve this unanimity is by manipulating the kinetic devices that convey this mimetic art. Indeed, if movies seize and hold our conviction in the mimetic experience with more hypnotic intensity than any previous art, it is because they possess the richest set of kinetic tools to intensify these experiences.

KINESIS

The pleasure of kinesis is perhaps easier to understand than that of mimesis. The physical stimulation and invigoration of the senses is one of the chief sources of pleasure. Although the kinetic arts begin by stimulating the senses, they do not necessarily remain an exclusively sensual experience—like the breath-taking ride on a roller coaster or the gentle relaxation of a massage. The massage of a kinetic art can go from the senses, through the nerves, to the brain, which can translate it into another, more abstract kind of human experience. Like the work of mimesis, the work of kinetic art is a surrogate for actual experience, yet a more indirect, metaphoric, and oblique surrogate. We do not witness specific events and figures that we *recognize* from natural experience; instead, we feel sensations that vaguely parallel and evoke the sensations, rhythms, and emotions of life. If the mimetic arts resemble the concrete elements of our dreams (the specific people, occurrences, and objects that we "see" in our sleep and can then see on the stage or screen or "see" in our mind's eye as we read), the kinetic arts resemble the abstract and associational elements of dreaming (the feeling that we are floating in a moody bath of sensation and emotion without any specific referents for those feelings).

Before the cinema, music was the most familiar, perhaps the only purely kinetic time-art. Like the waking dreams of mimesis, music is a highly controlled dream. It is controlled, first, by developing and intensifying its self-contained emotional moods to their purest limits. Although many musicologists deplore adjectival descriptions of musical passages—joyful, sad, triumphant, heroic, *pathétique, capriccioso*—the fact that composers themselves have applied such adjectives to works and movements indicates that there is some relationship between abstract human emotions and musical passages. This vague relationship accounts for the fact that the purely kinetic art of music plays a major role in three "impure" kinetic-mimetic arts (opera, dance, and cinema), all of which make the link between music and human emotion more specific and concrete than it is in the original, purely musical passage.

Second, music is controlled by the structural laws, the "logic," of musical composition, just as the mimetic arts are controlled by their "logical" laws of imitation. And like the modernist mimetic arts, music can break its familiar laws of logic for specific artistic effects which are themselves products of a different logic. Whereas in the mimetic arts the laws are known by such terms as causality, motivation, beginning-middle-end, probability, and so forth, in music the laws are known by such terms as major and minor, theme and variation, *largo* and *scherzo*, ¾ and ¼, C♯ and B♭. They are the laws of development, expansion, and progression, which control the relationships of the individual moments in this time-art. Like the laws of mimesis, their aim is to assemble those moments into a perfect microcosm of experience, a universe complete in itself and governed according to its own self-contained principles. There are probabilities of succession in music as well as in a mimetic art, but whereas the probabilities in a mimetic art are synonymous with "credibility" (what certain kinds of people in certain kinds of situations would believably do or say), probabilities in music are more related to a mathematical series of permutations.

Like mathematics, music is a closed system of terms, operations, and intervals; like mathematics, a musical composition is a series of deductions within that system. Perhaps for this reason, computer music has been one of the more successful forms of computer art. As with the mimetic arts, the value of our experience with a musical universe of art is dependent upon, first, its degree of internal perfection and, second, its degree of complexity (technically, emotionally, and/or intellectually) within that perfection. The successful universe of musical art removes us from nature and allows us to experience a surrogate existence of purified sensations, rhythms, and emotions that abstractly suggest the feelings of human experience without imitating them concretely.

The cinema extended the possibilities of the kinetic time-arts by being the first that could work upon the eyes in the same way that music worked on the ears. Of course, the drama was a traditional time-art with an undeniable visual (i.e., kinetic) appeal. Aristotle's "spectacle," by which he meant those things that an audience perceived directly by means of the sense of sight, was one of the two specific kinetic appeals that made the drama "superior" to narrative. (The other was "melody," which refers to a play's kinetic appeal to the ear.) For Aristotle, spectacle was the least important ingredient of the drama, and although there is plenty to see at a play (faces, costumes, gestures, stage movement, settings, lighting tones), one can still enjoy a play (and understand it almost perfectly) with the eyes closed (or just by listening to something, like the marvelous Laughton recording of Shaw's "Don Juan in Hell"). When we read a play we dispense with spectacle and melody altogether—except in our mind's "eye" and "ear." Which means that such a pleasure is identical to reading narrative fiction, where we only "see" and "hear" things according to the eye and voice of the imagination.

It is impossible, however, to read an opera or a ballet. Opera scores and Labanotation manuscripts are performing "scripts" for the professional expert. They cannot begin to approximate the experiencing of a work by a layman, as can reading the script of a play. These two varieties of theater simply mix Aristotle's dramatic elements differently by altering the proportion of kinetic effects.* For the sake of melody, the power of many other Aristotelian dramatic elements must be sacrificed or reduced in an opera—quantity of incident, complexity of psychology, subtlety and detail of characterization, intellectual ambiguity of ideas. A comparison of Verdi's *Otello* and Shakespeare's *Othello* reveals the opera's magnifying the characters' external expressions of passion and reducing the internalized texture of human events (precisely the kind of human texture that gives us our conviction in *Othello*). I once heard Christopher Isherwood claim that opera was inherently "camp," and what he meant in my terms was that for opera we willingly sacrifice total conviction in the mimetic experience for a limited conviction in the mimesis that allows us to marvel at the musical embellishments (the kinesis). However, an opera is not simply a drama that has *more* melody; it is a drama in which melody becomes a part of its diction (or "language," or semiotic codes), assuming many of the usual dramatic functions of words for communicating the feelings of the characters and the meanings of the events.

Precisely the same is true of spectacle in ballet. It is not simply that there is more to look at in a ballet, but that what we see (the physical movement of the human body in space) and what we hear (the music that underscores the movement) communicate what is happening (say, the death of a swan or the birth of Apollo), what the characters think, feel, and want (say, the varying emotional states of Petrouchka), and

* Comparisons between film and theater usually fail to get anywhere because the critic erroneously equates theater and "play." To realize that opera and ballet are certainly forms of drama (they satisfy Aristotle's definition entirely) is to suggest the range and variety of theater expression. Bazin's discussion of theater décor is so valuable because it applies to all forms of theater—not just to plays.

even the general emotional texture of the piece (be it the vague joy and élan of Arpino's *Viva Vivaldi!* or the vague *angst* and tension of one of Alwin Nikolais's cityscapes). The balletic movement can be as concrete, specific, and mimetic as a play or as oblique, general, and vague as the emotions in music itself. The kinesis of physical movement (accompanied by the kinetic power of the music) becomes the diction of the dance, its means of "saying" whatever it wants to "say," and our conviction in such a work is a product of our understanding what the movement imitates (if it imitates anything specifically) and/or our undergoing the sensual and experiential journey on which the movement-music takes us.

The interrelation of kinesis and mimesis in the dance brings us very close to their parallel connection in the cinema. However, in the ballet or a play the balance between mimesis and kinesis remains fairly stable for every instance of the art; kinesis is subordinate in the drama, but dominates the dance. But the balance between kinesis and mimesis is infinitely variable and inconstant in cinema. It can range from movies in which kinesis seemingly plays as small a role as it does in a play to a film that is as purely kinetic as a piece of music. And there are as many instances of important and effective cinema works at both these extremes as there are for every shade and gradation between the two. Arnheim's difficulty with the "impure" art of talking cinema was partially the result of this unstable and inconstant relationship between mimesis and kinesis in the cinema. In the final section of *Film as Art,* Arnheim uses opera and ballet as examples of successful "impure" arts, specifically on the grounds that their mixtures are so stable that a particular element necessarily dominates while others are subordinate.

Although Arnheim was quite astute in his observation of the instability of the cinema compound, his conclusion fails for two reasons. First, the same impurity and instability existed previously in the silent film, which also could mix the mimetic and kinetic in different proportions and which was never really silent. The addition of *synchronized* sound merely extended the cinema's range of both mimetic and kinetic effects. Second, his nineteenth-century assumption of a single dominant element for each art failed to fit the twentieth-century artistic condition in which the individual work was free to determine the ordering of its own elements.

Many experimental, or "underground," or abstract, or nonlinear films (no one can agree on a single label) are works of pure kinesis, as purely "musical" as a sequence of visual images can get. The films of Oskar Fischinger, Len Lye, or John Whitney are animated "dances" of color and form, precisely and hypnotically synchronized in their rhythms and colors with the tones and rhythms of the accompanying music. As if to emphasize the parallel with music, Whitney's films are spun by computers, which have also been most successful with music. The films of Robert Breer often dispense with a musical sound track altogether. Their "music" is often purely visual as he animates either a fluid succession of continuous and evolving forms or produces a sensation of collision and assault from a montage of related but discontinuous frames of forms and colors. The films of Stan Brakhage and Bruce Baillie are more elusive and metaphoric (like the fleeting, abstract sensations of music), partially mimetic (in that they imitate the personal feelings and states of consciousness of the artist), but essentially kinetic (in that, like music, they convey those feelings allusively, obliquely, and abstractly).

Perhaps another analogy for such films would be the short lyric poem —a Donne sonnet or a Blake song or a Yeats "voyage." Like the lyric poem, these films tend to be quite short (often less than ten minutes); they tend to be highly personal, charged with the artist's personal system of symbol, metaphor, and meaning. Because lyric poems often don't really "imitate" anything other than an internal feeling or sensation (they certainly don't imitate an action), they tend to use words themselves more kinetically, especially attentive to the musical sounds and to the associations of visual images that the words evoke. Given the difficulty in finding an acceptable and accepted name for these short, personal, kinetic films, perhaps "lyric film" would be as good as any (especially since another kind of poem, "narrative poem," is also a recognized and opposite type of poetry).

On the other hand, the films of Yasujiro Ozu seem as nonkinetic as an effective movie can get. Not that there aren't plenty of things to see and hear in an Ozu movie (the voices, the faces, the eyes, some sound effects —especially silence—and music, walls, furniture, colors, objects). But the kinetic contribution does not seem much greater than it does at a performance of a play. Ozu's camera quietly, unobtrusively, and intimately records a series of human conversations. Movies of this type *can* be read as books (Ozu was a consciously literate writer as well as maker of films) and have been published as books. Reading such a movie can never reproduce the complete experience of cinema (but the same is true of reading the script of a play, an operation we take for granted). Perhaps such a film script can serve only to refresh our memory of experiencing the movie. However, it is as absolutely impossible and unthinkable to read a Len Lye or Robert Breer or Stan Brakhage film as it is to read a ballet. The only possible "script" would be a synopsis of sounds and images, which, however accurate, could never even suggest the experience of such a film.

A Chaplin film would be one of the possible gradations between these two extremes. His films are dependent on the kinetic power of human movement in space (like the dance), but they deliberately restrict any obvious and powerful kinetic effects in the cinematic recording process. According to such a formulation, it would be inaccurate to say that Chaplin was "uncinematic" (since he made good cinema), or that he did not use any of the kinetic possibilities of cinema (since physical movement is necessarily kinetic). However, his cinematic (recording) process was not itself kinetic. Deliberately not, of course, for he instinctively perceived that the more he made space move around, the less interesting (and the less possible) it would be to watch him moving around in space. Unlike the dance, cinema *can* make space itself appear to move (Erwin Panofsky calls this potentiality the "dynamization of space"). In making space move, cinema can achieve unique and powerful kinetic effects (mirroring the frenzy of a chase on horseback with a moving camera; the assaultive effects of rhythmic or rapid montage; the mysterious tension of a bizarre, "Dutch" camera angle, and so many others). *If* a film wants or needs those effects. But cinema *can* also make space stand still so that things can move around in space.

Conversely, Eisenstein made good cinema by combining images that were, in themselves, more static and less rich than when they were combined. With a reduced inherent power in some of his individual images, Eisenstein gave them their power in his manner of making space jump around from image to image—the rhythms, tones, "collisions" (to use his term), pace of this moving space. And in manipulating these kinetic effects of editing, Eisenstein's montage also accomplished its mimetic (and didactic) ends—for example, conveying the brutal slaughter on the Odessa Steps or the slaughter of the workers in their tenements (which, in turn, implied what people would need to do to prevent such slaughters in the future).

One of the general trends of modernism in all the arts has been an increasing value in the effects of kinesis, both as a means to mimetic effects and as an end in itself. The collapse of representational painting necessarily emphasized the resulting purely visual effects of the color, shape, texture, and relationships of paint on canvas. Artaud's dramatic theory attacks language as the source of the rational in the drama; he calls instead for more primitive and irrational dramatic forms, closer to the dance than to the familiar play. Many of the most interesting theater works of the twentieth century are plays that reduce the power of language (Beckett's mime plays, Marceau's mime), or use language more as sound than as sense (Ionesco, Pinter), or convert the drama into the kind of assaultive, sensual ritual that Artaud urged (Genêt, Arrabal). Like those lyric films, most of these modernist plays are short (one act is the standard length), and when these playwrights expanded to longer forms they often reverted to more traditional kinds of mimetic constructions.

In cinema, the modernist trend toward kinesis shows itself not only in the lyric films specifically dedicated to it, but also in the commercial movies of the last decade that use kinesis heavily to serve mimetic purposes: the breath-taking "trip" that brings Kubrick's space voyage to its climax in *2001*, the slow-motion "rumbles" in his *Clockwork Orange* (in fact, the whole range of slow-motion effects in just about everyone's films, which can convey everything from idyllic love to idealized violence), the exciting automobile chases in *Bullitt* or *The French Connection*, the psychedelic rock-music sequences in so many films (or even whole films that are purely psychedelic rock concerts). Most of these examples of film kinesis (or of kinesis as mimesis) are explicitly sexual, and the "climaxes" of *2001, Bonnie and Clyde, Bullitt, The Wild Bunch*, or *Taxi Driver* are experiential orgasms toward which the films have carefully built (as did Ravel in his *Bolero* and *Daphnis and Chloe*, or Ionesco in *The Bald Soprano* and *The Lesson*). We film spectators are not only voyeurs; we also experience a kind of rape.

This taste for kinesis in films (especially the violent, assaultive, or sexual kinds) can be partially explained by the current attitudes of audiences toward these kinds of human pleasures. No longer do we consider the crudely and violently sensual as inherently base, low, or vulgar. At least the crude, raw experience is "honest"; it genuinely "grabs you." It isn't full of "a lot of jive" about the ideal and the sublime. It is impossible to understand the cinema's aesthetic values of the last decade without also understanding the new sexual and moral values of the culture. Perhaps the cinema is the true twentieth-century art; it is probably the most sensually assaultive of all the arts. The pre-twentieth-century attitude toward explicit sexual stimulation by works of art was that such stimulation was vulgar, animalistic, and subhuman. (Of course, the twentieth century has also redefined the human animal's evolutionary relationship to the "lower" animals.) Even Croce mocks this "vulgar current of thought":

> . . . some have tried to deduce the pleasure of art from the echo of that of the sexual organs. . . . This theory is seasoned with much anecdotal erudition, heaven knows of what degree of credibility, as to the customs of savage peoples. . . . [*Aesthetic,* p. 83]

And Croce was a contemporary of Freud's.

A second explanation for the new assaultively kinetic film styles is the existence of technology to produce the kinesis. The huge wide screen, the total conversion to color, the magnificent stereophonic (indeed, quadra- and quintophonic) sound systems, the dizzying zoom lenses, are all tools that either did not exist at all twenty-five years ago or were not as flexible, efficient, and functional. With its new machines, the cinema can "grab" an audience (and thereupon proceed to shake, bash, and smash the hell out of it, leaving it limp) more violently, more forcefully, and more directly than can any other art. This direct sensual stimulation has perpetually led moviemakers of the last twenty years to experiment with devices akin to *Brave New World*'s "feelies": the electric shocks in *The Tingler*, Sensurround in *Earthquake*, Smell-o-Vision for *Scent of Mystery*. But this kind of grabbing is merely an extension (easily capable of overextension) of a kinetic power that has always been uniquely cinema's.

This overt kinetic power of the cinema experience explains why and how the cinema has legitimized, indeed redefined and redeemed, that "lower form" of mimetic pleasure—melodrama. Although the cinema may have seized upon melodrama in its infancy because of melodrama's popularity on the stages of that day, many of the cinema's later and most stunning representatives are still melodramas—*Stagecoach* (indeed much of Ford), *The Big Sleep* (and Hawks), *Psycho* (and Hitchcock), *Rashomon* (and Kurosawa), *The Rules of the Game, The Seventh Seal, La Strada* (even Renoir, Bergman, and Fellini), *Citizen Kane, Chinatown, Taxi Driver,* and so many more.

Melodrama, which might be defined as the excitation and stimulation of crude sensations (such as fear, sorrow, horror, and suspense), may well have been less appropriate to the stage where the richer subtleties of intellect and personality could be developed by the play of words. Those melodramatic pieces that seize their audience's passions in the theater almost never succeed in seizing them upon subsequent reading, for they inevitably play well but do not read well (and our system of values in the drama has been determined by the reading of texts—primarily because it has been determined by those who read). But because our experience with a cinema work can be infinitely repeated (unlike productions of plays that pass away), and because the kinetic stimulation of cinema defies publishing films as books (although some have been published), and because those who determine the values of films are unanimously opposed to evaluating cinema as if it were a book (if there is any unanimity in film thinking, this is it), the excitation and stimulation of melodrama seems not only appropriate to cinema but inherent in much of it.

Although there would seem to be a kind of inevitable evolutionary trend toward a purer and purer kinesis and a modernist cinema, there is no evidence that this trend is not simply a matter of contemporary taste, easily reversible. (Just as modernist fiction reached a kind of high point in Joyce, but now coexists with more rational and traditional structures; just as modernist drama reached its high point in the mid-1950s, but has since returned to more familiar mimetic methods.) If the modernist and traditional cinema, the purely kinetic and purely mimetic, coexist and intertwine, perhaps it is because the cinema has telescoped the lengthy traditions of the older arts into less than a single·century. The parallel historical arguments may simply not apply to cinema's unique history.

When a contemporary critic or film buff dislikes a film for being uncinematic, he or she usually means that it does not have *enough* kinesis in its cinematic style (as if kinesis in the cinema were an absolute good in itself, like happiness, and the more of it, the better). To condemn Chaplin according to the cinematic style of Kubrick is to condemn Henry Fielding according to the style of Henry James (which, by the way, literary critics have done). The purely kinetic power of the cinema is another of its unique *possibilities,* which is not, however, one of the essential qualities of every effective instance of it. Although music is most crudely powerful when huge symphony orchestras play loud, not all music is symphonic and orchestras do not always play loud.

At this point let me compile a brief list of those qualities that are absolutely unique to cinema but demonstrably not essential to every instance of it. There are three uniquely cinematic qualities, each of which has had its developers and defenders. Because there are three unique qualities, yet because the qualities are not compatible, it is not surprising that no theorist has yet been able to synthesize them. First, cinema is unique among the arts in the assaultive power and wide range of the purely kinetic effects it can produce. Can—but not must (for *Rules of the Game,* Ozu, *The Seventh Seal,* and *Casablanca* do not). Second, cinema is unique among the arts in that it can make space itself move. Can—but not must (for Chaplin and Astaire do not). Third, cinema is unique in that it can capture nature whole. Can—but not must (for *Caligari, Singin' in the Rain,* Oskar Fischinger, and cartoons do not). Is there any unique characteristic of cinema that every instance of it must necessarily exhibit? Cinema is unique among the arts in that it has an infinitely variable range of possibilities for integrating kinetic and mimetic effects, and every instance inevitably determines for itself the proportions and the balance between the two.

4/Kinesis and Conviction

One of the common ways to talk about movies is in terms of their central themes: *Modern Times* contrasts the inhuman demands of immense machines with the natural spontaneity of one man's responses; *Citizen Kane* reveals the corrupting power of wealth and the poverty of a life without love; *Rules of the Game* notes the ironic and necessary contradictions between sincerity and form in human civilization; *Amarcord* affectionately chronicles the loss of youth; *Persona* probes the instability and indistinctness of familiar psychological definitions of human personality. And so on. Though these phrases are obvious simplifications, the simplest statements will suffice for this argument.

There are two primary objections to this kind of movie criticism. The first is that it is "literary" to discuss cinema works thematically, since literary works can be discussed in the same way: *King Lear* develops the perilous frailty of "bare unaccommodated man" who cannot survive in the immense and neutral universe without love; *Great Expectations* traces the development of boy into man by his learning what kinds of expectations are greater than others; and so on. The second is that such short and simple statements seem flat and puny ("reductive" in the critical jargon) in comparison to the two hours of our experience with a moving movie. (Isn't precisely the same true with a play or novel?)

Victor Perkins is especially unsympathetic to this kind of movie criticism:

> . . . significance is locked into the picture's form. We are taken beyond the realm of the language substitute which provides an *illustration* of messages, opinions, and themes. . . . We can summarize *Marnie*'s content and label some of its themes—dream and reality, fraud and self-deception, guilt and atonement, identity, isolation, and so forth—but this does not define the richness and complexity of the film itself. If it did, the film would be superfluous. . . . [*Film as Film*, pp. 119, 154]

There are a great many who think that *Marnie* is superfluous in any case. An opposite approach to thematic criticism is "structuralism" or "formal analysis," which pays strict attention to the formal composition and visual relationships of the individual frames rather than to their meaning and thematic/fictional content. Although this method is much practiced in France and in certain graduate cinema programs in America, it has not frequently found its way into American print.

Since I am one of those who practice thematic criticism that "does not define the richness and complexity" of movies themselves, I think it would be useful to set down what I believe such criticism claims and does not claim, and what exactly this thematic criticism implies about the work of movie art. Such short statements are merely a form of shorthand, a way of setting down the spine, the core, the kernel, the trunk, the nucleus (whichever metaphor you prefer) of the work that holds all its pieces together. The central theme of a work is its First Principle, the primary law of that artistic microcosm—the idea that binds together all the pieces of that artistic universe in the same way that gravity binds all of us and the objects around us and the air we breathe to the earth. There is more to the earth than gravity, but without gravity there isn't any earth. Precisely the same is true of the "gravity" of one of these microcosms of art (and Perkins believes, as do I, that the movie is a microcosm).

Now, it is quite true that many of these thematic statements are very trite (even if the movies seem quite complex). To boil *Citizen Kane* down to "What the world needs now is love, sweet love" is to distill it into the sappy gruel of a popular song. And that popular song was literally the theme of another movie (*Bob and Carol and Ted and Alice*), which indicates that these themes are "very old hat." The idea of love has been "done before" in *King Lear* and "done again" in *Bob and Carol* and no doubt "done to death" ever after. As the wife of a playwright said in Ionesco's *Victimes du devoir,* a play about playwriting, "There's nothing new under the sun—even when there isn't any." There aren't any new themes (nor, therefore, any old ones that no longer apply: isn't that the meaning of the "universality" of art?). What is the point of an artist's building (either consciously or intuitively) his universe of art around such old, trite ideas that we already know?

Because our surrogate life in the individual universe of art makes us *know* what we already know. And our experience of *knowing* these things, even in two different works that "say" the same thing when reduced to a simple sentence, is totally different, special, unique. The thematic statement is a distillation of the experience, although it is not the experience itself. However, unless we truly have conviction in the experience, we can have no conviction in the concluding thematic statements about it. When thematic statements run to paragraphs and pages (rather than short phrases), it is because the critic builds into the thematic statement the sources of his/her conviction as he/she experienced the work. For the critic, the thematic statements have genuine substance and body; they are not empty, trite, and old, but are filled with the conviction of the critic's personal experience with the work (hopefully, his/her arguments are also filled with it), which makes that precise experience unlike any other with any other work.

On the other hand, we have all had the experience of reading thematic distillations of movies that seem to have nothing to do with our experience of them. For example, some European critics see Jerry Lewis's *The Nutty Professor* as a comment on the puritanical contradictions in American sexuality that reduce male sexual responses to one of two stereotyped poses (the lecher and the eunuch), revealing the exaggerations and insufficiencies of both.[1] For me, the Jerry Lewis film has nothing to do with defining the qualities of bad lovers. That thematic issue does not seem to be the source of "gravity" for that film (Jekyll and Hyde is closer, and theme and variation on two contrasting stereotypes closer still). The relation of thematic summary and experiential conviction is, therefore, circular and paradoxical. Our conviction in the experience of a work of art produces a thematic conclusion about the source of unity in the microcosm, but the thematic conclusion can only be tested against our experience in living through the work. Perhaps this circular and dependent relationship between conviction and conclusion is parallel to Perkins's view that "significance is locked into the picture's form."

What produces our conviction in a work of cinema? Although the conclusions about film and literary works (the thematic statements) may appear similar, the experiences (the sources of conviction) for reaching these conclusions differ completely for the different forms. In cinema, the kinesis of picture and sound is the major (if not the sole) source of our conviction in the experience, whereas in the novel there is no kinesis at all, strictly speaking. True, the arrangement of type on a page produces a kind of kinetic effect (exploited by such novelists as Sterne and Joyce). But, as George Bluestone convincingly demonstrates in *Novels into Film*, the apprehension of narrative fiction is a conceptual process, triggered by the abstract sign system of words rather than the more concrete and physical sign system of sounds and sights. In the drama, the powers of kinesis are subordinate (which accounts for the fact that there can be different shades of experience in different productions of *Hamlet*, but all of them bear more resemblances to one another and to the experience of simply reading the play than differences). But our perception of cinema depends exclusively upon kinetic stimulation.

Those kinetic stimuli that produce conviction in a cinema experience cannot be easily categorized (for the same reason that semiotics cannot produce an "alphabet" of film effects). Indeed, this notion of conviction reveals the essential difficulty of the study of film semiotics. The semiologist confuses two questions that are paradoxically interdependent and yet separate: How does a sign communicate its information? and How does a sign communicate its information *effectively?* Our having conviction in a moment of a film implies both that we know (understand) what the moment means and that we *know* (feel) what the moment wants us to feel. Denotation and connotation in the cinema are inextricable.

Every effective moment in the work of cinema is the product of integrating several filmic, cinematic, and structural devices. The particular integration produces an absolutely original trope, not precisely identical to any other integration of devices that has been used before. And any effective film is an accumulation of these effective moments in which we have conviction, bound together by the central thematic source of "gravity," of unity in the microcosm. Perhaps I can give some sense of how these integrations of various kinetic devices produce (or fail to produce) conviction by specific discussion of how and why some have succeeded or failed to produce it for me.

In *Aparajito*, the second film of Satyajit Ray's Apu trilogy, the director wants to convey the precise moment of the death of the boy's father (to be mirrored and magnified, at the end of the film, by the moment of the boy's reaction to the death of his mother). To do this, Ray selects a simile which, stated linguistically, seems quite trite: the departure of a man's spirit is like birds flying off into the sky. Ray conveys the idea of "like" with the traditional means of cinematic simile—montage. He cuts from the father's deathbed to the birds (just as Eisenstein cut from workers to ox in *Strike*). But it is Ray's manner of cutting that brings this simile to life, making it quite unlike any other simile of death and birds I can imagine.

Ray's camera begins on the man's face, as it collapses on the pillow of his deathbed with startling suddenness. At the same moment as this sudden collapse of head on pillow, there is a startling sound of a crack on the sound track (which is, at that moment, a completely unmotivated crack). Ray cuts immediately and just as suddenly to a close shot of a

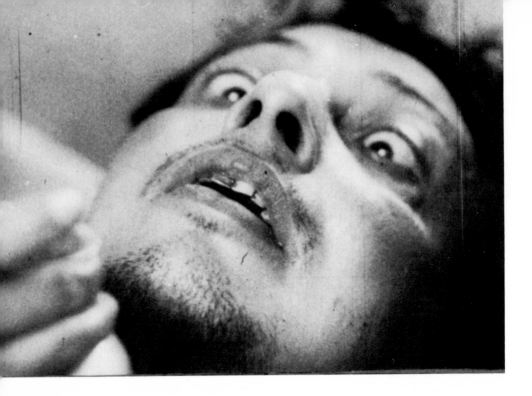

The kinetic tools of cinema simile in *Aparajito:* from the dead man's collapsing head, to scurrying birds, to their graceful flight.

flock of birds, suddenly scared off a rooftop and into flight, seemingly startled by the sound of the crack itself (the crack of a rifle, perhaps?). Slightly more than one second later (twenty-eight frames), Ray cuts again to a more distant shot of these birds. But after this technique of startling movement, startling sound, and startling cutting, Ray shifts into a more languid gear to watch the birds flying off into a sunset-streaked sky—the graceful, lyric calm of their liquid motion, swirling in circular patterns as they melt into the distance. But he lets us watch this flight and dwell in this languidness only briefly, perhaps five seconds, before he jerks us back into the story, cutting short our pleasure in the gracefully flying birds as life has cut short the existence of the father. The flight of the birds on screen is like the man's life itself, so beautiful yet so ephemeral, so short. The moment is not only exquisite in itself; it is a startling and effective depiction of the moment of death, of loss, of departure from life.

In *Pather Panchali*, the first film of this same director's trilogy, there is another, equally effective simile (I stay with Ray because he is a master of simile, and this mastery is neither occasional nor accidental). Let me first state the simile verbally again: Ray compares the battle against death to the battle by human beings to keep the storms of nature out of their houses. Death invades the human body as a storm invades the shelter of human homes. Ray personifies the forces of death as a violent wind which attempts to invade a human home to extinguish a fragile candle (a concrete symbol for the dying girl). Now, the metaphoric parallel of candles to human lives is a familiar film metaphor, which I have seen used far less effectively in at least two previous films (Lubitsch's *Madame du Barry* and Lang's *Destiny*). Ray, however, converts a potentially static and dead metaphor into a vital and dramatic battle of life against death, people against nature.

A mother sits a nighttime vigil beside the bed of her feverish daughter at the same time that a violent storm rages outside their home. Ray brings the simile to life by bringing the storm to life. Not only is there violent blowing on the sound track, but the storm rattles the creaky door, shakes the rickety windows, threatens to extinguish the flickering flame of the tiny candle that is the sole source of light in the dark room. With his cutting (from the various specific assaults of the wind against the feeble door, window, and candle to the figures of mother and daughter), Ray personalizes the storm into a concrete assailant (like the burglars invading the mother's house in Griffith's *The Lonely Villa*), against whom the mother is struggling. But since it is impossible to struggle against an immense natural force with such pathetic protection, Ray's mother can only sit, and wait, and hope. In the end, the storm wins, of course; the next morning we see the storm's wreckage all over the village. And we see the mother—sitting, staring, motionless—beside the inert corpse of her daughter. The tiny flame of the candle has gone out.

These two film passages are so mimetically successful in depicting the moment of death because they are so kinetically successful in their selection of sound and images and cutting, and in the precise visual and temporal relationships between them. On the other hand, there is a section of Abel Gance's highly praised *Napoléon* (ridiculously overpraised, I think—primarily because its extant fragments are highly uneven, and very few in America have ever seen them) that ludicrously fails to develop a similar simile. On paper, there is nothing intrinsically less interesting about Gance's simile: he likens the natural tempest that Bonaparte faces in a tiny boat adrift at sea (after fleeing Corsica) to the human tempest in the French Assembly, which will lead to the Reign of Terror. The implication is that both Napoleon and the French nation are in danger of sinking beneath the stormy sea of history and, further, only by Napoleon's remaining afloat can the French nation remain "afloat." To parallel the two "storms" Gance uses montage, as did Ray. He crosscuts between a shot of Napoleon struggling against the tempest and shots of the human agitation, anger, and chaos inside the Assembly chamber.*

How does Gance go wrong? First, he cuts back and forth between these two tempests at least ten times (that means ten of each), each cut lasting at least ten seconds (and most much longer). After the first series (and certainly after the second), it is clear that we see two tempests—one natural, one political—the two united by history and the single man whose survival guarantees the survival of the other. All right; since we understand the point of the simile after the first crosscut or two, we expect Gance to show us more if he continues to crosscut. He, however, shows us not more but more of the same—more tempest at sea, more tempest in the Assembly. Although the shots vary a bit (slightly different angles, distances, and subjects), they all signify the same information: miscellaneous turmoil.

And as Gance shows more and more of the same intercut shots, he unwittingly shows less and less. First, the shots of the little boat in the storm become ludicrous because man, boat, and sail are absolutely drenched; it would be impossible for any animate or inanimate object to stay afloat in such a deluge. And then we begin to see quite clearly that the whole tempest is rigged, that the boat floats in some studio tank, that the drenching rain is of the throw-another-water-bucket variety. Second, when Gance returns to the Assembly for about the fifth time, he starts rocking the camera back and forth—so we get the idea that this is like a boat rocking on the ocean (an idea we already got several crosscuts ago). And then Gance repeats this camera-rocking maneuver for several series of crosscuts (as if we did not get the idea the first time).

The idea may have been worth a fifteen-second series of two crosscuts. (How long does Eisenstein extend his classic crosscuts? Not very, since he realizes that with such a device less is more and more is less.) Gance gives us a five-minute sequence (it felt endless) out of a fifteen-second idea. Of course, an audience can easily lose conviction in the sequence (and, therefore, in the idea it tried to express): not only be-

---

* Let me qualify my critical remarks by mentioning, first, that this sequence of "The Two Tempests" was originally shot in "polyvision"—using three screens and not just one. Second, that the sequence, as it exists today, may not reflect Gance's original cutting. But whatever the sequence may have been is irrelevant to my point—which is the reason for its failure to gain my conviction as I saw it projected. Further, Kevin Brownlow, one of Gance's most avid defenders, finds the sequence "astonishing . . . even on one screen" (see *The Parade's Gone By,* p. 562). Such a judgment is another reminder of our unique thresholds of conviction. There were, however, both snickers and boos at the screening that evening in the *Cinématheque Française,* which indicates that there were others whose thresholds of conviction resembled mine.

cause our intelligence is insulted (a director ought to know when an audience will get the idea), but also because the kinetic appeal of the cuts is identical, therefore repetitious, therefore boring. And the kinetic rhythms of the cuts make no sense or impact whatever. The ultimate result is that the idea behind the crosscuts begins to seem trite and ludicrous, and that idea was the reason for Gance's making his jingoistic film in the first place. To use this puerile sequence to demonstrate either that montage is necessarily unconvincing or that film is necessarily inadequate at depicting abstract ideas is not critically cricket.

A comparison of the Ray and Gance similes leads to a general conclusion about simile in the cinema. The value of a simile in literature is usually dependent on the interest of the two terms separated by the "like." (My love is like a summer's day; dawn is like it has rosy fingers.) The "like" is a simple and neutral equation mark; sometimes it is so neutral that it is invisible and the simile is technically a metaphor. In literature, if the terms on either side of the "like" (stated or implied) bear an interesting, surprising, evocative, original, illuminating relationship, the simile is successful. But in cinema, the quality of *like*ness must itself be developed, and if it is interestingly, evocatively, powerfully developed (rather than under- or over-developed) by the film's kinesis, then the simile succeeds. The manner of making the comparison, rather than the inherent interest in the idea of the comparison itself, is at the heart of a successful cinema simile. This is perhaps another instance of significance "locked into" the form.

The kinetic manner of the cinema's conveying its mimetic matter controls our conviction in many other ways. Take, for example, the "ogre" scene in *Citizen Kane,* the one in which Kane destroys Susan's bedroom after she walks out on him. The scene is so effective in itself that it has been frequently excerpted as the one outstanding example of the movie's power whenever Welles makes an appearance on a television talk show. What produces my conviction in the scene and of what does it want to convince us? The scene represents Kane's nadir, the final stopping place on the journey we have traveled with him. It is his ugliest moment in the movie. Also his last (except for the quiet coda of the mirror-reflection shot, as he walks down the empty corridor of his castle and his life). And so our final impression of Kane reflects the ultimate barrenness and bankruptcy of the life he has led (partially of his own choosing, partially thrust upon him). What makes the scene so successfully brutal and ugly?

First, the man himself has grown physically ugly. The bald, barren scalp, the puffy eyes, the squashed nose, are grotesque and pointed reminders of the man we had seen as youthful and vibrant only an hour

The ogre destroying Susan's bedroom in *Citizen Kane*. The low angle and grotesque lighting accentuates the impression of a beast in the cumulative act of destruction. (Note the room's childlike delicacy with its tiny, painted animals on the ceiling beams.)
Courtesy Janus Films

earlier. Age does not necessarily make people look ugly and brutal, but Welles has made age turn Kane into a non-hairy ape, implying the brutal ugliness that had potentially lurked beneath the surface. Second, Welles's camera angle from below thrusts this apish presence upward in front of the lens, towering above us, his swollen but elongated body surmounted by that terrible, too-far-away head. The angle also pushes that head upward so that it threatens to ram the ceiling, which, in turn, appears to encage him (of course, the low camera angle dictated the low ceilings). The effect is of a huge animal in a tiny cage, in a rage to get out of it. Third, the sound track emphasizes the animality: no dialogue, no music, only the accelerating noise of crashing objects as we watch and hear a human beast in the process of cumulative destruction. Finally, the movement in the scene also emphasizes the enraged beast: it begins slowly, deliberately; then begins accelerating as the animal rage to destroy feeds itself and produces purer and purer destruction, until the human being has been completely transformed into a brutish and irrational force of animal destruction.

Even the end of this violently destructive orgy suggests the animal and the subhuman. Kane's grasping the glass ball stills his savage rage with irrationally sudden swiftness, like the vicious lion who suddenly recognizes Androcles or one of the mythic beasts suddenly hypnotized by the voice and lyre of Orpheus. The motion ceases altogether and the sound track suddenly becomes absolutely silent. I have great conviction in the end, the finish of Charles Foster Kane. Nothing remains inside the man, only an outer shell that can be reflected in an endless series of mirrors (like the newsreel refractions of his life and the refractive accounts of his friends and enemies).

In contrast, I recently read a discussion of an earlier scene in the film in which I have no conviction—or rather, I have great conviction in the scene but not the kind of conviction that the critic claims I ought to have.[2] The critic's aim is to develop an apology for Rosebud, which he, like many others, finds a banal and sentimental symbol if interpreted as a sign of Kane's "lost youth." He argues that Rosebud is not relevant to the story of Kane at all but to the search for that story by the newsreel reporter. According to the critic, the need to find a Rosebud is a rule of the newsreel game, and there is a tension between Rawlston (the newsreel boss), the kind of establishment figure who believes in such sappy sentimentality, and Thompson (the reporter doing the leg and talk work), who looks cynically at such perfect pieces that complete jigsaw puzzles. The tension between the two men is supposedly established in the projection-room scene, and the critic brings two pieces of evidence to develop this tension. First, he cites dialogue from the scene (which can indeed be read so as to suggest tension). Second, he compares the scene to typical newspaper-genre movies of the thirties (as did Pauline Kael), such as *The Front Page* and *His Girl Friday,* in which there is a central and similar boss-reporter tension.

Now, I have absolutely no conviction in the existence of this Rawlston-Thompson tension in *Citizen Kane.* Why not? First, if I explained the existence of such a tension in the preceding paragraph without the parentheses identifying the characters, you might well ask who are Rawlston and Thompson. Not Thompson, perhaps, but how many times did you see the movie before you knew the name of Thompson's boss? An infinity, perhaps, because his name is uttered only three times, flippantly and indistinctly. Is it likely that the film's "Maguffin" and central symbol would pivot around a virtual anonymity?*

Even if so, the problem with the analysis of this scene that sets up a "tension" between one anonymity and another is that it does not discuss whether the camera views this "tension" tensely. For me, the tension in the projection room is between being able to see and hear what's happening and not being able to do so. Because Gregg Toland knew how to take pictures and light sets, I feel that this tension is intentional (indeed, it is a tension in which I have great conviction), that the scene is supposed to look dark, shadowy, light-streaked, smoke-screened, that the dialogue is supposed to be half-audible, informal, not fully intelligible.

Why should Welles want us to feel this? Because he does not want us to see or hear very much in the scene. Why not? Because he deliberately wants the entire reporter process, the search for Rosebud, to be conducted by absolutely neutral, anonymous figures for the most obvious, least complicated human reasons. He does not want the newsreel to get in the way of the story of Kane; he wants it to be useful to get *at* that story (which it certainly is). Thompson remains a blank, a cipher throughout the film. He is a shadow in a phone booth. He is a half-silhouetted face, or a pair of wire-rimmed glasses, or the back of a hat, or the padded shoulder of the back of a suit. William Alland, who plays him, looks something like Charles Lane, I think. (Charles Lane, alias Charles Levinson, played the cynical reporter in the Capra newspaper pictures and others.) And I can't even conjure up a memory of what "Rawlston" looks like, for in the few shots that Toland takes of him his face is always deliberately engulfed by shadows.

---

* The "Maguffin" is the name that Hitchcock gave to the tiny detail that propels the entire complex plot of a film—such as the meaning of "the 39 steps."

Citizen Kane: the depiction of Thompson and Rawlston as perpetual blanks, shadows, and ciphers. (Note the hot spot of light on Rawlston's shirt and tie; it could just as easily have illuminated his face.)*Courtesy Janus Films*

If the dialogue is important in the projection-room scene, I ought to be able to see and hear it. In fact, I must be made to see and hear and pay attention to it. Because the opening dialogue scene of *His Girl Friday* is brightly lit, photographed straight on, in fairly standard American two-shots, we can and do pay attention to it. If the dialogue of the opening scene is supposed to stay with us throughout the quest for Rosebud, Welles has made a terrible error in shooting, lighting, and recording the scene in this manner.

I have conviction, however, in the easygoing, sloppy, informal, intimate professionalism of the talk in the scene (this is indeed one of the movie's legitimate relations to the newspaper genre). And the shadowy, smoke-infested, nonlit lighting increases that conviction for me. The only line of dialogue I take away from the scene is the final one (Rawlston's) about uncovering Rosebud: "It'll probably turn out to be a very simple thing." And I take it away because immediately after "thing," Welles assaults our ears with an overwhelming clap of Gothic thunder on the sound track (a reminder of Welles's radio apprenticeship), which one can interpret as either a sign of the film's trashy-Gothic origins (Kael) or an ironic laugh by its creator-gods, or both.

This Rawlston-Thompson theory could be developed only by a reading (indeed, a very careful reading) of the screenplay. Its problem seems to be similar to a lot of scholarly dramatic criticism: it smells too much of the lamp. The analytic conclusion is not the product of direct experience with the work, of personal conviction in it, but the product of study with the "text" (except the "text" of a film is even further from the actual aesthetic experience than the text of a play). Such criticism is more like fiddling with the pieces of one of Susan's jigsaw puzzles, rather than observing and delineating the careful configuration that the artist has "locked into the picture's form."

But an even more important question must be asked about the alleged banality of the Rosebud symbol, which began the critic's ingenious search for a less banal explanation. Even granting that Rosebud symbolizes "lost youth," and even granting that such an idea is inherently banal when reduced to words, I wonder if the symbol feels banal in the course of our experiencing the discovery of the sled whose name is Rosebud. Welles begins the process of our discovery with a workman treating this object of great importance as a piece of trash, carelessly and routinely consigning the junk to the flames. Only when Welles cuts to a close-up of the sled do we discover that the trash is really the all-important Rosebud, as we see its name and the rose on its face. (And with all our viewings and re-viewings of *Citizen Kane*, let us not forget the surprise of discovering that Rosebud was his sled when we saw the movie the first time.)

But even after our initial discovery, Welles does not permit our vision of Rosebud to remain still or static. Juxtaposed with the discovery, we immediately see the flames begin to lick away at this finally recovered mystery. Rather than conceptualizing "lost youth" at that particular moment, I am asked to participate in the death of this object. I watch the lacquered wood begin to peel, bubble, and crack with the heat. I recall that the natural environment of this object is cold and watery (snow), not hot and fiery. I recall the earliest scenes and imagery of the movie, when the object (like the boy who possessed it) existed in its natural environment rather than this present one. There is a terrible feeling of loss and destruction in the sled's demise, as well as the irony that the answer to the great mystery is gone forever, like Kane himself. Only after this experience has ended, well after the movie has ended, might I begin to transfer the kinetic stimuli into the static conception: "lost youth." And even when I do, I then reflect on the fact that only the audience and the camera discovered what Rosebud was. So whatever it means, that knowledge is the unique possession of storytellers, audiences, and the gods, not the mere mortals who came into contact with Charles Foster Kane. Kane knew Rosebud and believed in it as a symbol of his "lost youth," but need we do the same?

The test of success for any cinematic moment must begin with the specific way the moment is experienced, just as the success of a musical phrase can be determined only from experiencing it in a musical context rather than in translating it into an adjectival description after the experience. The Gance simile failed to produce conviction in a moment of the movie kinetically (it became repetitious and dull to watch) and, hence, it failed mimetically (I understood the simile, but I found it stupid and worthless). The *Kane* Rosebud discussion showed the failure of a conclusion about the film's mimetic intentions that was not supported (that was indeed contradicted) by its kinesis. The successful moments in both Ray and Welles display the perfect interworking and interdependence of mimesis and kinesis, in which what was imitated was inseparable from how it was imitated, and in which how it was imitated produced the conviction that we were intimately experiencing what was imitated. Because the issue is extremely difficult (and because our sense of conviction is an absolutely personal response), I would like to explore a few more examples. My personal experiences of conviction may not be yours, but by giving a few more of them, perhaps you can translate mine into yours.

Modern Times is a series of comic confrontations between man and modern society, business, and machines. One of its most famous confrontations is between Charlie and the mechanical feeding machine, a perfect statement of the movie's contrast between the artificial and the natural: the machine converts one of the essential, natural human functions—eating—into a mechanical process. However good the idea (and it is very good), the sequence would not be able to fulfill itself and occupy some five minutes of screen time without retaining our conviction for its duration. Chaplin does indeed retain our conviction in the entire lengthy sequence (as usual) and he retains it in his usual manner: by the supple and hypnotic kinesis of his movement. But wait a minute, you say. Chaplin doesn't move in the sequence. His body is strapped into the machine, which merely pushes food at him. Even his head has been clamped into a vise to keep his mouth from moving away from the spindly metallic arms of the feeder. Those arms move in the sequence, of course, and the comic delight of their motion (a combination of robot regularity and quirky jerkiness) contributes to our conviction. But how can Chaplin move?

In the eyes. The eyes (and eyebrows) are virtually the only part of him that can move (his mouth is also occupied—with the food), and it is the eyes that separate Charlie (and any human being) from a machine. The eyes show their greatest movement (and greatest wariness) in reacting to the food blotter, the wooden dowel that swings in to blot Charlie's lips and mustache after each course (even a food machine is concerned about etiquette). Each time the blotter moves toward his face, the Chaplin eyes watch the potential assailant with anxiety, puzzlement, defensiveness (we know Charlie's instinctual defensiveness against any aggressive movement toward his face or person). We can almost see his eyes changing focus as the wooden enemy proceeds toward his face. And as the dowel retreats, the Chaplin eyes follow its departure intently, making sure that it has actually departed without giving him a kick or a bash somewhere or other.

The Chaplin eyes give the sequence life by keeping our focus on its human center. Chaplin does not simply treat us to a screwy machine (as do some of the Snub Pollard films); he perpetually and pointedly reminds us of the fact that even unanimated humans are more supple, more alive, than animated but inanimate machines. The eyes also give the sequence its suspense, for it is the eyes that tell us of Charlie's doubts about the effectiveness of this machine, his suspicion that even this tasty meal (which he does not often get the opportunity to eat) cannot end well. It doesn't, of course, when the machine goes haywire and the blotter becomes the bashing assailant he always knew it would.

A completely different kinetic element is responsible for my conviction in one of the final sequences of Akira Kurosawa's *Dodes'ka-den*. The sequence is the movie's climactic coda; Kurosawa's camera explores a series of colored drawings for about ninety seconds, accompanied by a lyrical musical passage on the sound track. But this simple combination of drawings and music is a restatement and intensification of everything in the movie that has preceded it. Because very few people in America know this film (like Renoir's *The Golden Coach*, the film is the "sleeper" masterpiece of a master), let me summarize its issues.

Dodes'ka-den is one of Kurosawa's last movies (1970), a synthesis of his earlier *The Lower Depths* and *Ikiru*, but shot in dazzling Tohocolor. Like *The Lower Depths*, the movie is a study of a rather large social grouping (perhaps a dozen principal figures) who live in a wretched slum (not a single room, as in *The Lower Depths*, but a little "village" of slovenly shacks), and who have absolutely no hope for any better life in the future. Like *Ikiru*, the film is set in modern-day Japan and it examines the different kinds of possible human choices that exist in closed and determined circumstances where there are no genuinely good choices. One kind of choice is what Ibsen called "the Life Lie" in *The Wild Duck*—some kind of illusion that allows people to continue to exist (that life will be better; that their lives are not so bad; that they are in love or in lust; that they are doing something of value). The other choice is death (spiritual or physical). Kurosawa needed the large group of characters for precisely the same reason that Gorky did—to examine the different variations of response to the same experience.

The movie's title is essential to Kurosawa's thematic investigation. The word does not mean anything; it is a piece of onomatopoeia. It is the linguistic equivalent of the sound that a streetcar's wheels seem to produce as they roll along the tracks. (It rhymes with "Confess again," accent on the "fess." If you start saying dodes'ka-den slowly, and then gradually accelerate until saying it at top speed, you will hear what a good piece of onomatopoeia it is.) The character who uses the word is a young man (perhaps seventeen) who is mentally retarded. The boy thinks he is a streetcar driver. Whenever he goes anywhere outdoors, he "drives" his invisible streetcar, miming all the motions of a driver (the kinesis of cinema is brilliantly suited, of course, to this mime), chanting "dodes'ka-den" at top voice and top speed, halting his chant only when he needs to "blow his horn" (a high-pitched honk-squeal) at some pedestrian who has unsuspectingly walked onto the imaginary "tracks." Kurosawa's point here is that the streetcar obviously does not exist and the boy is certainly "tram crazy," as the normal children, half his age, shout. But what else does this human being have to live for? Even an imaginary streetcar is better than a real nothing, especially since that streetcar exists so vividly for the crazy boy.

Now, the drawings of which I spoke were made by this boy. They are drawings of streetcars; seemingly hundreds of them cover the walls of his room; they are his wallpaper. The drawings are childish, two-dimensional, out-of-perspective, poorly proportioned line drawings in multicolored crayon. They look very much like a display after one of those sessions when the second-grade class spends the entire day drawing streetcars. There are primitive lines and splotches of color, and the overwhelming first impression is of a series of pathetic-silly attempts to reproduce streetcars realistically, betrayed by the inability and immaturity of the artist (especially pathetic since the boy is roughly ten years too old for this primitive style). When Kurosawa's camera prowls over these drawings toward the end of the film, it is the second time it has looked at them. Toward the beginning of the film, he looks at them through the eyes of the boy's mother (who knows her son's affliction). Kurosawa uses an assaultive montage, accompanied by percussive sounds on the track, to examine the drawings this first time, producing a violent, threatening, aggressive effect. The drawings trouble the mother, and Kurosawa wants them to trouble us, too.

But when he returns to the drawings at the end, the effect is entirely different. Kurosawa's camera travels over them slowly and smoothly (no use of montage); it glides gracefully across their surfaces, accompanied not by percussion, but by a gracefully gliding piece of lyrical music. And as the camera lovingly glides across them, the lighting seems to flicker and pulse, making the pictures even more alluring and hypnotic. The effect is, first, of overwhelming beauty; the pathetically childish pictures suddenly seem exquisitely beautiful. Second, the effect is tender, gentle, and compassionate; the supple smoothness of music and camera softens our perception of the pictures. And, third, there is a feeling of consummate sadness, that such pathetic pictures should seem so beautiful, that such things are all that a human being has in life, that the life he lives appears the same to him as those silly, impossible pictures. And yet it is kinder to him and for him that he sees life as the pictures rather than as we see the pictures.

This exploration of the drawings means nothing in itself; it contributes nothing to the plot, no new information whatever. It is a coda, a summary of everything that has gone before, a prolonged moment of pure passion (and pure kinesis) in which Kurosawa opens the floodgates of our compassion and sorrow, which he has kept dammed in us throughout the development of the film, allowing our feelings to pour out and engulf us. (Kurosawa is a master of these climactic floodgates: recall the swing scene in *Ikiru,* another coda of pure passion, and the assassination of Washizu in *Throne of Blood.*) Without our understanding the issues of the film that preceded it, this moment of passion could never exist for us (could never gain our conviction). But without the slow languidness of camera and music and the visual beauty of the masses of color, the passion could never exist for us either.

Kinesis also controls our conviction in the experience of experimental films. Bruce Conner's *A Movie* (which is not a movie in the sense defined in the first chapter) is a satirical, twelve-minute compilation of stock footage, of fragments of movies (and newsreels, documentaries, etc.) that happened to be lying around in some film collection, library, or bin. The primary subjects of this footage are forms of violent disaster: Indians on the warpath, cowboys shooting pistols, animals stampeding, racing cars crashing, zeppelins aflame, aerial dogfights with the loser plummeting to earth in flames, political assassinations, firing squads, and the atomic bomb. But Conner interweaves several other kinds of subjects with these disasters that seem entirely consistent with them: daredevil acrobats perform stunts on the tops of city buildings (are we, like them, flirting with disaster?); a woman undresses in a snippet from a pornographic film (isn't all this destruction also a form of pornography?).

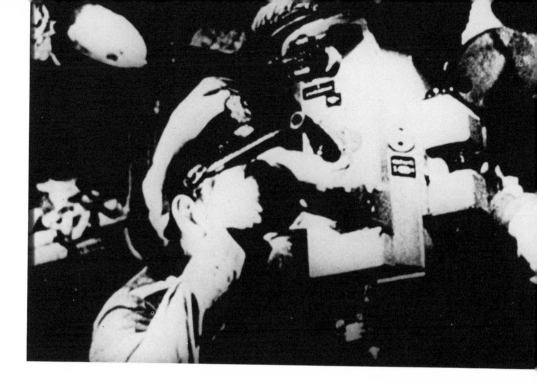

Two consecutive shots from *A Movie:* making meaning from miscellaneous pieces of found footage. The periscope of a B-movie submarine spies a porno pinup.

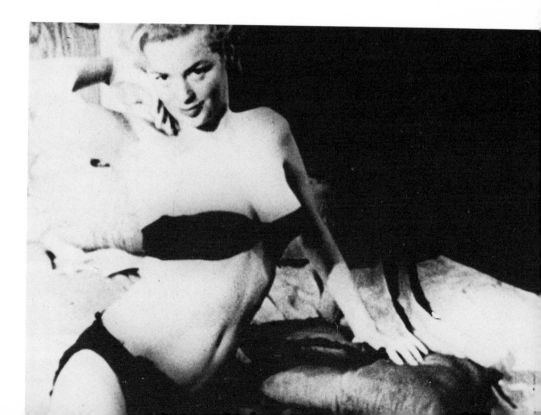

In one delightful sequence of clips, Conner yokes together B-movie footage, porno-film footage, and newsreel footage. A naval officer looks through his periscope (cheap submarine movie), spies a woman undressing (porno), fires his torpedoes (either from the submarine movie or from documentary footage), and produces the orgasmic explosion of the atomic bomb. The implication of the montage sequence is, clearly, that man's war drive is also his sex drive (did Kubrick see *A Movie* before he made his movie *Dr. Strangelove?*), and that man's movie machines, like all his other machines, are devoted to these two inextricable, destructive, and unnatural (indeed, anti-natural) desires.

This compilation of catastrophes is amusing, of course. There is such a plethora of death, war, and rapacity that the deaths of human beings before our eyes—in auto crashes, from aerial dog fights, before firing squads—become both funny and predictable. This miscellaneous "stock" footage is so unified in its catastrophic content that the extraordinariness of disaster becomes ordinary and commonplace, unremarkable and inconsequential. Disaster, like the footage itself, becomes "stock." Further, the coincidence of finding so much consistency in such miscellaneous and accidental footage seems to betray an inherent consistency in the cinema.

But even this amusing stunt would be worth only a minute or two without Conner's careful control of two kinetic appeals. The first is his visual sensitivity to the vectors, the directions of each catastrophe; the disasters occur in contrapuntal directions within the screen rectangle. Bombs fall *downward;* flames shoot *upward;* bullets fly from plane to plane *on the diagonal;* the horses gallop *right* or *left* or directly *toward* us; the autos careen around the *oval* track before *tumbling over* themselves; the zeppelins collapse *inward;* the bridge wobbles *up* and *down* before plummeting *downward*. The conflicting patterns of movement of these frenziedly destructive objects within the frame are a perpetual delight to the constantly exercised eye.

The second is Conner's rhythmic sensitivity to the pace of this destruction and his linking those rhythms to an ironically appropriate musical score. The film contains three "movements," each carefully synchronized to the tones and rhythms of Ottorino Respighi's *The Pines of Rome*. Conner's first movement, like Respighi's, is playfully exuberant, rhythmic, and fast. The disasters succeed each other at a frantic, *prestissimo* pace, which gradually accelerates throughout the movement. The gleeful music drives the visual rhythms while, at the same time, mocking, belying the catastrophic content. The *accelerando* is a common rhythmic device for experimental films since it provides a way to treat visual images as if they were musical phrases. But it is also a common rhythmic device for com-

Plates 1 and 2 (above). The color system of *The Red Desert:* for everyday reality, the drab neutrality of pale colors and weak light; for the fairy-tale story of escape, the sparkling brilliance of bright color and blazing sunlight.

Plate 3. Interiors in *The Red Desert* use the same light-color values as the outdoor scenes: the red walls of the orgy sequence.

Plates 4, 5, and 6. Three filmstrips: the succession of absolutely different frames in *Blazes;* the use of varying frames and tints to depict a child's-eye vision of experience in *Dog Star Man; Mothlight* is made of natural objects (rather than photographs of such objects) and there are no frames. (See page 117)

Plate 7 (left). *Playtime:* the apparition of Sacre Cœur on the glass door of the modern café. (See pages 196-199)

Plate 8. *Scenes From A Marriage:* the far shot of the separated and separating couple in "The Illiterates" sequence. (See pages 202-203)

Plate 9. *The Wild Bunch:* Pike's retreating back. (See pages 203-205)

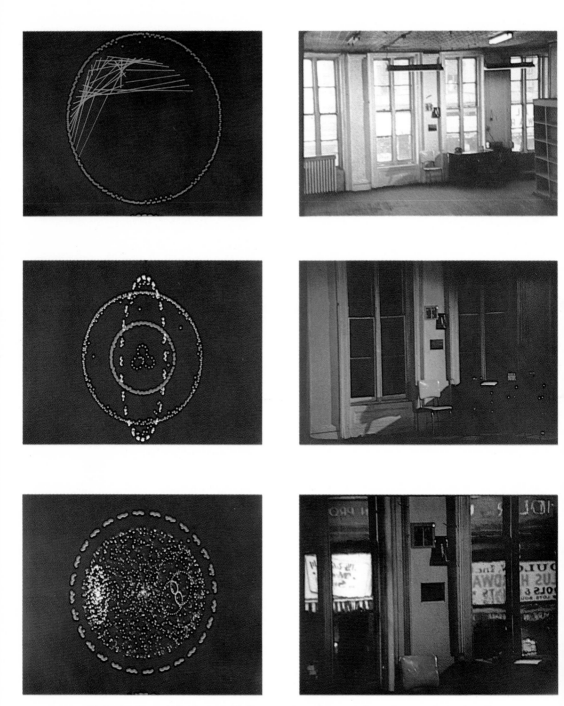

Plates 10, 11, and 12 (above left). *Permutations:* the evolution of computerized motion, shape, and color. (See page 262)

Plates 13, 14, and 15 (above right). *Wavelength:* changes in focus, focal length, exposure, and filters keep an unchanging room in perpetual motion. (See page 132) edy (for example, the feeding-machine sequence of *Modern Times* also uses the *accelerando*). To yoke this imagery with comic tempo creates both the energy and the significance of Conner's first section.

The movement ends when the familiar words that end all movies flash on the screen—"The End"—a static, flat image of white lettering against a black background that contrasts markedly with the sprightly movement of the preceding photographic images. Then the second section begins, a slower, more somber, less rhythmic series of visual images, controlled by the murkier, more mysterious Respighi passage ("The Pines Near a Catacomb"—even the movement's title suggests both Western civilization and death). Unlike the first section's counterpoint of deadly images with exuberant music, the lugubrious music of the second section seems to intensify, deepen, and sadden our response to the deadly imagery. This murky movement comes to its end, as did the first, with an announcement of "The End."

The final movement of *A Movie* returns to the ironic juxtaposition of images and music that opened the film. While the Respighi tone poem builds toward a triumphant, soaring, climactic explosion, the Conner images of devastation seem to run down like an old clock. Conner's *A Movie* ends more with a whimper than with Respighi's bang. Its final image of a diver beneath the sea, exploring a sunken ship (another reminder of destruction and death). He enters the depths of the wreckage and disappears from view—perhaps taking refuge in the only safe place under the sun (far under), perhaps being swallowed by the destructive fire that has invaded the air and the sea as well as the land. There is no "The End" at the end of *A Movie;* the images simply cease as, perhaps, life itself will cease. And there will be no movies or moviemakers to record that climax.

The very use of the Respighi music is itself an enriching irony for at least two reasons other than its underscoring the rhythms of Conner's editing and the implications of his visual imagery. First, Respighi is as close to "movie music" as serious music can get. Like "movie music" it is tonal, emotional, colorful, and loose.* It seems entirely appropriate (and ironic) that this parody of movies made up from bits and pieces of other movies uses music that parodies the music of movies. Further, this same Respighi music served as the score for an earlier (and very famous) experimental film, Kenneth Anger's *Fireworks;* the same climactic music that closes Conner's *A Movie* concluded that 1947 film. But in *Fireworks,* Respighi's musical climax accompanied the filmmaker-dreamer's sexual climax—the metamorphosis of his frustrated penis into a Roman candle and Christmas tree; the satisfaction of the dreamer's fantasies by finding

---

* I discuss the uses and values of "movie music" in Chapter 8.

another man to share his bed. Might Conner be using Respighi to parody experimental movies (especially sexual ones) as well as movie movies?

All these examples of kinesis have been drawn from sequences with powerful visual and/or aural stimuli, but without dialogue. Because I do not intend to imply that when a film begins to talk it necessarily becomes unkinetic (i.e., "uncinematic") and "literary," I think it useful to spend some time on the kinetic powers of dialogue in the cinema. The major difference between literary dialogue (in a printed play or novel) and dialogue on film is that film dialogue does not exist without a human voice to speak it. And the human voice is a musical instrument (especially since a microphone can get close enough to capture its nuances). The great stars of the sound film do not attract us solely with the visual magnetism of their faces. What would Dietrich be without her voice? Or Mae West? Or Gary Cooper? Cagney, Bogart, Bacall, Gable, James Stewart, Bette Davis, Cary Grant, Katharine Hepburn, Spencer Tracy, Jean Arthur, W. C. Fields? Just the names conjure up the sounds of their vocal music. Even Garbo.

Garbo was the only great star of the silents to remain as great a star in the talkies, precisely because the dark, mysterious music of her voice perfectly matched the visual "music" of that mysterious, unknowable face. Contrary to the opinion of Norma Desmond, the great stars of the sound film had faces. But they also had perfectly harmonious voices that suited and supplemented the faces, as well as unique habits of posture, movement (think of Cagney's bounce, Bogart's slouch, Davis's jerkiness, Hepburn's stride, Cooper's saunter), and comportment. The very greatest stars of the sound film are perfectly harmonious blends of multiple and striking kinetic appeals, both visual and vocal. Such perfect blends usually carry their own conviction (and ours) with them in their creating convincing archetypes of human behavior. The archetypal blends of the less great stars are simply less harmonious, less striking, or both.

What would Marilyn Monroe have been without her voice? Well, I was fortunate (only in the laboratory experiment sense) to be able to test this proposition. In Paris, during a Marilyn Monroe retrospective, I saw a print of *The Seven Year Itch* that, for some reason, contained as much as five minutes of dubbed (into French) footage at the end of each two-thousand-foot reel. Roughly 90 percent of the film was *version originale* and the remaining tenth was Marilyn's mouth moving while French came out in a voice that sounded like Martine Carol's (and perhaps was). Instead of the breathy, quavering, vulnerably tentative voice and hesitant vocal patterns that are so intimately connected with the star's wounded eyes, voluptuous but vulnerably soft body, and her cautious, hesitant sense of motion, I heard a hard, firm voice speaking fast, flat French. The woman's entire being seemed to change instantaneously as the sound track slipped into French without warning. And not just her voice had changed; she simply did not *feel* like the same person. She even seemed to look different. With that new voice in that same body Marilyn Monroe was not the blend that we know as Marilyn Monroe. Nor would that new blend ever have become a star. What a relief when that reel ended and Marilyn came to herself again in the new one.

The music of the human voice is not the only kinetic appeal of film dialogue. Pace, rhythm, and intensity are as important to film dialogue as to any other kind of cinema kinesis. Sheer speed hypnotizes (and convinces) us in the most effective screwball comedies. Some of the best Preston Sturges sequences (say, the projection-room sequence of *Sullivan's Travels*—now, there's a projection room where you can see and hear) gain their conviction from sheer speed alone. Frantic speed has always been the pace for the lunacy of farce (Plautus, Feydeau, Sennett), primarily because it has been an axiom of theater that a fundamentally incredible action gains conviction when played so quickly that no one has the time to realize that the action is incredible. The invention of synchronized sound allowed dialogue speeds that could not exist on the stage (for we are close enough to hear every word, we can see the speakers' faces perfectly, and we can watch the lips forming the words that they issue). On the other hand, a shamblingly casual and slow pace of conversation can solve other problems of conviction (for example, Bogart's effectively embarrassed and self-conscious admission to Bacall that he sort of loves her at the end of *The Big Sleep*).

Why do I have conviction in Howard Hawks's *Bringing Up Baby* and no conviction in Peter Bogdanovich's imitation-parody-travesty of it, *What's Up, Doc?*[3] First, pace. The sheer speed of the Hawks dialogue charges *Bringing Up Baby* with a musical energy, a feeling of both *presto* quickness and *scherzando* lightness. In contrast, the Bogdanovich pace is slow, lumbering, and labored. Hawks's speed, in addition to its musical zest, increases our conviction by eliminating our contemplation of any of the basic absurdities of this (or any) farce: that such a coincidental string of lunatic events is possible; that such characterizations are credible (for example, Cary Grant as scientist); that romance between two human beings could ever develop in such circumstances (indeed, be the product of such circumstances). The hard, crackling drive of both Hawks's stars perfectly matches and produces the breathless pace; their voices are hard and firm, their diction faultlessly clipped. And the implication is that their brains work as fast as their mouths, effortlessly leaping to the next stratagem in their love battle. For it is a love battle. Although the characters talk well and talk much, they don't tell as much as they feel. The crackling talk is also camouflage.

In contrast, the stars of *What's Up, Doc?*, Barbra Streisand and Ryan O'Neal, are soft, warm, and watery. They do not talk well (in fact, Streisand's stardom is partly a product of her charming inarticulateness, her nasal nondelivery of incomprehensible verbal phrases). They communicate with glances and glimpses, not words; their feeling for one another (and their appeal for an audience) can be communicated only by getting their "vibes together." To communicate these "vibes" takes time (time for close-ups, time to see the soft longings in the eyes, time to realize why they cannot speak of certain things). Bogdanovich needs a lot of reaction shots. So his problem is one of uniting these kinds of soft people and this kind of slow pace with a sequence of events and characterizations that are no less ludicrous and impossible than those of the Hawks film. The result for me is that Bogdanovich's film feels much more ludicrous, incredible, impossible—and unconvincing.

Hawks's control of his camera does nothing to detract from the vitality of the characters' talk. The analogy here is with Chaplin's style. Just as Chaplin does nothing with the camera or editing kinesis to disturb our concentration on the kinesis of his physical movement, Hawks's camera and editing do nothing with kinesis to disturb our concentration on the kinesis of the speakers' faces, bodies, and verbal music. Contrary to the *Citizen Kane* example, Hawks makes sure we can see and hear the talk, because the talk is both worth hearing and worth understanding. That Hawks has complete mastery over his camera style becomes clear in one of those brief moments when he uses a reaction shot, deserting the standard American two-shot to produce some special punctuation. For example, the first close-up of Katharine Hepburn comes almost thirty minutes into the film, right after she learns that David (Cary Grant) is about to marry someone else. Hawks's camera leaps to her face for her reaction; the talk suddenly stops for a breath; for perhaps five seconds we watch Katharine Hepburn's face, both reacting to the news and trying not to give anything away by making a reaction to it. Then Hawks leaps back to the distance of his two-shots, and the talk continues on its merry way, as if it had never stopped, as if Katharine had never made the reaction. Such a device is an example of a "sign" that is completely communicative yet convincingly subtle and understated at the same time.

Bogdanovich's film is so full of special punctuation (so many very long shots and very close shots and pure reaction shots) that it is all punctuation. Everything is punctuated and, hence, nothing is punctuated. The movie's lack of a strong, swift human center forces Bogdano-vich to concentrate on the peripheral—peripheral characters (like Madeline Kahn as the bitchy fiancée, who, as usual, steals the movie, partially because of her nasally rasping voice); peripheral incidents (the belabored chase that tries so hard to parody everyone else's chases—Sennett's, Keaton's, Hitchcock's, and Peter Yates's *Bullitt*). And yet the chase is also supposed to be kinetically exciting in itself—and it often is. But why should *this* movie about *these* people have a kinetically exciting chase sequence? The result is that the two movies produce adjectival reactions such as light as opposed to heavy, effortless as opposed to belabored, subtle as opposed to overstated, vital as opposed to artificial. All these terms are synonymous with my feeling of conviction in the experience of the Hawks movie and lack of conviction in the experience of Bogdanovich's.

And then, of course, *Bringing Up Baby* is in black-and-white and the "Golden Frame" (the old nonwide screen, with a 4 to 3 ratio of width to height), while *What's Up, Doc?* is in color and Panavision (which is as wide as the wide screen can go). The general point about this distinction is parallel to the earlier discussion of the projection-room sequence of *Citizen Kane:* a "little-screen" black-and-white film can concentrate our attention on dialogue; a wide-screen color film easily distracts us from the talk by attracting our eye elsewhere. Because this discussion of the two movies has brought us to the edge of one of the chief issues in the kinetic possibilities of cinema, we might explore it now.

COLOR AND MONOCHROME, BIG SCREEN AND SMALL

The rise of the assaultively violent kinetic cinema experience and the decline of the literate, elegant dialogue movie are contemporaneous with the rise of color, the wide screen, and stereophonic sound. The new style of cinema is not simply the result of the new audience's taste for rougher sensations, not simply of the development of the appropriate technology, but also of the particular kinetic possibilities of color, size, and stereo.

Rudolf Arnheim deplored the use of color because it was too real, too much like nature, removing yet another of the ways that the art of film could exploit its differences from nature. Stanley Cavell, conversely, found black-and-white a more realistic medium, and a more dramatic one. For years (particularly in the transitional 1950s and '60s) critics assumed that no intimate film could be made in color. Monochrome was the medium of the "art film," of neorealism, of the French "New Wave," of Bergman, Kurosawa, Buñuel, of the American realists (Kazan, Huston, Rossen, Dassin), of *Dr. Strangelove* and *The Hustler* and *The Pawnbroker.* Bogdanovich obviously felt some of the power of this argument himself, for he shot his two most intimate movies, *The Last Picture Show* and *Paper Moon,* in glorious black-and-white. However, *Red Desert, Blow-Up, Belle de Jour, Bonnie and Clyde, Stolen Kisses, Cries and Whispers, Thieves Like Us, Alice Doesn't Live Here Anymore, Taxi Driver,* and dozens of other films can prove that color can be just as intimate as black-and-white. For years, the same critics assumed that no intelligent movie could be made in the wide screen (despite Ophuls's *Lola Montès* of 1955), until along came *2001, A Clockwork Orange, The Wild Bunch, McCabe and Mrs. Miller, Fellini Satyricon, Chinatown,* and dozens of other intelligent wide movies. So the question can now be raised whether color and screen size have any inherent effects, strengths, and liabilities.

I remember once seeing a black-and-white work print of a student film that was being shot in color. There was one very distant, long-lens shot of a group of figures making their way slowly and laboriously across a field and toward the camera. In the black-and-white print I was struck by the variety of vertical forms—of reeds in the foreground, swaying gently in the wind; in the vertical forms of the figures, growing steadily but gradually larger as they approached the camera; of the immense verticals of distant trees in the rearground, which looked like dark shadows cut out of a pale sky. This sense of verticality disappeared completely in the color print, which I saw immediately afterward. My eye caught the variations of yellow-orange-brown in the reeds themselves, and the variations in the colors of the clothing of the figures, and the varying shades of green in the trees, which simply contrasted with the blue sky without seeming like dark patches almost cut out of it.

In that same film, I remember an interior scene which was lit entirely by harsh, bright sunlight, streaming in through windows, doors, and cracks in the ceiling (the house was a dilapidated ruin). The dominant effect in the black-and-white work print was of the intensity of the shadows, the intense patterns of light and darkness, and the varying rough textures of the walls, floors, ceilings, on which the light cast its glance or its shadow. The dominant effect of the color print was much softer and mellower. The colors of the walls and floors, rather than their rough textures, dominated my attention. Further, those colors softened the contrasting patterns of light and shadow by creating their own unity, which bridged the gulf between light and dark, making the walls appear a single entity with lighter and darker areas rather than a conflicting and contrasting pattern of light and dark forms. Although the views of these same scenes were both pleasing, the pleasure was not the same. Indeed, the views seemed not the same (like Marilyn Monroe speaking French).

Black-and-white is a medium of unities and contrasts; color, of individuation and proliferation. Black-and-white emphasizes line, shape, pattern, and texture; color calls attention to the minute diversities of objects and within objects themselves. Black-and-white reveals the operations of light upon its opposite, darkness; color reveals the operations of light in giving birth to all the colors of the spectrum. The word "shade" has two primary meanings in reference to light. Monochrome uses one of them—shade (shadow) as opposed to brightness. Color uses the other—all the shades of the spectrum. Black-and-white translates the shades of natural color into shades of gray, in effect translating color shades into different intensities of shadows.

On the one hand, black and white are more truly opposites than any two colors of the spectrum. Black and white are polarities; the film's shades are mixtures of the two opposite "primaries." Color is a trinity; its shades are mixtures of three primaries. Von Sternberg's beautiful effects with key lights (a streak of brilliant light on Dietrich's veiled face surrounded by darkness) are possible only in monochrome. What color would that light and that darkness be in a color film? Would the light be amber (the usual color of dimness—as in candlelight, oil lanterns, or low-wattage electric bulbs)? Would the darkness be bluish (the usual color of movie darkness)? But then would her hat and veil be black and the darkness blue (as opposed to the effect in Shanghai Express where her hat, veil, and dress are the same color as the surrounding darkness and seem to be a part of that darkness)?

Of course, one could shoot a scene on color film using only white and black (like the scene in the rich man's house in Terence Malick's Badlands, with pure white light, black clothing, and a background of white-sheeted furniture). Many of the Astaire color movies at MGM try to capture the effects of his black-and-white movies at RKO by shooting at least one sequence using only black-and-white costumes, lighting, and décor. Bogdanovich uses color similarly in At Long Last Love. Such choices in color films are simply admissions that color cannot translate the sharp antithesis of monochrome into colors. It can only copy them, as if color were monochrome film. Significantly, although it is common to discuss the effects of color in a color film, I cannot recall a discussion of lighting effects in a color film.

On the other hand, the shades of gray are all closer to one another

The beauty of movie monochrome in *Citizen Kane:* painting darkness with light.
Courtesy Janus Films

than any two different shades of the spectrum. Where in his black-and-white movies the awesome rock formations of John Ford's Monument Valley look like single entities that thrust themselves majestically upward against the light sky, in his color movies one notes the different-colored ribbons of marbled rock and sediment within those stone pillars themselves. When color film tries to produce the gentle and delicate shading of similarities that monochrome does so well, it is forced to produce its décor from different shades of the same color (for example, a scene in variations on pastels of rose, pink, and mauve—like "Think Pink" in *Funny Face*—or the murky aquatic green that bathes the "Deep Throat" garage scenes of *All The President's Men*). Although such effects can be quite effective, they are appropriate only to stylized settings (say, one of the onstage numbers in a Technicolor musical), since reality is not composed of pastel variations on a single color. Black-and-white, however, imitates reality by producing these kinds of visual simplifications—a simplifying both of natural similarities and of contrasting differences.

Because the cinema is a highly visual art, the "rule of five" applies no less to film than to painting. (The "rule of five" is an approximate formula for the number of stimuli that the eye can perceive and integrate simultaneously and instantaneously. Although the precise number may be disputed, the important implication is that the number of sensual stimuli that can be absorbed and assimilated at any one time is finite.) In the cinema, the finiteness of what can be simultaneously absorbed and assimilated is even more complicated and critical than in painting. First, the visual sensual stimuli are themselves not static; they move. Second, there are two kinds of sensual stimuli (sight and sound) acting at once. Third, there are mimetic elements (of plot, dialogue, characterization) to comprehend either through or in addition to the sensual stimuli. To take an extreme example, what would be the effect of watching the climactic "trip" sequence of *2001* (in its original Cinerama process) while listening to Laurence Olivier's recitation of Hamlet's "To be or not to be" soliloquy on the sound track (instead of the modernist *musique concrète* that actually accompanies this sequence)? My guess is that Shakespeare's complex poetry would be reduced to *musique concrète;* it would be a kind of buzzing, accompanying sound, but would make no discrete sense.

Black-and-white simplifies visual stimuli into harmonious unities and bold contrasts. (One might be tempted to claim that it exhausts only two of the possible five in the rule, but I think such exact quantification is shaky.) This simplification frees our concentration for such stimuli as the evocations of the faces of stars, the richness of verbal dialogue, and the complexity of narrative structure. That these were three complementary and corollary characteristics of black-and-white cinema can, I think, be demonstrated by the fact that all three are now in the same kind of decline as monochrome.

Of course, there are still great movie stars (Robert Redford, Gene Hackman, Jack Nicholson, Al Pacino, Faye Dunaway, and several others), but their total number now seems fewer than that at any one of the major studios in the Hollywood era. The disappearance of women stars is especially striking. In the annual poll of film exhibitors on the drawing power of stars (published in *New York* magazine, January 15, 1974), only one woman, Barbra Streisand, placed in the top ten. But she brought her stardom and her star personality with her from recordings and the theater, rather than by the camera's perpetual discovery and revelation of her unique, archetypal qualities in film after film (as it did with Garbo, Gable, Hepburn, Grant; as it does with Redford, Hackman, Nicholson, and a few others). The only woman in current films who seems to me a real "star" in this archetypal sense is Faye Dunaway. Imagine *The Day of the Locust* with Faye Dunaway as Faye Greener instead of Karen Black, who was incapable of parodying a star and being one at the same time.

Without the studios a star makes fewer pictures, of course, an industrial fact which also inhibits the creation of these compelling archetypes. The repetitive exposure of audiences to a star in the studio era not only fixed the archetype in the culture, but also produced expectations in an audience about what each archetype would do and be—even before the movie began. An audience came into the theater knowing things about the character that Katharine Hepburn, or Bette Davis, or Cary Grant would play (just as it knew that the Tramp, Charlie, could respond only to certain kinds of challenges in certain kinds of ways; just as we know today that Jack Nicholson will be loose, perceptive, and a "smartass" in every role he plays, and Faye Dunaway will be sensuous, vibrant, and vulnerable beneath whatever surface). These cultural expectations about an archetypal star make movie stars one of the "media" of movies for Stanley Cavell, one of their "ways of making sense."

But directors can undertake major movie projects now with unknowns, little knowns, or nonentities in the principal roles (*2001, If . . ., Thieves Like Us, Alice Doesn't Live Here Anymore, The Day of the Locust, Nashville*). For in addition to the commercial fact that there are now fewer movies (and, hence, fewer stars), the star as medium now carries far less communicative weight. The human beings now have more competition in the frame with them in color and wide-screen films—sensual stimuli to divert our attention from their archetypal presences.

The Wild Bunch: composition in the wide screen. The single-face closeup in the frame's center has been replaced by two balanced heads (William Holden and Ernest Borgnine) on either side of the frame.

Charles Barr describes a close-up in Nicholas Ray's *Bitter Victory,* a color and wide-screen movie of 1958:

> The close-ups do not wholly isolate the characters; we know where we are. . . . At the edges of the frame there is decor and space and perhaps some casual detail; thus when the camera is on . . . Richard Burton, we can see a couple dancing, and an Arab guard, and a general background of the room; we are completely situated at each moment . . . ["CinemaScope: Before and After," pp. 145–6]

This close-up style (single face at one side of the frame balanced on the other by rearground action or foreground object or a second face) is as common to wide-screen color movies as the isolated single face in center frame was to monochrome, "Golden Frame" movies. Whatever the advantages of keeping a face situated among its surroundings, the psychological fact is that the newer-style close-up puts less communicative responsibility on the isolated face.

Although Stanley Cavell noted that in the cinema human beings were not ontologically favored over anything else in nature, the view has not really been demonstrated until the last decade. For in black-and-white and the "Golden Frame," human beings (in practice, if not necessarily in theory) were very much favored over everything else in nature. Nothing in the frame competed for our attention with Greta Garbo, Clark Gable, Bette Davis, and the rest of them (especially when the frame got two of them together). One of the subtlest effects of the studio era (subtle because it was not perceived as a visual effect) was that of sculpting the light around the stars' faces so that nothing could be favored over him and her. That principle of lighting has gone with the studios, for the natural locations that movies now prefer not only negate the idea of star lighting, but make it impossible to achieve.

This same concentration of attention on the star gave more power and control to the scenarist, for he wrote what issued from those sculpted heads. If the stars are fewer and dimmer now than they were, the professional scriptwriter is virtually extinct. (Robert Towne, Mario Puzo, and Paul Schrader are among the few survivors of this lost species.) The most important and capable scriptwriters today are the directors themselves— Coppola, Bergman, Truffaut, and so forth. In the black-and-white era, the two potential values of a screenplay—richness of dialogue and complexity of structure—were developed by talented men who formed a group that today seems as numerous and as important as that of the best directors of the era: Jacques Prévert, Charles Spaak, Herman J. Mankiewicz, Ben Hecht, Dudley Nichols, Samson Raphaelson, Robert Riskin, Garson Kanin. The result could be verbal sparkle (*Bringing Up Baby, Woman of the Year, Pat and Mike, Trouble in Paradise, All About Eve*), evocative verbal imagery (*Port of Shadows, The Children of Paradise*), or a complexly literate narrative structure (*The Children of Paradise, Bizarre, Bizarre, Rules of the Game, Citizen Kane, The Big Sleep, Boudu Saved from Drowning*).

Structural complexity has been easier to preserve in today's color movies: the labyrinthine journey in Robert Towne's *Chinatown*, the overlapping and enmeshing lives in Joan Tewkesbury's *Nashville*, the two symmetrical triangles formed by Travis Bickle, the unattainable woman and the fulfilling male in Paul Schrader's *Taxi Driver*. It is the dialogue that has gone—partially because our culture delights less in good talk, partially because sharp talk clashes with the communicative power and beauty of color and the wide screen.

Not that black-and-white was not visually beautiful. It is easy to forget how beautiful black-and-white can be, for we rarely get a chance to see it properly. Prints of older films are almost inevitably poor or poorly projected in classrooms, film societies, and run-down revival houses. To see a black-and-white film on television is a guarantee not to see it, for the ultra-low fidelity of the reproduction washes out the deepest blacks and brightest whites, not to mention blurring all the gradations between. On a color television set, black-and-white looks more like purple-gray-and-pale-pink, since the color dots still produce faint hues without any stimulus. The beauty of black-and-white is a cool, quiet, detached beauty, a beauty that perfectly suited the elegance of the classical movies that used it.

Why did Hitchcock make *Psycho* in black-and-white, sandwiched between almost a decade of color films before and after it? Not simply to evoke memories of the Gothic and horrific film genres. The movie's mixture of horrifying violence and ironic psychology required the coolness and detachment of monochrome. Can you imagine the famous slaughter in the shower, with its black blood swirling down the drain, in color? For one thing, red blood dissipates and turns pink in water. It is the *darkness* of the new liquid in the water that evokes our response. For another, the sight of "real" red blood splattered against the side of the tub and swirling down the drain might well have been too loathsome and noxious to watch. The "broken glass" sequence of *Cries and Whispers* is a deliberately nauseating visceral attack precisely because the resulting blood is so really and richly red. To "derealize" the climactic murder sequence of *Taxi Driver*, Scorsese's blood looked more maroon-brown than blood-red, a choice that suited deliberately the dreamlike mode of that final slaughter.

The conversion of red blood into black lines and spots in *Psycho* troubles our imaginations, not our stomachs. In this cinematic blood bath, the two opposite opinions of Cavell and Arnheim are united. The black-and-white film removes the shower scene from the strictly natural world, increasing its appeal to our imagination and heightening our emotional participation in what seems a "real" and dramatic event. Despite the critical concern about the movie's violent brutality when it first appeared, the remarkable quality about *Psycho* is its cool restraint—and its use of monochrome is both a symptom and a source of that restraint. As always, Hitchcock is the master chef when it comes to mixing nature and artifice so that the result is a genuinely horrifying, or suspenseful, or sexual *fantasy* (and usually a combination of all three).

The few monochrome films I can recall of the last five years comprise a small and select group (*The Wild Child*, 1970; *The Last Picture Show*, 1971; *King Lear*, 1971; *Paper Moon*, 1973; *Lenny*, 1974; and *Young Frankenstein*, 1974). They share two traits that reveal the current assumptions about monochrome. First, they all depict the distant or the immediate past (eighteenth-century France; a savage, pre-medieval Britain; American decades of the thirties through the sixties; and "today's" Transylvania set in a nineteenth-century Gothic novel). Ironically, Renoir once remarked that for him color was the inevitable means of depicting the costumed past. Color is now the medium of presentness (*Taxi Driver*) and pastness (*Chinatown*). Second, five of these monochrome films self-consciously refer to the visual look of the monochrome past: in *Wild Child,* Griffith's silvery orthochrome; in *Paper Moon,* the dusty aridity of socially-conscious "dust bowl" films like *The Grapes of Wrath* and Lorenz's *The River;* in *Lenny,* the documentary-commentary or *cinéma vérité* of the early 1960s like *The Savage Eye, The Cool World,* and *Chronique d'un été;* in *Young Frankenstein,* the James Whale–Tod Browning horror films at Universal. Black-and-white (like the mute mime of the silent era) is no longer a means for depicting contemporary social reality.

Color can obviously be very beautiful, but if it is to be visually beautiful and dramatically effective (rather than simply colorful) at the same time, it must be carefully tuned. Color can be tuned to parallel monochrome (say, Antonioni's *Red Desert* with its pale gray-brown-green factory sequences punctuated by the striking oranges and blues of the pipes); it can produce kinetic metaphors to enrich our conviction in the experience of the film's events (as in *2001, Rosemary's Baby, Lola Montès, Cries and Whispers,* and *Taxi Driver*); it can produce thematic and symbolic contrasts that underlie the film's microcosmic system (as in *Mon Oncle, The Golden Coach, Juliet of the Spirits*). But in so many films, because directors lack the time, the budget, or the eye, color is simply there.

In films in which color is simply there and black-and-white is simply there, the black-and-white seems much more beautiful. Black-and-white permits our observation of so many more of those lovely accidents ("leaves rippling in the wind") that Lumière first noticed, since its concentrated harmony and diversity call our eye's attention to such accidents more easily. Given the existence of filmmakers who cannot select visual beauty for the camera, monochrome film *selects* accidental beauties of necessity, since it "sees" shapes, shadows, forms, and textures that the human eye cannot. Perhaps this is one valid application of Arnheim's theory of the gap between nature and art: if the filmmaker cannot exercise artistic choices, black-and-white film can. Perhaps for this same reason, black-and-white continues to be the primary medium of still photography, which is more purely interested in the operations of light and the juxtapositions of forms, shapes, textures, and lines. Color photography is the medium of advertising, travel folders, and picture postcards; often the "prettiest" color movies (say, *The Sound of Music, Death in Venice,* or *Ryan's Daughter*) are close cousins to the picture postcard.

There is no point in lamenting the death of black-and-white, for there are too many good color films to compensate for it. Like the death of the silent film, the death of black-and-white marked the end of a style that made artistic virtues of its limitations, and the end of the kind of artists who excelled in that particular style. *Le style est mort. Vive le style.*

The evolution of the wide screen has paralleled the evolution of color. In the small screen, color was conceived as something to be looked *at:* as if it were black-and-white, but in color. But the years of practice have convinced the most talented directorial eyes that color is less an element of composition than it is an affective element that can leap out of the frame to control an audience's emotional responses. The multiple and diverse optical stimuli of the moving color image were not well suited to harmonious and unified observation; they were well suited, however, to appealing to the eye directly and sensually in the same way that color imagery in poetry appeals indirectly to the imagination with its associations of color and emotion (white as snow, white as purity, white as death, yellow fog, golden warmth of the sun, the green of envy). If monochrome produces a more unified observation, color can produce a more unified and intense sensual impression of emotional associations.

So, too, the original wide-screen movies applied the compositional values of the "Golden Frame" to their new, huge expanse. Because the screen was so big, the first tendency was to use its bigness as a kind of immense container, filling it with huge spectacles and vast panoramas and casts of thousands. The combination of the huge screen that could "contain" so many objects and the use of color, which proliferated the diverse effect of individual objects, tended to fracture and disintegrate the dramatic and visual unity of the image. In his article on the visual virtues of CinemaScope, Charles Barr apologizes for this fractured image in Bazinian terms. The huge screen allows the frame to "contain" *more* nature and allows the eye to wander about this vast expanse on its own, picking out significance for itself and thereby producing "real conviction." By applying Bazin's principle of composition-in-depth to the wide screen's composition-in-width, Barr makes the strongest possible argument for the "scattered" compositional values of this first era of the wide screen. Indeed, one obvious parallel with Bazin's principles was the hesitancy of early movies in the wide screen to use assaultive montage or any strikingly noticeable camera movement. They feared the discomfort and visual disorientation they might cause an audience by leaping about in space with such a huge image.

The difficulty with such a "scattered" image is that it seems to sacrifice concentrated power for the subtlety of randomness, gaining a kind of "conviction" (in that we do not feel an event is a contrived piece of symbolism), but losing another kind of conviction (in that we do not feel the event very deeply). Barr, for example, discusses a sequence in Otto

Preminger's *The River of No Return* (1954), which the French consider the first artistic achievement in CinemaScope. In one sequence Marilyn Monroe loses all her dance-hall clothing to the power of the river, which sweeps her goods downstream.

> As Harry lifts Kay from the raft, she drops the bundle which contains most of her "things" into the water. Kay's gradual loss of the physical tokens of her way of life has great symbolic significance. But Preminger is not over-impressed. The bundle simply floats away off-screen while Harry brings Kay ashore. . . .[4]

Since I have recently seen a near-perfect CinemaScope print of this film, let me say that Preminger is not the only one who was not overimpressed. As I watched the bundle of "things" make its way toward the right-hand edge of the screen, a mere footnote to the main action of Marilyn Monroe's leaving the raft, which dominates screen left and center, I realized that this loss was more than of a bunch of clothing, that the loss was of a whole former way of life. Her whole life had changed direction, swept away by the course of events and by the uncontrollable and irresistible course of the river itself. Although I knew (in the conscious, rational sense) what this loss meant, I did not *know* (in the emotional, internal sense) how she felt about the loss. Nor did I feel anything about that loss myself. The "subtle" device was, for me, less powerful, more purely intellectual, than one of Eisenstein's "obvious" montage sequences.

Compare that scene of end and loss to the spectacular (and spectacularly beautiful) fire sequence that closes the first movement of Terence Malick's *Badlands*. The young girl's father has been killed by her boyfriend. He is about to dispose of the evidence and her house by burning it down; she is about to leave with him for her new life of crime in a Rousseauesque nature. Her youth, her innocence, her respectability, are lost—burned to the ground. To capture this loss, Malick uses a languid montage series of shots of the fire eating away at the various rooms of the house in which she lived as a young, innocent girl. Perhaps the most striking (and the most symbolic) of those shots is of the room that contains her doll's house—a house-on-fire within a house-on-fire. We watch the beautiful movement of the flames (the motion and color of the flames are the dominant kinetic sources of our conviction in the sequence), licking away at the wallpaper of the doll's house, even as it licks away at the walls of the big house, which we see through the windows of the little one. This is a sequence in which I feel powerfully and personally exactly what it means to lose a part of one's life, to see a period of a life come to an absolute and irreversible end.

If space can be "dynamized" in the "Golden Frame," it can be doubly dynamized in a frame that is twice as big. Rather than using the screen's size to construct these organized disorganized images, directors realized that the hugeness of the screen had a kinetic power itself, and that composition, as with color, could leap out of the frame rather than simply be observed within it. The wide screen has resuscitated Eisenstein's theories (and their implications) after over forty years of contrary Hollywood practice and Bazinian principle. The wide screen has once again demonstrated the kinetic possibilities of the cinema as visual "music" and metaphor rather than as the passive recorder of a literal reality.

The two seminal films in the combined and kinetic use of color and the wide screen are Ophuls's *Lola Montès* and Kubrick's *2001*, both of which used their dazzling, overpowering visual effects as the kinetic means to their mimesis, aided by the spectacular assault on the ear of multichannel sound recording (six channels for *2001*). The films still remain the two ultimate examples of the raw power of cinema kinesis, yet that power was merely the servant of two superior artistic intelligences who knew exactly why (as well as how) they wanted to manipulate it. Significantly, these two modern masterpieces share a surprising trait in that neither required the magnetism of a star's performance. The most interesting person in *Lola Montès* is a supporting player (Peter Ustinov); the star's performance (Martine Carol) is a disaster that is mitigated only by our awareness that she is irrelevant, and that we need neither to look at nor listen to her to see and hear the movie. The most interesting performance in *2001* is by a machine; Kubrick chose the movie's two nominal "stars" specifically because they were the blandest, most colorless players he could find. The star is no longer the star of this kind of cinema.

Although all movies today use color (with the exception of those I noted, of course), there has been some retreat from the widest of wide screens. But even in today's films of standard width (that use neither anamorphic lens nor wide-gauge film) the frame is wider and less square than it was in the "Golden Frame" (closer to 5:3 than 4:3). That is why classic black-and-white movies don't fit the screen at top and bottom when 35-mm prints of them are projected with today's projectors on today's screens in commercial movie houses. Even today's standard-width films use the kinetic effects of color, camera, montage, and sound for many of their communicative "signs," rather than dialogue and the kinetic effects of the human face, voice, and figure. The exceptions, of course, are the "movies" and series programs made for television, which combine color with the very small screen and, hence, concentrate on faces, talk, and voices as much as movies in their monochrome days. If kinesis distinguishes the cinema experience from that of all the traditional arts, how can cinema be distinguished from television, this even newer medium which also communicates kinetically?

TELEVISION AND KINESIS

The question What is television? has been no more precisely answered than the companion one about cinema. As a result, comparisons of the two "media" have also been imprecise and incomplete. For some, television is merely small cinema—especially since television is our major "revival house" for American movies, since so-called movies have even been made especially for television, and since television programs fit into many of the same genres as movies (and have even been adapted from movies). For others, television is completely unlike cinema because it comes into the home, or it has commercials, or it is heavily censored, or it is mediocre, or it is electronic, or it is small, or it is "live." By returning to the three-part division of material, process, and form, I think we can more precisely examine how television is and is not like film, cinema, and movie, and what this reveals about film, cinema, and movie.

Whereas the material of cinema is film, the *material* of television is a glass screen that is bombarded by electrons. Television does not project light *through* anything; it shoots electron particles against a sensitized surface with an electrode gun, causing that surface to glow. One major difference between these two materials, then, would be the comparative qualities of "resolution" of the resulting visual images, the clarity, crispness, and malleability of the two different visual materials and methods. As of the time of this writing, light passing through celluloid is capable of much greater sharpness and detail and, at the same time, much softer and mellower visual effects than electrons shot against a glass screen (which is why black-and-white films have no blacks or whites or subtly variegated grays on a television screen). Television is visual and aural "low fidelity," and although technology could certainly raise this fidelity (for example, television sound could be transmitted now with the clarity and purity of FM stereo), there seems to be little impulse toward improvement in this direction. The subtlety and clarity of film as a visual material in comparison to television becomes especially clear if you watch a film on a Steenbeck or Moviola viewing machine. Although the screen is no larger (indeed, even smaller) than the typical television image, the resolution produced by the usual filmic method of projecting light through celluloid is much sharper than television can presently produce.

A second difference between the two material bases of these "media" is that the material of television reception is not the material of television recording (unlike celluloid, which both photographs and is projected). The recording material of television can be one of three kinds of things. A program can be shot "live" (say, a football game), which means that the action passes directly through the camera's lens and is instantly relayed into the electronic process for viewing at home. A program can be a videotaped recording of a previously "live" performance or event (like most soap operas, comedy and variety shows, talk shows, and game shows), which means that a "playback" machine sends the delayed event into the electronic process. Or the program can be recorded on film (like movies on television, most series dramas, and commercials), which means that the program must be projected into the electronic process. This difference means that, although television transmits all these materials with equal instantaneity, its recording materials produce three different tenses: the now, the a little while ago that looks like now, and the some time ago. Although you can always distinguish a filmed program from a live or taped one by simply observing the resolution, it is impossible to distinguish visually between live and tape. Television transmits all three of these tenses with equal instantaneity.

A final consequence of the different materials of the two "media" is that television does not produce the same *illusion* of movement (or succession) as film does. Unlike film, television has no frames in its recording process; in its transmission process it shoots thirty pictures per second (in America; twenty-five in Europe) onto the sensitized screen. All the arguments about film's ability to capture nature whole are even more applicable to television, for it is less of an optical illusion than film inevitably must be.

As a *process*, television satisfies every one of the definitions of the "cinematic" that we have examined. Those unique qualities of the cinema as a medium are not so unique after all. Television *can* capture nature whole (even more wholly than cinema since its material is not film) and *now*. Television *can* make space move; Panofsky's dynamization of space applies no less to television. And television has an infinitely variable range of possibilities for integrating kinetic and mimetic effects. It is not surprising that television can do what movies do since it can do movies.

But can it do them as well? Although television has a theoretically "infinite range of possibilities for integrating kinetic and mimetic effects," in practice its infinity is quite finite because the range of its kinesis is so severely restricted. With television one simply cannot see or hear as much or as well as one can with cinema. Television's sights and sounds are not only reproduced in very "lo-fi," but in very tiny "lo-fi." We are no longer overwhelmed by something very much bigger than we are, by life that is much larger than life, distant views that are more distant, close-up details that are more close and more detailed, sounds that are much louder, or much softer, or much more selective than the range of our visual and aural experiences in life. Instead, we watch life shrunk into a box that we can carry around, life reduced to a toy or a piece of furniture, life that loses its mysterious immensity (like the earth reduced to a globe) because it is something we can so easily grasp (literally and, hence, figuratively). Although we cannot really see black-and-white dialogue films on television, we can see a lot more of them than we can of the huge wide-screen, stereophonic, color movies that get shrunk into the box because their huge width and their sharp color and their surrounding sound are what they *are* and are the primary source of our conviction in experiencing them.

I heard Ken Russell say that frequently when he watched a movie on television that had moved him in a theater, he saw flaws in it that he had not previously noticed. He felt he had not seen the same movie on television as he had in the theater. And he hadn't. It is not simply that his mind had been diverted from the movie's flaws by the cinema's overwhelming manipulation of huge sights and sounds. Nor that his experience had been magnified by the communality of sharing it with an audience. Nor that the movie touched a chord in him or in the culture that no longer sounded. The "flaws" were not flaws when he saw the movie in a theater because they were not there. The hypnotic kinesis of the film experience made those "flaws" invisible. To notice such flaws in retrospect is parallel to realizing that no one actually heard Kane say "Rosebud," since no one came into the room until after he had whispered it and dropped the glass ball in death. In the process of experiencing this shattering (literally) moment, who notes such contradictions? It is comparable to reading a melodramatic thriller at home (say, *Sleuth*) and noting incongruities and incredibilities that we never noticed in the theater, where we were being thrilled by the thriller and had no opportunity to notice.

Because television slavishly copies movie styles, it has also begun to use the cinema's assortment of visual effects: distorting lenses, rack focus (changing focus within a shot so as to capture only the foreground and then the rearground, or vice versa), split screens, rapid montage, color tinting, psychedelic strobe effects, and so forth. But whereas in cinema these devices (effectively manipulated) produce almost tactile, sensual effects on the nerves, stomach, even skin, on television they remain occasionally interesting visual effects. In the cinema, the kinetic effects go from eyes to nervous system to (perhaps) brain, whereas on television the same effects go from eyes to (perhaps) brain, producing reactions such as: "Oh, he's supposed to be drunk because things look blurry, tipsy, and distorted." Cinema's kinetic effects produce the internal, emotional responses themselves (blurry, drunken tipsiness); television produces an awareness that an effect is intended. In this sense, experiencing sensations while watching television is perhaps closer to the experiencing of a novel than it is to the cinema experience. The television devices invite us to conceptualize the feeling or meaning of an event or emotion rather than induce us to experience it physically.

Because we can see and hear so much less on television, the dominant shots are facial close-ups and human-centered medium shots; the primary communicative devices are faces, dialogue, voices, and music. Except for its color, television style is almost identical to that of the cheapest and quickest filming methods of the 1930s (in fact, it is B-movie style). Television producers spend neither time nor money on what cannot be perceived.

Could television become as kinetically effective as cinema with sharp resolution, stereophonic sound, and an immense wall screen?* Perhaps. (But then it would not be television as we know it today and contrast with the kinesis of cinema as it presently does.) However, television's limp and limpid kinetic effects not only suffer from the feebleness of the sights and sounds that come out of the box; they also suffer from the feeble command that the box exerts over our attention.

We sit comfortably in our own homes; perhaps the television offering must compete with sounds and sights and conversations and events that are not inside the box. The experience is much less compelling than in a theater, where we sit in darkness and cannot see or hear anything else. The voyeurism of the cinema experience takes advantage of the paradox that we are both alone and together in the movie theater—both among others and in our fantasies, both safe in a seat and endangered by the dream or nightmare of the screen. The "rape" of the cinema experience is an act done both privately and publicly.

The cinema not only demands our concentration; it also automatically gets it. We must make a supreme effort not to concentrate on a movie. Conversely, we must make a supreme effort to concentrate on a television program; and once we have done so, it purposely breaks that concentra-

---

* These wall screens presently exist. A four-foot-by-five-foot screen costs $2,800. How much would a thirty-foot-by-forty-foot screen cost?

tion (with a commercial, station break, or some kind of interruption). This issue of concentration is one that links the television process with television's forms, its temporal succession with its structural principles.

Virtually all of television's *forms* are built around interruptions. However, these interruptions are most acute (and most theoretically interesting) in their effect on fictional programs, television's analogue to movies. (Like cinema, television has forms that could be called documentary, animation, narrative, or informational). Each hour of television contains twelve minutes of commercials, and each hour-long program is inevitably built in six parts to allow for them: the "tease" (this is the "preview of coming attractions" that precedes each show, accompanied by the program's musical theme, intended to arrest the viewer's hand in the process of twisting the dial); four "acts" (often labeled "Act I," etc.); and the "epilog" (often labeled—but almost never with a "ue").

The one advantage of this structure is that it takes account of the fact that the commercials exist and can therefore build each segment up to a mini-climax (the analogue of the "curtain line" in the theater). Conversely, when a movie is shown on television, the station frequently breaks into the work in the middle of a scene (or a line, sometimes), since the movie was not constructed to allow for commercial breaks. However, it can be legitimately asked whether a dramatic work can accommodate so many climaxes and curtain lines, no matter how carefully built, within an hour (in a play, there tends to be only one curtain line in an hour). The artificiality of this television structure is even more apparent when one sees the same shows without the commercials (as on British television), but with the structure that allows for them. Ironically, the feeling of climax about each of these television "acts" is partially the result of the commercial's breaking our concentration altogether. Precisely the same observations apply to thirty-minute programs and those longer "made-for-TV movies" (which are simply poorly disguised television programs which take a bit more—but not much—time, care, and money to shoot).

The inevitable conclusion is that because of its weaker kinesis and of its constant disruption of concentration, television's attempts to ape the cinema and its forms necessarily produce a feeble counterfeit. The conclusion is not the result of the usual argument about the stupidity and banality of the *content* of television programs, for even when the content is as good as a movie (for example, when the content *is* a movie), television can present only a weak copy (like the souvenir postcard of a Goya painting that can be bought at the Prado).

But when television presents one of its forms that take advantage of its presentness, of its simultaneity of transmission and reception, it presents something that not only is absolutely unique, but that also circumvents its feebleness of kinesis and concentration. Talk shows, sports events, and news programs (either regular newscasts or special events like press conferences and congressional hearings) take advantage of television's instantaneousness by being spontaneous, actual, informational, and immediate. They are not controlled microcosms that require our conviction. They are all forms of news because they are all forms of nows. They are in no way dependent on creating an illusory, surrogate world for us to experience deeply and fully (which television does so poorly). Our interest in these news programs stems from the fact that they are as unpredictable, as uncontrollable and uncontrolled, as subject to accident and chance, as life itself. Anything might be said (the unintentionally revealing remark of a personality on a talk show or the revelation of a secret tape-recording system); anything might be done (the assassination of an assassin or the last-minute "immaculate reception" of a deflected pass). There was an earlier television era when comedy and variety shows were also presented "live" (the Sid Caesar *Show of Shows,* for example), and they gained spontaneity, energy, freshness, and freedom from the demands and the *danger* of live performance. Now, with the exception of *Saturday Night,* these forms are all videotaped (in front of an audience, perhaps), so although they look "live," they are as safely edited and packaged as any filmed television series.

The only narrative form that seems especially appropriate to the television process is soap opera. These butts of so many jokes take advantage of many unique characteristics of the television experience. Until recently, most of them were shot and transmitted live. Now that they are taped, they are produced quickly and cheaply—as if they were live—without editing and without erasing any but the most disastrous mistakes. The repetitiveness of their stories, the fact that they are perpetual, open-ended middles without beginnings and ends, and the slow development of those middles take advantage of the fact that their viewers do not so much watch them as live with them while doing other things. Despite the superiority complex of the nighttime network programs, the soap operas seem to display some of the most interesting acting on television, writing that is not many cuts below the nighttime scripts (how could it be?), and one of the most aesthetically valid uses of a medium that is more like a piece of furniture with which we live than an artistic experience which takes us totally out of our lives.

When television attempts to compel us with a hypnotic illusion of human experience (which the kinesis of cinema does so well), it betrays the limitations of its material, process, and forms.

EPILOG

The role of kinesis in the cinema is essentially what distinguishes its effect, appeal, and pleasure from that of the other time-arts. Unlike music, cinema makes its kinetic appeal to the eye as well as the ear, and that kinesis is also capable of complex mimetic functions. But unlike the mimetic literary arts, cinema uses kinesis as an essential element in its diction, its "language," as a means of both making itself understood and making itself felt. As opposed to narrative fiction, in which there is no kinesis (words alone conjure up whatever sights and sounds the reader might imagine), and as opposed to a play, in which there is a limited kinesis (the appeals to the eye and ear supplement the communicative power of words), the cinema's appeal to eye and ear is the primary source of our understanding the action and of our having conviction in its experience. As opposed to opera, which makes a powerful kinetic appeal to the ear, cinema works forcefully on both eye and ear. As opposed to ballet, which indeed works powerfully on eye and ear, cinema is capable of working more subtly with sound (because of the microphone) and of working more forcefully with sight (by making space itself "dance"). Finally, as opposed to television, which would seem to display the same kind of mixture of kinesis and mimesis as cinema, the force of cinema is so much greater because its kinetic tools are so much better developed and so much more powerful.

It is the sheer physical power of an effective cinema experience—be it with a lyric, experimental film or with a revealing documentary or with a movie—that separates the pleasure of cinema from that of the other arts. Our apprehension of the experience is so much more immediate, direct, concrete. Cinema conducts us through the surrogate existence that is the basis of all the mimetic arts more concretely, more sensually than any other art. It is as close as the surrogate existence can be to life itself and yet not life at all. It is as tactile and as concrete as a dream can get. It makes more demands on our senses and nerves and fewer demands on our imaginations than any other art.

It is for this reason that many theorists and critics (even those who love the cinema) note that the pleasure of the art is less "sublime," less complex, more shallow than our pleasure with the greatest instances of the other arts—with Shakespeare, Proust, Mozart, and the like. They have also noted that the staying power of the cinema experience (even of the best films) is weaker than that of the less kinetic arts; the memory of our experience with a film does not haunt us as long or as deeply as the memory of our experience with a complex and moving novel. Perhaps.

On the other hand, with no other art are we so shaken by the immediate experience with the work as in the cinema. With no other art does the world look so different and do our lives feel so different immediately after the work ends (and the lights come on) as with *Rules of the Game*, or *Chinatown*, or *The 400 Blows*, or *Red River*, or *2001*, or *Open City*, or *City Lights*, or whatever movie happens to move us. It is the direct, stunning immediacy of the cinema experience that makes those who love movies love them so deeply and those who argue about movies argue about them so vigorously (and perhaps so irrationally). It is that experience of the overwhelming conviction in an artistic experience and the shattering submission to an immense artistic force that those of us who love the cinema all share, even if we do not share it with the same cinema works.

II/An Integrated Succession of Projected Images and (Recorded) Sounds

5/Succession

A work of cinema is an *integrated succession of projected images and (recorded) sounds*. Although this definition is terribly simple (even transparently obvious), a close examination of each of its terms reveals some relevant categories, distinctions, and values.

A cinematic work is necessarily a series of frames that succeed one another. Even the scratch film, with its scratches etched directly into the emulsion of black leader and then immediately projected (without processing and printing), works in principle as a succession of frames, despite the fact that it has no clearly demarcated frames. The projector makes each unit of the scratch film stop in front of the light source for $\frac{1}{24}$ second, treating the scratch film *as if* it had frames. The work of cinema moves forward through the projector at twenty-four frames per second,[*] ineluctably, ceaselessly moving from beginning to end of the reel even more obligatorily than the eye moves across this page from left to right and from top to bottom. Although the solitary reader can take his eyes from the page to rest them, or can go back to read certain passages over again, more slowly if need be, the viewer of the cinematic work is the prisoner of the remorseless, steady forward movement of film through the projector. (Unless, of course, he is a solitary viewer operating an analytic projector or viewing machine—a condition that is not the usual one for experiencing cinema, but corresponds to the usual one for reading.)

This steady succession of frames parallels the operation of time itself, which is similarly unstoppable and inevitable. The closest parallel to the reel of film is the hourglass, the one side filling up with material in the

---

[*] I am using the number of frames per second of the sound projector rather than the many variant speeds of the silent era. Although the numbers differ, the principle does not.

irreversible process of evacuating the other. And you can estimate time as easily from the operation of a reel of film as from an hourglass. For example, the unspooling of a fairly full 1,600-foot reel of 16-mm film will take about forty minutes, and you can glance periodically at its remains during the unspooling to estimate how many of these forty remain.

This parallel between the succession of cinema frames and the flow of time underscores the fact that cinema is essentially (in Lessing's terms) a time-art. Although film has an undeniable spatial dimension (for the organization of space is the primary characteristic of the still photo-graph), the cinematic process subjects that space to the will of time. Space exists in the cinema only as it undergoes temporal operations and can be perceived as static only when the temporal succession of frames permits it (i.e., when an identical frame repeats itself successively, as in a "freeze frame," or when the cinema camera shoots still photographs). Perhaps the cinema is the truest time-art of all, since it most closely parallels the operation of time itself. Its experience is exactly as long as it is, and no one (not the audience, not an interpreter, not even the artist himself) can tamper with its ceaseless flow once it has begun.

The reader of the novel can put it down to stop its flow whenever he or she needs or wants to do so. The fact that novels are organized into chapters implies that stopping is an anticipated characteristic of experiencing them. The conductor or soloist can alter the pace of musical passages or of the pauses between them. The actor and director can alter the pace of scenes, the audience at a play can alter the length of pauses by filling them with laughter, the theater manager can alter the length of the performance by altering the length of the intermissions. But the cinematic work moves ceaselessly forward. Cinema *fugit*.

The apparent exceptions truly prove this rule. One is the possibility of *studying* a film, viewing it alone (or in a classroom)—stopping, starting, reversing, slowing, speeding it, as the kind of study demands. But studying a film is not experiencing it as it was intended; it is a dissection which, at best, reveals how and why it is experienced. Of the time-arts, only the purely literary (novels and poems) allow for the possibility of long and unregulated interruptions during the experience itself because that experience is personal rather than a public exhibition or performance (as in cinema, music, drama, dance, and opera). All these time-arts that manipulate kinetic effects produce an inevitable distinction between experience and study, but the contemplative and purely mental experience of reading a novel is very much a kind of study itself (for example, you can read it in your study).

The second exception is the not so unfamiliar event of some kind of interruption—either planned (as with the intermissions for very long spectacular movies like *The Birth of a Nation, Gone With the Wind,* and *Ben Hur*) or unplanned (as when the projector breaks down, or the film breaks, or the commerical comes on, or the use of a single projector necessitates pauses for changing reels). The unplanned intermission is truly wrenching and traumatic, the sudden snapping of the cinema's kinetic hypnosis, which can feel both sickening and withering. The planned intermissions are usually irrelevant, necessitated by the length of the movie (the producer's opinion that "people can't sit that long") rather than by any structural demands of the work itself. Even when the movie's intermission has some structural basis (say, the Reconstruction following the Civil War of both *Birth of a Nation* and *Gone With the Wind*), the intermission is itself irrelevant. The structural point (that one unit has ended and another has begun) can be made with a title card or some other visual cue and without an intermission (as in the falling of the curtain that separates the two halves of *The Children of Paradise*). Indeed, when the spectacular movies leave the road-show houses for the showcase theaters, they inevitably leave their intermissions behind them. But in the drama, intermissions are not simply "rest periods"; they are an intrinsic element in dramatic construction, which assumes that characters spend much of their time onstage reacting to events that have taken place offstage (some other place) or during the intermissions (some other time).

The appeal of the cinema is the *cumulative* kinetic hypnosis of the *uninterrupted* flow of film and time. Because the art of cinema most closely parallels the operation of time, it imprisons the attention within a hypnotic grip that becomes steadily tighter and stronger (if the work is properly built) as the film progresses and it refuses to let go until it has had its way. As I mentioned earlier, the cinema experience is a kind of rape, and no successful rapist lets his quarry escape for an occasional breather.

The flow of film moves steadily, successively forward, but within that forward flow one can distinguish between three kinds of "movement," three kinds of succession: a literal succession (the succession of frames); an imagistic succession (the succession of shots); a structural succession (the succession of "events"). Any time-art presupposes that one moment in time follows another in a work, and that there is a reason for moment B's following moment A, and not the other way round. Why does moment B succeed moment A in a work of cinema? There are three answers to that question, and to neglect any of the three is to neglect an essential feature of this time-art.

LITERAL SUCCESSION

The first reason is that frame 2 necessarily succeeds frame 1, frame 3 necessarily succeeds frame 2, frame 4 frame 3, and so forth through the nth frame, which marks the termination of the strip of film. This literal succession of frames is both automatic and impersonal. The frames succeed one another automatically, regardless of the content of their images. This literal succession exists in both the recording and the projection processes and is the essential cinematographic operation. All the steps leading to the invention of the cinema were attempts to surmount the problem of recording a theoretically infinite number of frames that successively produced an impression of continuity when projected. The crucial steps in that process were: (1) the invention of the photographic (still) camera; (2) the development of "faster" photographic materials; (3) the invention of the camera shutter; (4) the invention of celluloid; and (5) the refinement of intermittent projection.

But just because this succession of frames is the essential cinematographic operation in no way implies that it is the only one. The first ten or fifteen years of cinema history powerfully demonstrated the limits of this single operation. To record an action automatically and then to project that same literal succession of frames—as did Edison or Lumière —became boring for audiences that had seen it before. The success of the Méliès fantasies was, however, a surprising variation of the same literal succession of his contemporaries. Méliès intuitively perceived that the literal succession of frames in the projection process made the action appear absolutely continuous, even if it had been halted and something added or subtracted in the recording process. The projector pushed the film steadily forward, erasing any previous stops and starts, making the "magical" appearances, disappearances, and conversions seem absolutely fluid and, therefore, natural and real.

From this early Méliès discovery it was a short leap to animation, and an animated cartoon is the one kind of cinema that is completely dependent on the literal succession of frames through the projector. By definition, animation is the recording of a single frame at a time (each frame capturing a particular phase of movement). The literal succession of frames through the projector—which is both unaware of and unconcerned with the way the frames were recorded—makes sequential sense

Two consecutive frames of *The Conjuror (Méliès,* 1898). The magician (Méliès) turns into his female assistant in mid-air by using the inevitable successivity of projection to erase the stops and starts during filming.

out of the disparate pieces. It might be useful to a define a category of *synthetic* film effects that would include Méliès, animation, pixillation,* and any others in which the action is either stopped, or analyzed, or altered in the recording process, but resynthesized to become continuous and whole in the projection process as a result of the literal succession of frames through the projector.

Two other familiar synthetic effects are the commonly known fast and slow motion. Both these effects are dependent upon the variability of the recording process and the implacable unalterability of the projection process. A scene recorded at eight frames per second will still be projected at twenty-four and will appear three times faster; ten seconds of thus recorded action will contain only eighty frames and will, therefore, be projected in 3.33 seconds. Conversely, a scene recorded at seventy-two frames per second will appear three times slower; ten seconds of thus recorded action will contain 720 frames and will take, therefore, thirty seconds to project. The projector is a kind of mathematician; it automatically reduces all images to $\frac{1}{24}$.

In the silent era, of course, the projection process was often no more automatic than the recording process. The skilled projectionist had to know how to turn the crank to make the action seem fluid and natural, just as the skilled cameraman did. The projectionist with artistic and rhythmic sensitivity could lyricize or comicalize scenes by cranking too slow or too fast (in fact, silent films were often released with cranking instructions to the projectionist for doing so). The coming of synchronized sound ended all that, transferring all synthetic effects to the recording process, leaving the projector to unspool the film electrically and, hence, constantly.

Several makers of lyric (or experimental) films exploit this literal succession of frames exclusively since these filmmakers are frequently sensitive to the puristic possibilities of a single one of the cinema's many variables. These experiments take this literal succession in two opposite directions. Robert Breer makes films that are very close in style and spirit to animation; many of his films are indeed animated films in the most familiar sense, such as his *Horse Over Teakettle, 69,* or *Jamestown Baloos.* That Breer's roots lie in animation is not surprising, since one of the primary influences on his work is that of Émile Cohl, the first maker of surrealist animated films. But several of Breer's other films (such as *Blazes* or *Fist Fight*) reveal a very unfamiliar use of animation, since they

---

* Pixillation is the recording of natural movement one frame at a time, as if nature were a drawn cartoon. The result is a comical, jerky, extra-fast rendering of natural motion.

are composed of a succession of absolutely different frames. The projector shows us twenty-four different frames per second rather than (as in a typical animation film) related frames that contain only a slightly different phase of movement.

But Breer's bizarre technique is still very close to animation, for *Blazes* does not give us twenty-four frames of just anything at all (i.e., one frame of Mickey Mouse, the next of the Eiffel Tower, the next of a spot of color, the next of Spot the dog, the next of Dick and Jane, the next of Nancy and Sluggo, the next of Nixon and Checkers, and so on). Breer's different frames are all of spots, lines, patches, and swatches of color—with many of the colors and shapes recurring over a series of several frames. So what Breer really does is to animate color and shape itself. His goal is not the Dada film described above, but to reveal how our eye perceives connections and linkages (a "dance" of form and color) where no actual connections exist, simply because the literal succession of frames through the projector makes us connect. *Blazes* is a theoretical investigation of the essential cinema illusion—the fact that literal succession converts separate entities into apparently continuous unities.

In a completely opposite direction, some experimental filmmakers take advantage of the literal succession of frames by making a film that is only an uninterrupted (i.e., uncut) succession of frames. This kind of lyric film, called either a structural or minimal or absolute film, is a kind of regression to the pre-editing era, to the earliest films of Edison and Lumière. With some major additions.

First, the camera or perspective can move or change—tracking, panning, tilting, and zooming—adding the interest of new viewing angles and distances within the unedited succession. Most of these minimal films use a maximum of zoom. Second, there is a carefully controlled sound track—perhaps speech (either conversation or narration), or natural sounds, or music, or *musique concrète,* or some combination of all four. And third, the unedited film strip can be subjected to any number of laboratory and printing effects, such as superimposition, color tinting, or switching from positive to negative.

Perhaps the most famous (and longest) of these minimal films, which uses all three devices, is Michael Snow's forty-five-minute *Wavelength,* and among the most noted of the independent filmmakers who have experimented in this style are Bruce Baillie (*All My Life*), Andy Warhol (*Sleep, Empire State*), and Hollis Frampton (*Lemon*). To some extent, the goal of these structural films is precisely opposite that of Breer's use of the opposite principle of literal succession. Where Breer revealed our perception of unity in a deliberate diversity, Snow, Baillie, and the others reveal our perception of diversity and variety in what is theoretically a unity. The structural films reveal how different the same thing can look, even without our being aware that this sameness is constantly changing.

To some extent, the classic narrative filmmakers who relied on the extended take and the visual interest of the unedited shot (Chaplin, Keaton, Renoir, the Astaire films, von Stroheim, Wyler, Welles) held a parallel view of the literal succession of frames. For these moviemakers, the uninterrupted flow of closely related frames that did not constantly require the viewer to make both visual and mental adjustments to a new field of vision allowed the viewer to perceive more in that constant field of vision. In a film in which the different images succeed each other as often as they do in Breer's, nothing can be perceived but the motion and the impact of the succession itself.

Of the classic narrative filmmakers closest to Breer, Eisenstein, experimenting in *October,* produced the assaultive effect of battle by alternating images of men and gunfire that were each two frames long. Dziga-Vertov's *Man with a Movie Camera* produces similar effects with clashing shots that are frequently one to four frames long. Such clashing images produce not Breer's assaultive dance of colors, but what has been labeled the "Phi" effect—an impression curiously close to superimposition but kinetically different from it. The two images seem almost to melt into one, but their alternation produces a more dynamic, clashing, jangling rhythm than the fluid melding of a true superimposition. But these Eisenstein and Vertov devices were as closely related to the effects of montage as to the effects of the simple succession of frames. And Eisenstein's theory of montage is one of the fullest treatments of the issue of joining shots, not joining frames.

IMAGISTIC SUCCESSION

If you hold a strip of film up to the light to examine it with the eye alone, you can see how easily it splits into clearly demarcated units. By holding the celluloid at a distance, you might perceive one strip of similar-looking patterns that goes on for, say, fifteen inches, and then another strip of patterns similar to each other but different from the first that extends over, say, forty inches, and then another strip of patterns similar to each other but different from the second (although not necessarily from the first) that extends over, say, twenty-four inches, and so forth. If you run your fingers along the celluloid, the strip feels perfectly smooth (unless

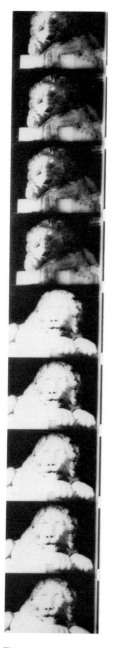 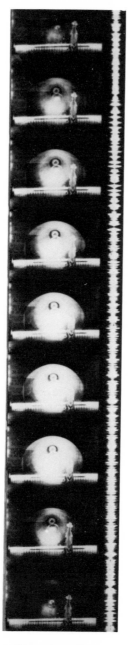 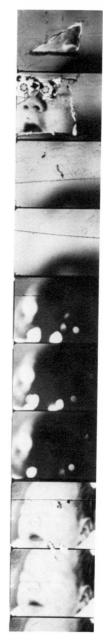

Three filmstrips. *Potemkin:* the sitting stone lion succeeds the sleeping one automatically. *Citizen Kane:* the opera montage sequence with its newspapers, theater activity, the blinking lightbulb, and cacophonous sound (evident from the patterns of the sound track that accompany the images). *Courtesy Janus Films. Dog Star Man:* some "shots" are only a single frame.

this is a work print, or unless the film has broken and been spliced). There is no textural difference between the different strips of patterns, just as the projector does not indicate any place where the frames of two different shots join one another (unless the splices still exist in the print, which makes the projector jump and give the game away). The first frame of a new shot follows the last frame of the previous one in as smooth and automatic a manner as any other frame succeeds any other.

The decision to end one image and begin a new one is a creative decision, made during the assembling of the film, and its result is projected automatically during a screening. Most films are indeed sequences of these shots, joined one to the other, rather than a simple succession of frames in a single shot (Edison, Lumière, minimal films) or a succession of absolutely different frames (Breer, animation). It would certainly be valid to argue that the single shot and not the joining of shots is the essential cinematic operation (as did Bazin), simply because it is possible to make a cinematic work that is merely a succession of frames (i.e., a single shot) but not possible to make one that is merely a succession of shots (since all shots contain frames that succeed one another). But not very many interesting films can be made with only a literal succession of frames, nor can the technique produce much variety. A second answer to the question of why moment B succeeds moment A in a work of cinema is that B is a shot that follows A in the unspooling of the reel of film. A film is usually as undeniably an imagistic succession of shots as it is a literal succession of frames.

Because both image and shot bear many different definitions in English, it might be well to state how I use them here. An image (or shot—I use these terms synonymously in this sense) is a unit of frames in the final print of the film that was originally exposed consecutively and continuously by the camera. Or if the camera stopped, it did so without changing position, so that no stop is perceptible. With such a synthetic effect, the image *appears* continuous and consecutive even if it is not. It is this definition and notion of a shot with which Keaton's famous montage sequence plays in *Sherlock Jr.* The brilliantly funny sequence manipulates the paradox that we are watching different shots (because the location constantly changes) and the same shot (because Buster's position in the frame never changes) at the same time. Conceivably, the continuous unit that makes up a shot could be as short as a single frame (as in Vertov or, for example, if the frame fell between two lengthier shots of a man's face, representing a mental "blip" of some kind). In practice, however, even a very brief shot lasts some eight frames, unless the creator intends some special effect (like Eisenstein,

Vertov, the experimental filmmaker Gregory Markopoulos, or the mental flashes forward or backward in *Easy Rider* or *The Pawnbroker*).

This sense of "image" clearly differs from other familiar English uses: for example, in *Rules of the Game* Renoir presents an image of a decaying society. This much looser and literary use of "image" is merely a synonym for metaphor, symbol, vision, view, or any number of other terms which could be substituted without changing the meaning of the assertion. My use of "image" refers to a single, unedited sequence of frames that is physically single on the strip of celluloid (although an image can last so long and become so complex—as in Hitchcock's *Rope*—that it is single only in physical fact, not in function or effect). In its original form, the single image was a single strip of celluloid in the editing bin that remained intact in the final editing process and was spliced between two other intact pieces.

This sense of "shot" is equally different from other familiar English uses: for example, Renoir shot much of *Rules of the Game* on location. It is quite close, however, to: Renoir planned the opening sequence of *Rules of the Game* at Le Bourget as a single shot. Without question, the single shot of radio cable, the airport, the radio reporter, and the milling throng that opens the finished movie is a trimmed and tightened version of the single one that Renoir blocked in space and shot with his camera.

An animated film cannot truly contain shots in this sense—for every frame is exposed individually. But a cartoon organizes its assemblages of individual frames in a way that is analogous to the shot. Whenever the main "cel" (or background "cel") of a cartoon changes (i.e., we no longer see a distant view of Roadrunner skimming across the desert, but instead see a close view of the coyote holding a stick of dynamite), we see something analogous to a different shot, despite the fact that the animation camera simply continues to expose individual frames.

There are three primary principles of imagistic succession, three general reasons for one shot's succeeding another: visual, rhythmic, and structural. In practice, a film's imagistic succession may use two or even all three of these successive principles at once, for they are in no way mutually exclusive or contradictory. To clarify their uses and effects, however, it is functional to treat them as discrete entities.

If we return to examining the strip of celluloid with the naked eye, we might discover three things about the unprojected film by simply using a pair of rewinds and an ordinary light bulb between them. First, it may be apparent that there is a consistent pattern of light-looking images, succeeded by darker ones, succeeded by light ones, succeeded by dark ones, and so forth. Tony Conrad's *The Flicker* is precisely such a film, an alternating succession of units composed of pure white and pure black frames. Second, it may be apparent that each of these succeeding pieces is slightly shorter than the one preceding it. Indeed, the visual alternation of black and white in Conrad's film is perceived as rhythmic flicker rather than alternating visual pattern. Third, it may be apparent that at the beginning of the strip the color tones of the image are a light pink (let us add color to Conrad's black-white opposition), but it becomes apparent (as one quickly winds the film forward) that there is a tendency for the colors to change gradually from the pale pink to a deeper pink, to a rose, and finally, at the end of the film, to a deep red.* These three possibilities are examples of each of the possible principles of imagistic succession.

Shots can succeed one another for purely visual reasons. A light image can be succeeded by a dark one, succeeded by another light one, then a dark one, and so on. Or a light image can be succeeded by an even lighter one, and then by one lighter still. A close shot can be succeeded by a far one; a shot of a circular object can be succeeded by a shot of a horizontal mass. A shot of motion from right to left can be succeeded by one of motion from left to right; or it can be succeeded by another of motion from right to left; and still another after that. Of course, the different possibilities of visual succession cannot always be determined by simply examining the celluloid's successive pattern of shots with the naked eye. Unlike the pureness of the Conrad flicker film, most shots manipulate internal visual values that are dependent on the objects or the motion within the image. To translate this observation into the terms of this discussion, the visual effect of the imagistic succession of shots may also be dependent on the continuous motion that has been captured by the literal succession of frames.

Perhaps this discussion of visual succession seems very close to Eisenstein's discussion of the possibilities of montage, and of course it is.[1] Eisenstein is the one classical film theorist who built his theory on the premise that the imagistic succession of shots (rather than the literal succession of frames) was the essence of the cinema art. (This is the Bazin-Eisenstein "debate" in a parenthesis.) The rhythmical effects of imagistic succession are also Eisenstein topics. The effects of rhythmical succession are felt rather than seen; one can describe them not in visual terms (i.e., light-dark, big-little, right-left), but in temporal ones (short-long, fast-slow).

Rhythmical principles of succession proceed from the fact that film is a time-art and, like music, it has effects that can be felt in strictly tem-

---

* The experimental films of Paul Sharits (*Ray Gun Virus* or *T,O,U,C,H,I,N,G*) combine these flicker effects with color.

poral terms. Because time in the cinema can be translated into a mathematical expression (the fraction 1/24), its effects can also be translated into mathematical expressions (for example, 8 frames requires 1/3 second, 48 frames requires 2 seconds). A successive series of film strips, each 48 frames long, can produce the feeling of a steady, 2-second beat. A successive series of film strips, each shorter than the one preceding it (say, 48 frames, then 40, then 35, then 30, and so forth) can produce the *accelerando;* the opposite principle of steadily longer ones can produce the *decelerando.* The rhythmic succession of images is the cinema's closest approximation to the abstract kinesis of music; although visual images can be quite concrete, the rhythms of their succession are not. Cinema thinking and writing are much poorer for a lack of practitioners who are both sensitive to and skilled in the principles of musical structure.

It is even less possible to divorce the rhythmic, "musical" possibilities of imagistic succession from the action in the literal succession of frames than it was with the visual possibilities. There are two ways in which the literal succession of frames obviously influences the effects of the rhythmic succession of shots. First, the rhythm of the movement within the shot itself contains its own kind of visual "music," which necessarily influences our response to the succession of images. If one views a succession of images, each a languid ten seconds (240 frames) long, but the action of the literal succession of frames is that of the Keystone Kops giving chase on foot, car, boat, and horseback, the dominant rhythm of the sequence will be the *presto* of the chase. On the other hand, in the final sequence of *Intolerance,* D. W. Griffith combined the frantic movement of train, automobile, and chariots racing to their rescues with the dizzying motion of a moving camera racing along with them. He then combined this frenzied motion with a steadily shorter succession of images, producing the breathtaking excitement of the climactic *accelerando.*

The other way that literal succession influences the rhythms of imagistic succession is its determining the precise point at which the director (or editor) decides to make a cut. Perhaps the filmmaker wants to induce a feeling of mellow slowness by consistently prolonging the literal succession of a shot before cutting to the succeeding image. Ozu works in precisely this manner (as does Satyajit Ray), prolonging the image, for example, of a vacant room after the characters have deserted it, slowing down the action deliberately and, in the process, defining the texture and meaning of "vacancy." Leo McCarey also tends to stay with his shots for a while after the comic facial reaction has hit a climax and faded, an easy rhythm that makes Andrew Sarris find him supple and mellow—but a rhythm that make me prefer the snap of Capra or Hawks, who usually make the opposite choice. Their consistent cutting to the succeeding image immediately after the action in a shot has hit its climax or ended imparts a rhythmic urgency and bounce to the feel and texture of each scene.

This discussion of the imagistic succession of shots has inevitably introduced the issue of cutting. There is a tendency for both Eisenstein and Bazin to discuss cutting as if it were an applied science, a preplanned strategy of attack that influences the shooting of a film and is then carried out in the cutting room according to some kind of theoretical formula. A great moviemaker like Hitchcock tends to support such an attitude when he claims that he precuts entire films in his head as he shoots them. Well, perhaps he does. One major difference between John Ford's shooting methods and Frank Capra's was that Ford shot very little footage so the editor could cut the film in only one way (the way he wanted it), whereas Capra shot a lot of footage so he could play around with it in the cutting room (because he had won the right to cut his own films).[2]

The editing of the exposed footage is perhaps the most improvisatory, the most experimental, the most informal stage in the entire process of shooting and assembling a movie. It is not surprising that the editing process should be so improvisatory; it is one of the rare moments in a huge and expensive project when one person (or perhaps two or three) can sit alone in a quiet room with a lot of time and a cup of coffee. Unlike the shooting process, there are not hundreds of people hanging around, waiting to earn their salaries. There are no producers and assistant directors watching their watches, no temperamental stars to coax out of their dressing trailers and into a performance, no huge machines to drive, fly, shake, rattle, and roll. (Editing machinery, though extremely refined, can be manipulated by a mechanical incompetent.) In the editing process, the assembler (be he director, editor, cutter, or some team of all three) has the opportunity to take time and take chances—trying different takes of the same shots, trying to cut shots in a different order, or to intercut them, or to extend them, or to tighten them. It is a time to try because there is time to try.* In the terms of this discussion, the assembler can experiment with the duration of the shot's literal succession of frames, and with the order and selection of the imagistic succession of shots.

---

* I do not mean to imply that the editing process is completely free of such extra-artistic pressures as the bad taste of producers, the demands of stars' contracts that limit the number of close-ups for everyone else in the movie, and the simple necessity of making choices between lousy footage and less lousy footage. The editing process is *comparatively* free of such pressures and comparatively more instinctual than the scripting of a movie.

The really good director (or editor-cutter-assembler) makes a cut for only two reasons: (1) he or she finds the shot no longer interesting, or (2) he or she finds the shot interesting enough, but feels that the cut would be more important or more interesting. Cutting film is as instinctual a talent as working with actors, and the best directors cut film well not because of science and theory, but because of sensibility and instinct. Chaplin did not cut infrequently because he reasoned that infrequent cutting would enable us to watch him better. (That is the kind of deduction that critics legitimately make.) He cut infrequently because he *knew* (in that second, intuitive sense of knowing) that what he was looking at was worth looking at; he cut when it wasn't worth looking at or when something else was more worth looking at.

It is interesting that two youthful and instinctual talents, Eisenstein and Welles, made later movies that had occasionally fine moments, but were disappointing, stilted, even silly shadows of their early work. At least one of the reasons for their atrophy, I think, is that Eisenstein started to read Eisenstein (he made his greatest films before he began theorizing about montage) and Welles started to read Bazin (the opening sequence of a later film like *The Trial* seems an unintentional and grotesque parody of both his own early technique and Bazin's theory). Eisenstein's complex graph for *Alexander Nevsky*—integrating the musical score, bar by bar, with the visual composition, shot by shot—is an amazing exercise in mathematical and theoretical rigor. But that very precision is symptomatic of the movie's leaden lack of spontaneity—almost as if it were made to serve the complicated graph, and not the other way round. This is not an indictment of the critic, the theorist, or the processes of reason. It is a simple assertion that the most useful tool an artist can possess is talent, not a theory.

Which returns us to the theoretical issue of the third and most complicated principle of imagistic succession: structural succession. Structure is the most complex successive principle for two reasons. First, it is extremely unlikely that a film's structural principle has a basis in concrete, physical fact. The literal succession of frames has a basis in concrete, physical fact (one can see the precise point where one frame ends and the next begins). So can a film's visual and rhythmical principles of imagistic succession (one can see the contrast of light and dark strips or short and long ones; one can count frames and come up with an interesting inference). But a film's principle of structural succession can rarely be discovered by counting or by examining a strip of celluloid with the naked eye. (Notice all the words I needed to explain that pink-to-red example above. And how many films are structured so simply?)

Second, even in films that are extremely attentive to the imagistic succession of visual and rhythmic elements (for example, Eisenstein's), these values are secondary and subordinate to its general structural strategy. *Potemkin* contains magnificent sections that could be discussed (and have been discussed) solely as examples of visual and rhythmic successions of images. But the underlying reason for every image in *Potemkin* is to reveal something about the growth of unity and brotherhood in response to an evil and alien force. Its secondary systems of imagistic succession (visual and rhythmical) may indeed be the means to support and develop its primary and dominant system (the overall structural pattern), but there can be little question about which is primary in this film, which is the means and which the end.

It is easier, of course, to discuss rhythmical successions of shots (for example, here Eisenstein links a shot of 26 frames with one of 23, then one of 18, then 13, then 9, to produce an *accelerando*)—easier because it is so precisely mathematical and because the very question guarantees the result. To discuss why shot B succeeds shot A structurally is necessarily to introduce such imprecise, "impressionistic," unmathematical notions as function, intention, and effect. It requires leaving the physical effects of cinema's kinesis, by which it is initially perceived, to discuss the way our minds synthesize all that diverse data.

And yet how else to discuss an essential feature of a time-art in which there is moment the last and moment the first and all the moments between? The last moment is last (the deepest red, in my example) because it concludes whatever it was that began in the first moment (the palest red). Very few films, even those organized on purely visual and rhythmic principles, are organized so simply. Robert Breer's *Blazes* (to return to an old friend) is so unique precisely because its literal succession of different frames is identical with its visual and rhythmic succession (to assault with clashing colors), which is identical with its structural succession (a steady assault that forces us to perceive the illusory connections that are the basis of cinema). There is a similar identity of all three principles of succession in Tony Conrad's *The Flicker*. So, too, Hans Richter's *Rhythmus 21* uses its visual and rhythmic successions as the sole bases of its structural succession. In brief, Richter's film begins with a few geometric shapes moving slowly and simply and builds to a climax of many geometric shapes moving quickly and complexly. Its visual principle (variation and proliferation) and its rhythmic principle (*accelerando* and *crescendo*) are its structural principle, too. But such an identity of successive principles in a cinematic work seems dependent on stripping the visual images of their concrete referrents, indeed eliminating the differences between the pure abstraction of music and the potential concreteness of visual images.

Other films that use the same proliferation, variation, *accelerando,* and *crescendo* of Richter's film, and are no lengthier, are far more complex precisely because they combine these visual and musical principles with concrete images. Bruce Conner's *A Movie* (another old friend) uses these same successive principles visually and rhythmically, but its structural succession is complicated by the fact that its images contain concrete depictions of death, slaughter, war, and disaster. Ralph Steiner's H_2O uses Richter's proliferation and acceleration as well. Its structural succession is complicated by the fact that although all the shots of the film capture the movement of light upon the surfaces of water, as the film progresses the light-on-water tends gradually not to look like light-on-water at all, but some bubbling canvas of abstract forms. The structural principle of Steiner's film is the gradual dissolution of photographic concreteness into musical abstraction.

To discuss the structural succession of shots in a film requires leaving the imagistic succession of individual shots to discuss the structural succession of the whole work. There is one specific device of structural succession, however, that properly belongs to a discussion of the imagistic succession of shots: the several kinds of structural punctuation marks in cinema that seem analogous to an individual shot. These are not strictly part of a work's visual or rhythmic succession of shots, but they form a kind of unit that is seen as visual effect and felt as rhythmic respite. The most common of these punctuation units is the fade (or dissolve) to black, a short unit of blackness, and then the fade up (or dissolve in) again.* The meaning of such a punctuation mark is clearly that something has come to an end and then something else is beginning.[3]

The fade demarcates the major structural sections (the scenes, or sequences, or "movements," or "acts") of a cinematic work, and the need to use it is a consequence of the cinema's literal succession of frames. Because the projection process is unrelenting and unceasing, it makes no distinction between structural segments (or "movements") within the "content" of the work itself. So if the maker wants to notify an audience that one structural unit has come to an end and another is about to begin, he must build something into the literal succession of frames itself that will signify the shift of emphasis or attention.

---

* The opposite of the fade to black is the "burn to white"—another kind of punctuation device that substitutes the hotness and brilliance of white for the inkiness of black. It is extremely popular in experimental films.

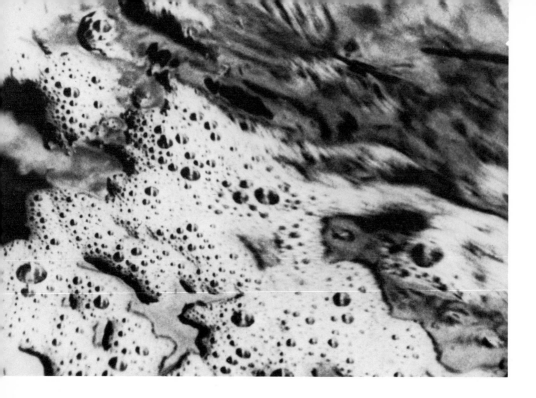

The structural succession of H_2O progressively dissolves concrete images into pure abstraction. The early and identifiable images (bubbles on water) evolve into less clearly discernible ones (the wooden pilings which disappear into strangely wavy reflections) and finally into unidentifiable abstract patterns.

In this sense, the cinema is completely different from the other time-arts, all of which arrest the flow of time to signify structural shifts. In literature, our eye informs us of such shifts and structural units as clause, sentence, paragraph, and chapter. In the theater, the stage lights dim or the curtain falls. In music, the kinetic flow of sound climaxes and then stops to signify the end of a movement and the beginning of the next (although the structural demarcations in musical works are frequently very subtle, so that they are musical rests rather than full pauses). But since there is no way for the cinema literally to stop (except for the artificiality of the intermission), it must build something into the imagistic succession of shots that looks *as if* it were a stop despite the fact that it is clearly not. The fade to black is, paradoxically, a moving stop.

A parallel punctuation mark in the cinema is the lap dissolve, the gradual appearance of the new image seemingly "on top of" the old one, growing steadily stronger and clearer while the old one fades away. This punctuation mark implies not just that something is ending and something else beginning, but that something is beginning at the same time that something else is ending. In comparison to the fade-out and fade-in, the lap dissolve is usually a lighter kind of rest, more like the end of a paragraph than a chapter. But because the duration of the lap dissolve can be prolonged indefinitely by the literal succession of "overlapping" frames, the device can imply an even weightier shift or pause than the fade. Of course, the "weight" of the fade or burn can also be increased by prolonging the literal succession of the fading or burning process (or of the period of blackness or whiteness)—as in the agonizingly slow and lyrical fade that closes our view of plowing the fields in D. W. Griffith's *A Corner in Wheat*.

Two formerly popular kinds of punctuation marks are in disfavor today, both because of their overt trickiness and because their "weight" and tone cannot be effectively manipulated by the rhythmic alteration of their literal successions: the iris-in (and iris-out) and the wipe. The iris implies the same thing as the fade, with perhaps the connotation of something closing down and something else opening up. The wipe implies the same thing as the dissolve, with perhaps the connotation that something new is pushing the old thing out of the way (or flipping it over, or turning it inside out or upside down). Both these marks seem decidedly comic today. The iris-out has become the standard ending of cartoons and the wipe has rarely been used for other than satiric purposes (e.g., *Young Frankenstein*) since about 1960.

These four kinds of structural punctuation marks are analogous to the succession of frames that forms the unit of a single shot, although, strictly speaking, the fade, burn, and iris contain three images (shot 1, black or white, shot 2) while the lap dissolve and wipe contain the two images at once.

STRUCTURAL SUCCESSION

The most common answer to the question of why moment B succeeds moment A in a work of cinema is that B represents some later or more developed stage in a film's sequence of "events." I use "event" rather than the more familiar term, "action," for the same reason I use "structural succession" rather than "plot." Although the literary notion of an action or plot can be applied to movies, lyric and nonfiction films often do not tell stories and, hence, do not have plots. Nevertheless, they contain clear structural patterns of "events" which shape their temporal progression and development as carefully and consistently as plot shapes the narrative structure of movies.

For example, two films as different as *Citizen Kane* and *Wavelength* manipulate strikingly similar structural assumptions. Both films are built on the structural principle of penetration, of approaching a subject as close as possible to uncover whatever lies beneath the surface. And with both films one can argue that there is a deliberate ambiguity about whether the steadily increasing closeness ever really gets anywhere, whether the surface is indeed penetrated or not. *Citizen Kane's* use of closeness is, of course, more metaphoric than *Wavelength's*, although it supports the metaphor with concrete visual images and camera strategies.

The movie begins outside a fence, then outside a house, then outside the window of a room. The camera moves steadily closer in the opening sequence, leaping over, past, and through the physical obstacles to its inquiry, until it arrives for a dying man's last word. The camera tends to begin each sequence by tracking toward its object—seemingly boring closer to an elusive center. The film's second sequence is the totally externalized account of the dead man's past life, reduced to a piece (indeed a parody of a piece) of film journalism. Its third sequence moves a bit closer to the man, since it is narrated by a human being who came into contact with Kane. But Thatcher is locked inside his own views and prejudices (just as his views are locked inside his memoirs, and his memoirs are locked inside a library, and the library is a mausoleum). He is never able to pierce beneath Kane's surfaces. The fourth sequence moves closer still by examining the testimony of a business acquaintance, but Bernstein is locked inside his respect for "Mister" Kane, just as Thatcher was locked inside his conservative contempt for him. The fifth sequence probes deeper because Jed Leland, although locked inside his smug self-righteousness, knew Kane well; and the sixth, Susan's, is that of a person who knew Kane even better (but had even more reason to detest him).

But after this steady succession of movings closer, the camera begins to pull back again, forced to retreat because it has gone as close and as deep as it could, but it still has come up empty. It has not discovered the private meaning of that last word which it (and only it?) caught at the beginning of the quest. Our final discovery that Rosebud was Charles's childhood sled (and our making connections between that concrete object and the glass ball, the snowscapes, and the other sled in the film—a gift of Thatcher's) is equally ambiguous. For only the camera discovers what Rosebud is, which perhaps implies that only a camera (i.e., an artist or a god) can penetrate the surfaces of human experience. But the camera pulls away and pulls backward, setting us down again outside the fence with the "No Trespassing" sign. Although we know we've trespassed and gone closer, we cannot be absolutely sure how far or how deep.

Wavelength takes its structural principle of closeness and penetration quite literally. It begins as a far shot of a part of a single room and then moves ceaselessly (like the succession of frames itself), but very slowly, toward the wall and windows of that room. Eventually (after some foreground diversions, which are deliberate and playful diversions from its true progress), the camera reveals its interest in some pictures on the wall; still later we move close enough to those pictures to be able to see them. We discover that what we first thought were the more important pictures (the two higher on the wall) are not at all the center of the camera's concern. We discover things about those higher pictures (that, for example, both are really two pictures, not one as we previously thought). We see that one of the pictures seems to be two black-and-white, identical photographs of a boy.

But we desert these upper pictures to move closer still to the lower one, which appeared to resemble mountains or clouds or waves or women's breasts from a distance, but which now looks like waves when it fills the frame. But as the camera continues to scrutinize this static photograph of the "waves," even it refuses to remain static or the same. Slight changes of the camera's focus attract our eyes to different details of the "waves"; then the camera blurs out of focus altogether (again altering our perception of these apparent "waves"; are they waves?) and the film comes to a highly inconclusive conclusion. Is it the end? And of what is it the end?

It is obviously the end of the process of moving close to the wall and the lower picture, but we both do and do not know anything more about this space and its artifacts and its occupants than at the beginning. Whose loft is it? Whose pictures are they? Who is the person in the picture? What is the significance of the "waves"? Who are the people that wander in and out during the shot (except that one of them may still be there on the floor)? Although we may be able to discover some answers to these questions from information that is not in the film (say, from our knowledge of details of the artist's life or his use of parallel objects and motifs in other films), the film itself is deliberately neutral and blank about them. We have indeed moved close to something and some things, but we know not what, except that we have moved close and, in the process, seen the appearances of various somethings change before our eyes without resolving or revealing what or why they are. We have moved close to surfaces without penetrating them, only discovering how mysterious and complex are the surfaces themselves.

In the process of a film's structural succession, "something is taking its course" (to use Vladimir's purposefully vague description of the even vaguer plot of Beckett's *Waiting for Godot*). But there are many kinds of somethings and many kinds of courses. To codify and classify all variants and types of structural successions would be a task even less useful than possible. But we might distinguish among three broad classes of successive structural patterns in works of cinema.

First, there are patterns built on the interrelationship of a course of human events and the personalities of those who perform the events or are influenced by those events. This is the familiar pattern of movies and it offers three principal variations. The movie can depict a course of human events that results from the consistent and unvarying characteristics and personalities of the human participants: Huston's *The Asphalt Jungle*; Lang's *You Only Live Once*; Renoir's *Rules of the Game, Grand Illusion*, and most of his others; Carné-Prévert's *The Children of Paradise* and most of their others; Ford's *Stagecoach, Fort Apache, The Informer*, and most of his others; Hitchcock's *The 39 Steps, Vertigo, Psycho, Strangers on a Train*, and most of his others; Godard's *Breathless*; Fellini's *La Strada* and *Nights of Cabiria*; Polanski's *Chinatown*; and virtually all of Chaplin, Keaton, Griffith, von Sternberg, and von Stroheim.

Or the movie can depict the way that a course of human events produces changes in the characteristics and personalities of the human participants: Capra's *Mr. Smith, Mr. Deeds, Meet John Doe*, and most of his others; Hawks's *Red River, Bringing Up Baby*, indeed, most of his films; Ray's Apu trilogy; Truffaut's *Shoot the Piano Player, Jules and Jim*, and *The Wild Child*; Antonioni's *L'Avventura, Eclipse*, and most others; Bergman's *Wild Strawberries, Persona, The Seventh Seal*, and most others; Murnau's *The Last Laugh*; Menzel's *Closely Watched Trains*. (So many major directors tend to fall either on one clear side or the other of this dichotomy, which reveals their attitude not only toward narrative structure, but toward the relative power of character and circumstance in determining the human condition.)

The final of these narrative possibilities is the interplay and interdependence between changes in events and changes in character: *Casablanca, The Big Sleep, To Have and Have Not* (indeed, isn't this the Bogart pattern?), Renoir's *Boudu Saved from Drowning*; Lubitsch's *Trouble in Paradise, The Marriage Circle*, and most of his others; Ophuls's *The Earrings of Madame de . . .* and *Lola Montès*. Can you think of a movie that doesn't fulfill one of these three shapes?

A variant form of narrative structure is that of certain experimental, lyric films which manipulate a clear pattern of human personality and events, but do so within a system of personal symbol and metaphor. Kenneth Anger's *Fireworks*, for example, has a clear narrative beginning (a young man, played by Anger himself, feels sexual frustration), middle (he goes out seeking to ease it), and end (he suceeds). But each event in that pattern can only be felt and understood by our responding to Anger's contextually defined symbols.

As he lies in bed in the opening sequence, his penis has been replaced by a primitive religious icon (erect beneath the sheets, but made of wood not flesh). A series of photographs of a strong sailor holding the boy's own limp body lies beside his bed (pornographic pictures? projections of the boy's desire? or both—since that is what pornography is?). He begins his quest for companionship by leaving his room (on the door, a sign marked "Gents"), observing a series of automobile headlights (cruising?), admiring the muscles of a man in a two-dimensionally painted bar, and, eventually, meeting a gang of sailors who beat him with chains, rip his flesh with broken glass, probe inside his innards (revealing a highly ironic symbol at his essence—a metered dial), and pour milk over his passive chin and chest (all of which obviously imply his masochistic submissiveness).

He returns to his room for the film's climax, where a Christmas tree has replaced his head (the wooden icon has become fertile and joyful) and an exploding Roman candle has replaced his penis (coupled with that climactic Respighi music). In the film's final shot, the boy has returned to his bed where he rests comfortably, for there is another male torso lying beside his own. The face of his male companion has been scratched out—ringed by circular scratches on the film emulsion. This personal symbol implies both the mystical beauty of their meeting (for the scratches look like a nimbus) and the fact that his companion is a body without a face. He is anybody. For any body will satisfy the boy— and has satisfied him.

Second, a work of cinema can be built on purely kinetic patterns, either analogous to musical forms (theme and variation, acceleration, deceleration, counterpoint, intensification, expansion, repetition) or dependent on translating visual values into temporal terms (proliferation, decimation, contrast, parallel, direction) or some combination of the two kinetic systems. Most of the lyric films devoted purely to visual perception and rhythmic stimulation are indeed built exclusively on these structural principles (Breer, Fischinger, Whitney, Steiner, Jordan Belson).

And third, a cinema work's structural succession can be built on expository, rhetorical or logical principles (cause and effect, comparison and contrast, process, procedure, induction, deduction). These are the common structural patterns of nonfiction films, primarily because they are the common structural patterns of nonfiction writing. The classic documentary *Night Mail* is structured around the process of receiving, transporting, and transmitting the mail, supported by the train's geographical journey (from London to Scotland), which mirrors that process precisely.

These common nonfiction patterns are not confined strictly to nonfiction cinematic structures. *Wavelength* is a classic example of a "structural film" since its structural logic is its essence—and that structure is the process of zooming closer to the wall and photographs. Bruce Conner's *A Movie* combines its kinetic principles (of direction, proliferation, and rhythmic variation) with an implied induction about movies, machines, and death. It is the specificity of this *Movie*'s images that makes it more concrete (if less pure) than an abstract work of cinema "music" and produces this induction. Stan Brakhage's *Window Water Baby Moving* combines kinetic principles (of theme and variation, repetition, contrast, and parallel) with an overall description of the process of birth—both the way the process occurred objectively and the way the artist felt about the process as it was occurring. Eisenstein's *Potemkin* straddles the three traditions of movie, kinetic abstraction, and nonfiction (it has been claimed as a representative of all three traditions by the critics and historians of each) precisely because it combines the structural patterns of all three. This narrative of an action taken by a group of sailors against an alien social system also fulfills an overall kinetic pattern of expansion and intensification (in addition to the many patterns of kinetic "movements" within the major pattern), all of which is intended as a kind of induction about the proper methods and valid reasons for revolutionary struggle.

The something that takes its course in movies can best be charted by comparing the beginning and end of the movie's course and then observing (or deducing) the strategy, significance, and stopping places in traveling between the two poles. A few specific (and highly concentrated) examples of the principles of structural succession that operate in some familiar movies may be useful. *Pather Panchali* (and the Apu trilogy as a whole) chronicles the maturing process of an intelligent and sensitive boy by exposing him, on the one hand, to a steadily broadening series of experiences with an ever expanding world and, on the other, to the emotional loss of an equally steady series of personal contractions through the deaths of those he loves.

Bringing Up Baby chronicles the eventual discovery by a man and a woman, who previously thought that they hated each other, that they really love and need one another, using the very bizarrely comic difficulties that made them think that they hated each other as the basis of their discovering how much fun they have together.

Rashomon contrasts the way that four different human beings—three intimate participants and an outside observer—view the same violent human event, each of their views colored by his (or her) own ego, personality, needs, and perceptions, concluding that the only solid truth lies in present action, not in perceptions of the past.

Stagecoach follows the perilous journey of a stagecoach, filled with extremely disparate human beings, through a wilderness where both man and nature are savage—a journey which is ultimately successful because the passengers can overcome their differences to work together in civilized fellowship against the savagery.

Never Give a Sucker an Even Break parodies the clichés of Hollywood studio life, the idiocy of Hollywood studio practices, and the fake but shiny conventions of "well made" Hollywood studio movies by making a movie-within-the-movie that is a ridiculously ill-made pastiche of romantic, operettic movies and by making the main movie itself an incoherent, rambling, and deliberately unstructured mess that is not about anything at all.

Closely Watched Trains chronicles the growth to maturity of a comically inept and impotent young man, who eventually proves his manhood both sexually and politically by destroying a Nazi train.

Persona is a sustained attack against the notion that human personality is easily defined and distinguishable, revealing the inadequacy of simple psychological definitions in both art (hence the patient's occupation of actress and the movie's self-conscious references to itself as a work of cinema) and science (hence the other woman's occupation of nurse and the societal assumption that the patient is indeed mentally ill).

These structural statements do not, of course, tell everything about these movies, but they tell something about them. They may seem dangerously close to being thematic statements, indeed, almost identical to thematic analyses of some of these very films. This kinship should not be surprising since in movies, as well as in literature, thematic inferences arise from a work's structural pattern of events: what happens to whom and why.

The cinema purist can react to this kinship between structural succession and literary plot in two ways. He can deny the existence or the importance of structural succession in cinema, concentrating exclusively on its literal and imagistic successions. Unfortunately, the significance of an event (such as the suicide attempt of Susan Alexander in *Citizen Kane*) often makes no sense at all exclusively in terms of the succession of frames or of shots. We bring to such events our knowledge of what we have seen the characters do in all the previous scenes of the work, as well as our personally and culturally defined senses of proper human behavior.

Or he can deny the importance of movies altogether as impure borrowings from the literary arts, a position that denies the value of so many rich and important works of cinema. It also fails to realize that even the structural successions of non-narrative films are analogous to structural patterns in the other arts, such as music, painting, and nonfiction prose, and there seems no reason why one borrowing is inherently purer than another. Finally, it fails to respond to the fact that narrative cinema is still narrative *cinema*, that movies are perceived and felt as works of cinema (not as books or plays), and the reason that they are so perceived is because structural succession (despite its importance) is only one of three kinds of cinematic succession that exist in every work of cinema, and succession itself is only one of the three primary sources of cinema's effects and information.

Visual succession in a film is an optical illusion, the illusion of wholeness and continuity produced by the movement of celluloid through the projector. Cinematic succession makes wholes out of mere pieces: (1) an apparently fluid whole out of obviously disparate frames; (2) an apparently spatial or temporal or imaginative whole out of obviously disparate shots; (3) an apparently structural whole out of obviously individual "events."

6/Projection

An obvious assumption of the preceding chapter is that the *aesthetic event* of cinema is the projection of the finished work—analogous to the reading of the type that is a novel, the attending to the motion and conversation that are a play, the listening to the sound that is a piece of music, or the looking at the color on canvas that is a painting. The creative process of shooting and assembling film is certainly a worthy subject of study—as are the notebooks of Henry James or the Georges Seurat sketches for *A Sunday Afternoon on the Island of La Grande Jatte*. To study this process reveals both the artist's specific choices and the general way he viewed his art and his craft. But it nonetheless studies the means to the end, and that end is experiencing the work of art itself, which remains its own testament and as solid a piece of evidence as any. With the cinema art it is perhaps an even solider piece of evidence than its maker's recollections of the creative process, since the memories of moviemakers are at least as prone to error as any, since the movie business encourages self-congratulation, and since the creative process of moviemaking is such an admittedly collective one.*

This emphasis on projection necessarily excludes certain interesting kinds of questions, among them some of the classic problems of film, cinema, and movie theory. It denies the notion of "the cinematic" altogether, since it assumes that any finished piece of cinema is indisputably

---

* Movie directors are notoriously unreliable. Frank Capra claims he watched Leo McCarey direct Laurel and Hardy at the Hal Roach studio in 1924 (L & H never worked together until 1927); Mack Sennett went to his grave claiming Buster Keaton was one of his Keystone Cops (never); Groucho Marx is under the impression that there are no musical numbers in *A Night at the Opera* (poor Kitty Carlisle and Allan Jones; or rather, poor us—because Groucho is unfortunately wrong). One of the consistent mistakes of film historians is to quote the recollections of moviemakers as gospel; the American Film Institute has invested both time and money in the recording of some four-hundred "oral histories" of their recollections. To preserve these thoughts and voices for posterity is undeniably valuable, but gospel it isn't.

a piece of cinema. The precise meaning of "cinematic" is "of or pertaining to the cinema," and its essence is merely that a succession of frames moves forward through the projector. You can, of course, then discuss whether that succession of frames is interesting or boring, beautiful or ugly, good or bad. True, the primitive film strips of Edison, Lumière, and most of their pre-Griffith contemporaries might properly be called "uncinematic," simply because they had no notion at all of one of the three principles of temporal succession (imagistic succession) and a very clumsy and undeveloped notion of another (structural succession). One of today's experimental, minimal films is certainly not uncinematic in the same way, for its maker was aware of all the possible principles of succession, but deliberately tried to extend or eliminate the use of some of them.

The insistence on projection has certain theoretical advantages. First, it clearly distinguishes cinema from a live theatrical performance, on the one hand, and from television on the other. The fact that film is projected alters its tense (it must necessarily *have been* photographed and processed in the past), whereas the tense of a live theatrical performance (dance, drama, opera) is the now. The fact that film is projected also means that it will be perceived and received differently from a live performance, particularly since projections are perceived and received as a series of different kinds of successions. In a live performance, although plot might parallel structural succession, there are no equivalents to the literal and imagistic successions of cinema; the stage movement is continuous, not successive. The visual power and concentration of cinema's successiveness (coupled with the kinetic power of the individual images) give the force of the spoken word a different (and lighter) "weight" in the cinema than in the drama (as noted and developed by Bazin).[1] Television transmission is not a projection at all; nor is its literal succession identical to cinema's. These differences produce the reduced clarity, subtlety, luminosity, density, and (for the present anyway) size of the television image. This reduction also guarantees a different emotional response and reaction to our perception of the weakened kinesis of the television image.

Indeed, the emphasis on projection as the aesthetic event consistently forces our attention on how a work of cinema is received and perceived rather than what cinema is. Arnheim gets into all kinds of trouble with this problem since he constantly explores the ways in which the cinema image differs physically from natural vision. What he never unscrambles, however, is whether the cinema makes us perceive its differences from nature or whether it fools us by erasing those physical differences so that we perceive the image as apparently quite natural. For example, Arnheim's first principle is that photography converts three-dimensional space into a two-dimensional plane.[2] He then develops the ways that this "fact" can be exploited artistically, some of those exploitations based on the way that the focal lengths of various lenses can alter the way we perceive relative distances between objects. One of his examples is that a newspaper appears to be "cut out" of the face of the person reading it; the converse effect would be the way that a wide-angle lens can make a hand holding a gun in the foreground appear ten times larger than the assailant's face, only an arm's length away.

But do we perceive the projected image as two-dimensional at all? The very fact that we call one object in the projected image apparently close to or far away from another implies that there is some kind of mental translation of the two-dimensional image into three-dimensional terms. In the cinema, when we see large and small, we translate our perception either into close and far (based on our awareness of relative distances and the sizes of objects in life) or into not so close or far but deliberately distorted for some effect by the lens (as in that hand-face example, which we know is based on an impossible relationship of size and distance in nature). We perceive the projected image as a kind of three-dimensional system, once we have learned to translate it (which means that we must learn to watch cinema, just as we must learn any system of translation—and just as we learn to translate sizes into distances in life).

The occasional 3-D movie (or the re-release of one from the Great Flurry of '52) proves that our perception of the projected three-dimensional image is nothing like that of the natural three-dimensional one either. The whole tendency of the 3-D image is to push the action and motion at us; not simply the deliberately hurled objects that sail toward our heads, but even the horizontal movement of walking from left to right feels as if it were thrusting toward us. Even the stationary walls seem to loom out at us, in a way that I do not usually perceive walls to do in life.

The projected cinema image does not appear to be flat; light on a screen is not perceived the same way as paint on canvas. Why not? First, paint is itself a hard, physical material that refracts light. That refraction is the physical stimulus that produces the effect of the painting (since light produces our perception of color by refraction); but it also reminds us of the flatness of the canvas and the material on it (because light bounces off the paint material itself, and that bouncing is perceived as a kind of surface refraction). Those painters who became self-conscious about the flatness of paint on canvas (for example, the evolving rough-textured brush strokes of Van Gogh) simply called attention to the essential flatness of the art by trying to avoid or exploit it. And what else was the development of perspective but a response to the flatness of canvas and paint? It was not the modernist response, however, as was Van Gogh's.

But the "material" of projected images is the immaterial operation of light itself; the images of cinema are produced by light's bouncing off the beaded surface of a screen, a refraction that is not, however, perceived as a refractive bouncing of light off a surface, but as the images themselves. The screen seems more to absorb the images (like a sponge) than to refract and bounce them, although such a refraction is literally what we see (but not perceive). The immateriality of light itself and the perception that the screen is a kind of translucent sponge (yet another cinema illusion) militate against the flatness of the projected image, convincing us that the image has a kind of depth (which it obviously does not).

Second, paintings are still and projected images are not. The two physical forms of cinema succession work upon the eye by keeping the photographed subjects constantly in motion. Not only is this motion a further diversion from any consciousness of the screen's flatness, but it is also a way of defining distance and dimensionality. The enlarging or shrinking of an object over a period of time or the length of time required to travel between two points are two familiar ways of defining terms like "close" and "far." One of the striking effects of halting the cinema's motion—of the "freeze frame"—is the sudden reduction of the screen's apparent depth. Only by freezing the movement that is the essence of cinema's succession does one convert the photographed image into a truly two-dimensional plane.

The projection of successive images does not convert three-dimensional nature into a two-dimensional pattern, but changes three-dimensional nature into a different three-dimensional system using two-dimensional symbols. As always, there are exceptional films that attempt to make the projected image appear as flat as possible (the Zagreb animation films, any experimental films that deliberately use the static flatness of lettering and title cards, the films of Len Lye, Norman McLaren, Robert Breer, or anyone else who uses drawn figures of any kind). Walt Disney's entire career in animation can be chronicled as a progressive war against the flatness of cinema cartooning, as a struggle to make the drawn image as apparently three-dimensional as the photographed one. Like so many valuable cinema experiments, these uses or denials of two-dimensionality are ironic reversals or revelations of traits that seem inherent to cinema.

This insistence on projection also addresses whether cinema is or is not an "automatic" art (is for Bazin, Kracauer, Cavell, and their followers; is not for Arnheim, Eisenstein, and theirs). Projection is obviously "automatic," but is the shooting of a film equally "automatic"? And these theories of film as "automatic" art are all based on the recording, not the projection, process. There is *something* about the shooting of a film that is certainly automatic—the precise moment of etching the light on the film material itself. Other than that moment of recording, however, almost nothing about the shooting of a film is automatic. The creators control the intensity and quality of the light; even outdoor sequences use key lights, floodlights, reflectors, and scrims, as well as selecting the precise type and time of day for shooting—as Antonioni did in *Red Desert* or Mizoguchi did in all his films). They control the action within the shot, the setting, the colors, the objects, the details of décor. They control the specific lens that will be used, and the filters for it (if any), and the speed and type of film itself. To reduce the question to the absurd, could you call the shooting of an animated film automatic? Yes, the film captures the light automatically when the single frame is exposed. But no, the entire world that is so captured is the product of a human imagination.

The primacy of projection also solves the nature-nurture controversy in the cinema, since that controversy is a corollary of considering the shooting process as automatic (i.e., cinema automatically records the integrity of nature) or not (i.e., cinema is the artificial product of human choices, not a mechanical recording of nature). Obviously, the projection of a reel of film has nothing to do with nature—no more than does the reading of a novel or the looking at a painting. There may be a good deal of nature (or human life, or natural experience) in the work's succession of frames, images, and events, but there may also be a good deal of this same kind of nature in the content of a novel or the subject of a painting. To emphasize projection is to reiterate that the work of cinema is necessarily as artificial as any work of any art.

To emphasize projection is also to reiterate that an essential condition of the cinema experience is viewing flickering light in an enveloping darkness. This piercing of darkness by projected light is the source of cinema's hypnotic power, paralleling the way that the professional hypnotist entrances a subject by focusing attention on a bright and rhythmically flickering source of light. This light-in-darkness also generates several paradoxes that infuse and influence our experiencing of cinema: we both sit in darkness and are bathed in light; the experience is both private and public at the same time; the projected images both speak to our personal dreams and fantasies and seem to depict the most public and familiar realities. Projection gives us both the concreteness of visual images and the abstract play of light itself.

7/Classification of the Image

The projected image presents an arrangement of forms in space, despite the fact that this space undergoes the remorseless operation and influence of temporal succession. Because film space is subject to film time, the smallest spatial unit in cinema is not the frame, which has no independent existence and endures for only ¼₄ a second. This fact should serve as a reminder that examining a frame blowup from a movie is no more like the experiencing of that shot than is the reading of a scene like seeing it. The smallest significant spatial unit of cinema is the shot: an unedited succession of projected frames. A single shot might be extremely simple (perhaps a single frame), just as a word in language can be composed of a single morpheme and phoneme (a, I). Or the shot can be extremely complex (Snow's *Wavelength*, Hitchcock's lengthy tracking shots in *Rope* and *Under Capricorn*), just as a word can be composed of many morphemes and phonemes (antidisestablishmentarianism). But the shot remains the smallest indivisible unit of significant meaning.[1]

In *Citizen Kane*, to take one example, there is a single shot that lasts two minutes, twenty-five seconds (3,984 frames), and that is a complex integration of narrative information, character introduction, and choreography for the moving camera which mirrors the emotional intensity of the scene precisely. The shot begins with a close-up on Thatcher's newspaper; headline: "Galleons of Spain Off the Jersey Coast." Since this is Thatcher's version of Kane's biography, and since this newspaper headline follows a montage of newspaper headlines which show Thatcher's growing infuriation with Kane's journalistic policies, we expect that this is simply another headline in the montage series. (*Citizen Kane* is brilliant at alternating montage sequences that encapsulate huge chunks of time and lengthy scenes that reveal the essence of the characters at a single moment; it is precisely this alternation that allows it to cover so much time and yet in so much depth.)

Then Thatcher drops the paper to reveal the youthful Kane sitting behind it at his editor's desk; it is the first time we have seen the adult Kane in the movie (except in his death or in the newsreel). As Thatcher admonishes Kane, Bernstein and Leland enter the frame, jauntily and breezily, to discuss a story that *The Inquirer* is attempting to cover (or to make); this is the only time that Kane's two important partners appear in Thatcher's version of Kane's life. When Leland and Bernstein leave, Thatcher continues his lecture—increasing its intensity, sitting down near Charles to talk both more personally and more closely with him. As Thatcher moves closer, the camera also moves closer. The tightest composition of the shot is Kane's reply—that he has moral obligations to his readers and fellow citizens, that he cannot be swayed by financial interests (even if they are his own interests). The tight composition mirrors his intensity, his commitment, and his coming of age as a human being. The camera then pulls back as the interview ends, as Thatcher takes his leave and Kane helps him with his coat. And suddenly we notice in the background that the other workers at *The Inquirer* have been a party to this scene, that they are both confused and worried about this confrontation, and that Kane has proved himself both worthy and able to be their leader. Such a shot is single only in physical fact, not in information or effect.

On the other hand, in a single frame of *Dog Star Man* Stan Brakhage makes a collage of an infant's face, the eyes replaced by what looks like a combination of snowflakes, snow balls, and Christmas-tree bulbs. The metaphor implies the innocence of a child's vision, that it responds to pure shapes, lights, and colors, uncorrupted by the culturally defined ways of seeing properly. The infant sees without recognizing, without attaching a meaning to the sights but simply enjoying them as pure sights. As such, the child automatically has the ability that Brakhage, as an adult artist, strives to attain—the innocence of pure seeing. Brakhage makes this statement in a shot that is one frame long; the baby with the snowflake eyes is one frame ($\frac{1}{24}$ second) of a seventy-five-minute film.

The spatial and visual characteristics of each image can be defined in terms of all those variables in the shooting, processing, and printing of a shot that are not "automatic." By manipulating these variables, the filmmaker can control our perceptions of the projected images and our responses to them. And by failing to manipulate and control these variables, the filmmaker will also fail to elicit the response he wishes (regardless of the other information in the shot), unintentionally producing either our failure to understand the moment or our lack of conviction that the moment means what it purports to mean. In Christian Metz's

A single shot of *Citizen Kane.* The newspaper headline gives way to the young Kane, whose white face looms out of the darkness behind his desk. Leland and Bernstein enter the frame. Thatcher lectures Charles and sits down.

The camera tracks closer for the intimate interview, moving closest to Kane for his most intense statement of commitment. The interview ends as Thatcher rises to get his coat (followed by the camera) and delivers a final sally. *Courtesy Janus Films*

terms, the moment can fail to produce either its denotative information or its connotative effect.[2] It is impossible for a single shot to manipulate all these visual variables; in practice, one visual stimulus usually dominates a shot, supported by several others in varying degrees. Experimental films (again by virtue of the fact that they are experiments) frequently isolate a single variable, to the deliberate exclusion of the others.

There are three broad categories of these visual variables, three classes of visual stimuli which can be distinguished in every shot: variables in (1) the filming of the image, (2) the toning of the image, and (3) the content of the image. Each of these major classes contains several subclasses, and this chapter now turns to the classification of these species and subspecies.

THE FILMING OF THE IMAGE

The filming of the image includes all the operations that light performs directly on the film material itself—both in the camera and in the laboratory. Although "filming" could be seen as two separate categories (the shooting of the image and the developing-printing of the image), the unifying element of the class is the material of film itself—the varying ways of affecting its exposure to light, its printing with light, and its consequent projection by light. The visual variables controlled by the filming of the image are the effects of lenses, filters, exposure, film stocks, camera angle, and camera activity (all of which pertain to the relationship of lens, film, and photographic object), and the effects of film developing and printing (which pertain to the final treatment of the film material after shooting).

Lens and Film

The camera's *lens* organizes the beams of light into images, which then travel through its barrel to be etched onto the film itself. The most important variable of the cinema lens (assuming the same high quality of materials and manufacture) is its focal length, the distance (usually expressed in millimeters) that light must travel between the glass surface of the lens and the film itself (where the images are recorded). Describing the camera's "lens" in English is complicated by the word's bearing two different meanings: (1) the full piece of apparatus, including the lens barrel and focusing ring; and (2) the glass surface which is literally the lens that organizes the beams of light. The precise definition of focal length is: the distance between the center of the glass lens (because lenses are convex) and the film, when the focusing ring is set at infinity (because focus affects focal length).

The focal length of a lens affects our perception in several important ways: by determining the apparent relative distances between objects; by determining the relative sharpness of focus between fore- and rear-ground; by determining the apparent width and depth of the image; by determining the amount of light required for varying degrees of depth, focus, and brightness. A so-called normal lens is one that preserves the approximate relationships of distances between close and distant objects as the eye sees them; this lens is, by tradition, a 50-mm (or two-inch) lens for 35-mm filming, a 25-mm (or one-inch) lens for 16-mm film. Because 35-mm film is approximately twice as wide as 16-mm film, the lenses that produce comparable effects are inevitably twice as long. Lenses that are "shorter" than this standard are called wide-angle lenses; lenses that are "longer" are called long lenses or (in their extremest lengths) telephoto lenses. The shorter the lens, the less distance the light must travel between glass surface and film material. Hence, the less light required to etch a suitable image. And the less light required to expose an image, the deeper the focus of the scene recorded by that lens.

An extreme wide-angle lens (say, a lens of 20 mm or less with 35-mm film) will provide several kinds of visual possibilities: it will cover a very wide field close to the camera itself (for this reason, amateur cinematographers often must use a wide-angle lens to shoot all of, say, Buckingham Palace without panning); it will introduce apparently huge relative distances between objects fairly close to the lens and one another (the large-hand/small-head example above would require a wide-angle lens; relative distances between foreground objects increase geometrically as they approach the lens); it will provide an absolutely enormous depth of field with an enormous amount of light (say, everything would be in perfect focus between six inches and infinity from the lens) and a fairly large depth of field with even a moderate amount of light (say, everything between one foot and one hundred feet would be in perfect focus).

The style of *Citizen Kane* could have been produced only with short lenses: the immense depth of the film's compositions (both indoors and out); the way that human figures seem to loom in front of the lens like mountains. Shot from below, the wide-angle lens makes human beings seem very broad at the base, rising to a peak at the top of the head. It was always possible to use extreme screen depth for outdoor shots (for example, Keaton's depth of field is a significant element of his style).

The integration of lighting and camera angle in *Citizen Kane*. The low angle and grotesque lighting magnifies the force of Leland's argument with Kane.

Citizen Kane pioneered in achieving these effects indoors—where slow film, slow lenses, and weak lights previously made them impossible. The mysterious tensions of Polanski's *Knife in the Water* can also be traced to his use of wide-angle lenses (and bizarre camera angles), which make small objects close to the lens seem to dwarf and dominate the larger people who stand farther from the lens. The close-up with the wide-angle lens has the advantage of feeling very sharp; short lenses are capable of very detailed resolution, and the extreme depth of field keeps the background equally crisp, fitting the human head into its surroundings, never divorcing the figure from the background, which can be perceived quite distinctly.

The extreme long lens (say, a lens of 200 mm or more with 35-mm film) produces the exactly opposite effects: it covers a very narrow field close to the camera, but can produce the feeling of closeness from great distances (for this reason, amateur cinematographers must use a long lens when trying to shoot, say, the action of a football game); it will introduce apparently small relative distances between objects quite distant from the lens and from each other (relative distances between objects decrease geometrically as they recede from the lens); it will produce a fairly limited depth of field, even with a significant amount of light (allowing the image to emphasize some objects by blurring others). The long lens tends to "flatten" the appearance of the image, often emphasizing the middle ground while blurring and flattening both extreme close and far.

Perhaps the most famous long-lens shot is the one that propels the climax of *The Graduate:* Dustin Hoffman runs doggedly toward the camera, but never seems to get anywhere—emphasizing his frustration with the useless marriage his girl wants to make and his determination to stop it. Although his running indeed carries him closer to the church (and the camera), the distance he traverses is not significant enough to register on the 600-mm lens. And so he appears to run doggedly while standing still—converting the natural universe into a kind of treadmill.

The close-up with the long lens has the advantage of feeling fairly soft; long lenses are less capable of highly detailed resolution and necessarily blur the background when concentrating on a single face. In *Red Desert* Antonioni consistently uses the short lens for his objective shots of everyday reality and the long lens for his close-ups of Giulia (Monica Vitti) trying to perceive and understand that reality. The contrast of Monica Vitti's crisply focused face or the back of her head with the blurry, ominously unclear background that surrounds her is a translation of her internal psychological problems with reality into concrete visual terms. Unlike the grossest distortion lenses for subjective effect (which will be discussed shortly), Antonioni's subjective use of the long-lensed close-up distorts reality not grotesquely but very slightly. That slightness of distortion and blur becomes a precise visual metaphor for the slight but significant gulf between Giulia's reactions to everyday human experience and the "normal" reactions of everyone else.

Although these are issues of optics, they have considerable influence on the effects of art. All shots must be photographed with some lens or other, and the lens that the maker selects will determine the way the shot looks and feels. Between the two extremes of very short and very long lenses lies a whole series of not-so-short and not-so-long ones, all of them producing subtler variations of the same pronounced effects.

A handy tool of the last twenty years has been the development of the lens whose focal length is not fixed, allowing the cinematographer to use any focal length between, say, 25 mm and 250 mm without changing lenses. This is the commonly known zoom lens, which is often used to

The long lens mirrors Giulia's point-of-view in *The Red Desert*. While her crisply focused head dominates the foreground, she sees the faces of others in the same room as a blur. A ship apparently sails through the forest, the long lens reducing all these distant objects (trees, truck, and ship) to a flat plane, blurring the focus into an impressionistic effect strikingly close to pointillism.

shoot scenes even when it is not busy a-zooming. The cinematographer can select the focal length he wants by simply looking through the view-finder and adjusting the focal length until the image looks right. The zoom lens made the reflex camera a necessity, of course (i.e., the kind of camera in which the cinematographer views the image through the camera's lens itself). The old Mitchell Studio camera was not a reflex camera, but used a separate viewfinder with its own viewing lens (that paralleled but was not identical with the shooting lens). The only disad-vantage of this newer method and apparatus is that the resolution of the zoom lens (and the reflex camera) is slightly less sharp and detailed than that of any lens of fixed focal length.

When the lens does zoom during a shot it introduces a visual effect that parallels several earlier ones but is quite different from them. The two variables of zooming are, obviously, toward or away, fast or slow. To zoom quickly toward an object or subject can produce the exciting rush of a feeling or a discovery; it is an emotional exclamation point, the "light bulb" of an idea suddenly snapping on. To move slowly toward it can express a slower, surer, steadier emotional effect—the impression of an idea or emotion sinking in slowly but deeply. To zoom away from an object or subject slowly and steadily can reveal its surroundings, the causes of whatever effects may have first registered on the subject. To zoom away quickly can reduce the object or subject to minute smallness with great suddenness, leaving it tiny and isolated amid vast surround-ings that seem to dwarf it.

The final sequence of Robert Altman's *California Split* provides a revealing example of the differences between zooming toward a subject as opposed to zooming away from it. After Billy's fantastic streak of luck, he suddenly feels tired, leaves the crap table, walks into a deserted bar, and disgorges himself of the chips he has won. He sits down on a bar stool at the deserted bar. Altman's camera then begins to zoom slowly toward the solitary figure (George Segal). As it does, it seems to sink into his feelings, revealing not his joy (for the moment, though victorious, is strangely sad), but his emptiness. Billy has achieved the gambler's dream; and so his future is now devoid of dreams. He will never again succeed so ultimately. And so even gambling—the one passion of his life—can now offer him no more joy or excitement or elation. His Godot has arrived; the gambler is truly empty. And the slow zoom of the lens is the primary sign of the nothing he has left inside him.

Charlie (Elliott Gould), Billy's partner, is not empty at all; he is elated. But Charlie has not performed any of the feats of gambling and winning. He has not even been permitted to watch (bad luck). And so

Charlie feels pure elation with the fact of winning $82,000. But when he tries to share the elation with Billy, Billy simply confesses to being tired and walks away—leaving Charlie alone. Altman then zooms slowly away from the puzzled Charlie—leaving him isolated in the bare room, revealing his confusion with Billy's reaction. Charlie realizes that there is some gulf between Billy's feelings and his own, but because the zooming away has slowly left him solitary in space, he has no one with whom to share either his elation or his confusion. Zooming toward Billy probed his internal condition; zooming away from Charlie revealed his inability to make a human connection.

Such zoom effects are vaguely parallel with the Griffith-era effects of irising in and out, which also tended to escape the surroundings to concentrate on a single subject (the effect of a cause) or to reveal suddenly the surroundings that are the cause of some emotional response (the cause of an effect). Griffith's irising out from the weeping mother in *The Birth of a Nation* to the panorama of Sherman's army marching to the sea, the cause of her weeping, is one of the most famous early uses of the iris which parallels one of today's zooms. The advantages of the zoom over the iris are that, first, you do not arbitrarily blacken any areas of the frame, but preserve the screen rectangle; and, second, the zoom transfers its kinetic feeling of movement to the intensity of the emotional event that is the reason for zooming in the first place.

This kinetic feeling vaguely parallels the sensation of the familiar traveling shot when the camera (and not just the lens) moves toward or away from its subject. The specific circumstances for preferring the zoom, however, are, first, for reactions or effects that require a much greater and striking suddenness than can be achieved with any camera movement (for the camera can travel only by being pushed or pulled through space). Second, certain reactions or effects require the physical sensation that only the zoom can produce. The eye perceives that the relative distances of objects and their varying planes of focus shift during the zoom maneuver, for the focal lengths that determine relative distance and focus are shifting. In a simple tracking shot with a lens of fixed focal length, the eye travels through the world perceiving the same relative distances, proportions, and focus of the objects moving past it. As a result, the traveling shot is more effective at depicting physical traveling in space, while the zoom more effectively evokes the sensation of emotional "traveling" in some kind of mental "space." Traveling shots convey movement; zoom shots convey realizations.

A totally different principle of camera or lens movement accounts for the increasing use of the jiggling, hand-held camera in narrative movies.

This borrowing from documentary, experimental, and *cinéma vérité* styles is a means of increasing the informality of the movie's feeling, of decreasing the impression of artifice and calculation, and of attempting to gain the viewer's conviction in the "realness" of the fiction. In many documentary and *cinéma vérité* films, the jiggling and bouncing of the hand-held camera is an inevitable result of the film's subject matter and/or shooting methods. The subject could simply not be studied or the material could not be recorded in any more planned or artful way. When a movie exploits the style (where both the subject matter and the shooting methods could easily smooth the camera's bumpiness), the moviemaker claims authenticity by pretending it could not have been shot more artfully under more artful conditions.

Another kind of lens movement that has become more popular in the last decade is a special use of rack focus (the changing of focus during the shot itself, either to follow the action clearly as it moves farther from or closer to the lens, or to discover different actions or faces at different distances from the lens). We rarely perceived a racking of focus in a studio-era shot, for the focus changed imperceptibly with the movement of the action itself; we would have noticed the racking only if the focus failed to change quickly enough and the shot's central figure suddenly walked into blurdom. But a more intrusive and interesting use of rack focus is the shot in which we first see, say, a husband and his mistress eating dinner in a restaurant surrounded by a blur of other patrons, only to observe the focus shift to reveal his wife and her lover eating dinner in the now crisp rearground of the same restaurant, while the first couple has blurred into semi-invisibility. The implication of such a use of rack focus is usually the irony that two related activities share the same space without realizing it (and the shift of focus makes us feel how possible it is for one to seem invisible to another in the same space). Another familiar subject of rack focus is the crisp close-up of a leafy tree, followed by the blurring of the leaves and the discovery of the young lovers walking in the distant rearground. Such a device would seem to link a romantic subject with its romantic surroundings.

This very use of rack focus is itself a consequence of modern technology, which has created faster lenses and film stocks and more powerful light sources, thereby making it possible to keep almost everything in every shot perfectly in focus. As Bazin noted, soft focus (in which some things look hazy and blurry) has steadily lost favor since the silents. But then the slow film and lenses and weak lights that produced soft focus have also lost favor and practice. To produce the effect of soft focus in a contemporary shot (and an assumption of rack focus is that some areas of the frame are necessarily "soft") requires very deliberate choices—especially the use of a long lens, and perhaps of slower film and weaker light (both of which would necessitate a wider lens aperture, reducing depth of field). The use of rack focus is a deliberate and intrusive reminder that the filmmaker has taken the trouble to use soft focus for certain artistic ends.

Another familiar use of rack focus (favored by movies in the 1940s but now much favored by television) is the blurring in or out of focus at the beginning or end of a shot—inevitably a subjective device to depict a character's waking up (from an accident, a fight, a drug, or a drunk) or blacking out (from the same causes). Similarly subjective effects can be achieved by various lenses that are prismatically arranged to distort the beams of light before they reach the film. One such distortion effect parallels the mirrors of the fun house in which straight lines all bend grotesquely, distending or shrinking heads, limbs, and bodies into bloated or gnarled shapes. This distortion effect of anamorphosis serves the subjective function of displaying the drunken, doped, or groggy man's view of the world itself, as in Murnau's *The Last Laugh,* Metzner's *Überfall,* or Sidney Peterson's *The Cage.* Another distortion effect breaks the wholeness of the visual pattern into a series of kaleidoscopic prisms, resembling the possible way that a schizophrenic might see a disconnected vision of natural experience. (The "ripple" effect, in which the image on the screen seems to be reflected in a pool of rippling water, is parallel to these other distortions in its subjective intent, but is produced by the printer and not the camera lens.)

Another familiar distortion effect is produced by a lens that registers a clear, sharp image in its center which then blurs into nondistinctness as the image moves outward toward the edges of the frame. This effect (which can be achieved both by printing and by filters, as well as with a lens) often implies that the character is undergoing a dream, nightmare, or some other subjective fantasy—as Mia Farrow does in her nightmarish copulation with the devil in *Rosemary's Baby* and James Stewart does as he follows Kim Novak through a cemetery in *Vertigo.* Ironically, both of these "nightmares" are "true" human experiences that only *feel* like nightmares (for both us and them). The implication of this kind of subjective device is that the world has not gone totally blurry; there is still something clearly discernible in the experience; but there is something fuzzy and abnormal and otherworldly about the experience at the same time. All these distortion lenses attempt to translate psychological phenomena into strictly visual terms, using the metaphor of sight in a way that has traditionally served as a link between sight and insight (blind Tiresias and "blind" Oedipus; Kent's admonition, "See better, Lear!").

Another lens that genuinely distorts the recorded image, though we often do not perceive a distortion when the image is projected, is the anamorphic lens, the basis of CinemaScope, VistaVision, and many of the other scopes and visions, which can squeeze an immensely wide image into a standard frame of 35-mm celluloid. We perceive no distortion when that frame is projected because the camera's lens has a companion for the projector which unsqueezes the image. These anamorphic lenses are the bases of the visual effects of CinemaScope—the huge, horizontal image; the increased depth in the center of the image; the tendency (in the earliest CinemaScope lenses) toward flatness, blurriness, and distortion as the image spreads outward to its right and left edges; the slight sacrifice of resolutional clarity and detail for the larger image and increased depth. Indeed, one early reason for coupling the anamorphic lens with the wider gauges of film (65 mm or 70 mm) was to increase the power of the resolution as well as the size of the image. With the newer anamorphic lenses—particularly the crisp perfection of the Panavision lens—both the distortion and the wider gauges of film have virtually disappeared.

A final series of visual effects also manipulate the relationship between the lens and the light striking it; these are effects in which light literally and directly strikes the lens. The two most common of these are lens flare (a prismatic streak of light across the image, caused by a direct ray of the sun or a studio light striking the glass surface of the lens) and lens halation (the impression that a bright light source in the darkness— for example, the automobile headlights in the climactic dance scene of *Badlands*—has a glowing halo around it, like a "ring around the moon" on a misty night). In earlier eras, both these "effects" were carefully avoided or excised as technical mistakes. Studio cameramen either circumvented such shooting conditions, or used a film with special anti-halation backing, or used a lens hood to reduce flare. Neither flare nor halation can be duplicated by natural human vision; both are specific consequences of the difference between the eye and brain as a visual system and the lens and film; both were carefully avoided in the polished studio era because of their strident proclamation of unnaturalness and artifice.

They seem to have two primary uses today: metaphoric and atmospheric. The outdoor flash of lens flare seems an increasingly obligatory way of depicting the flash-flush feeling of heat and warmth while spending a bright day on the beach or in the forest. The indoor flash of lens flare seems increasingly obligatory for the backstage musicals of the Bob Fosse–Liza Minnelli sort (also for rock-music TV specials), invoking (I suppose) the glittering, flashing, but ephemeral excitement of show-biz intensity for the performer. The halation effect is dreamier and mistier, indicating, perhaps, the magical softness of such moments.

Underlying both effects, however, is the aim to produce an atmosphere of informality and spontaneity—as if everyone, including the audience, knows that these "effects" are mistakes, but the shooting was so spontaneous and ramshackle and natural that it was impossible to avoid them. Such lighting "mistakes" parallel the bumpy informality and casualness of the hand-held camera, and their origin is the same—the inevitable sacrifice of polish and perfection for the authenticity of newsreel, documentary, and *cinéma vérité* filming. Ironically, it is difficult to determine whether such effects in movies are more or less natural uses of the cinema—in Bazin's terms. On the one hand, they are intrusive reminders that we are watching cinema, not life; on the other, they try to convince us that the shooting of that movie has been as natural and as spontaneous as possible.

A *filter* is a device that, as the name implies, filters something out of the beams of light before they reach the film. In practice, the filter is usually attached to the lens itself during shooting and seems almost a part of it; but its function is to strengthen or tone or alter or delete some potential visual element of the image before the film captures it. The most familiar kinds of filters are pieces of colored gelatin or glass that can be attached directly to the lens for the purpose of filtering out the light rays of that specific color. The most frequently used filters in monochrome filming are yellow and red, both of which increase the visual effectiveness of deep shadows and of a blue sky. The yellow filter (or a graduated filter—yellow at the top, fading gradually to colorless at the bottom) turns a clear and bright blue sky, which would photograph as white, into a deep shade of gray by filtering out the yellow light. A red filter (or a graduated filter using red instead of yellow) deepens the contrast between a bright blue sky and the white puffs of clouds, turning the blue into a velvety almost-black by filtering the red light from both sky and clouds. The purpose of the graduated filter is to achieve the effects of filtering on the sky without altering the color values of the objects on earth. The striking landscapes of earth, sagebrush, mountain, and sensuous, cloud-filled sky in John Ford's Monument Valley movies could have been achieved only with the intensifying effects of filters. In color filming, a polaroid filter deepens the blueness of the sky by filtering out the whitish haze.

One of the most spectacularly terrible uses of filters in color filming was Joshua Logan's decision to accent the secondary colors (yellow, magenta, and cyan) in his filmed version of *South Pacific,* undoubtedly to parallel the way that stage lighting (especially the follow spots) tones a scene emotionally with subtle shades of color. Logan's filmed use was anything but subtle, as the screen world suddenly went yellow, magenta, or pale blue-green. Although the device seemed inexplicable, hokey, and vulgar in general, its most specific ugliness was its conversion of human skin into the most gangrenous shades, including an ashen gray (in the cyan-filter scenes) that turned a human face into the approximate color of newsprint. A much more defensible use of garish color filtering, however, can be seen in the Roger Corman horror films (especially *The House of Usher* and *The Tomb of Ligeia*), which use the strikingly unnatural and grotesque color shades as a means of transposing the action out of the key of predictable human reality and into a realm of fantasy and super-unrealism. The garish, color-mad world becomes the cinematic equivalent of Poe's narrative style, which similarly transports us from the familiar world of psychological rationality into the aberrant and surreal world of the diseased or oversensitive human mind.

In contrast to color filters, the neutral density filter (as its name implies) is colorless. Its primary function is to reduce the *amount* of light that reaches the film, permitting some of the softer effects of underexposure—soft contrast between dark and light areas, soft shadows, dimness, and dullness. This neutral filter comes in varying degrees of density, permitting varying degrees of soft dimness.

Scrims or solids can also serve as filters, functioning exactly as do color or neutral filters—to screen some quality of light from lens or film. Erich von Stroheim shot sequences of *Foolish Wives* through a scrim, particularly the isolated shots of the mentally retarded child. The device converted the visual image into a kind of latticework, both flattening the child's world so that it looked like a kind of painting (or newspaper photograph) and emphasizing her separation from the world of ordinary perceptions and experiences.

Scrims often serve as what is colloquially called a "haze lens," its intention being to soften the visual image by making it appear hazy. The "haze lens" is a standard tool to soften or glamorize the leading lady's close-ups, often to eradicate the ravages of time, which has not been as kind to a star as her fans and the plot might wish. In many of the 1920s

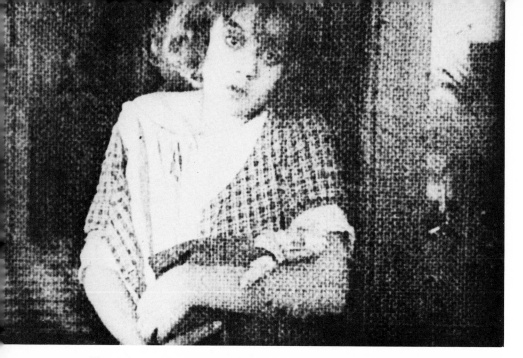

The scrim as filter in *Foolish Wives:* a curtain between the mentally retarded girl's world of innocence and the corruption of adult reality.

and '30s films, the male and female stars seem almost to inhabit different universes. Whereas his close-ups are usually shot in crisp detail, the reverse shots of her seem to have been recorded in some deep mist. Perhaps the device was intended as a subjective translation of the way he saw her, but its fuzzy gauziness seemed more related to the abstract glamorizing of women than to any internal psychology. A similar and even more blurry effect can be achieved by smearing a coat of vaseline on a piece of glass in front of the lens; in such scenes the "first-aid kit in a jar" functions exactly like a filter, applying first aid to the ruined visage of yesterday's sweetheart. But these vaseline effects are also popular (and even effective) in producing the blurred distortions of certain experimental films. In *Étoile de mer* (1928), Man Ray used blurry and distorting panes of glass as filters, which acted similarly to the smeary coat of vaseline.

Solid masks and mattes also function as filters, blocking out the light completely from certain areas of the frame. The use of mattes is one of the primary means of achieving special effects, of producing the convincing impression that two elements share the same framed space when those elements obviously do not or could not (for example, the rowboatful of survivors who watch the waves swallow the *Titanic*). Such an effect might be produced by shooting the rowboat in the studio, with the precise pattern of the background disaster matted out, and then shooting the sinking ship (undoubtedly in miniature) with the precise pattern of the foreground rowboat matted out. The two precisely calculated shots would then be superimposed with equal precision by the optical printer without betraying any superimposition.

A parallel use of the matte or mask is for what were once called split-screen effects—in which Bette Davis talks to herself as her own evil sister, or Larry Parks as Al Jolson talks to Larry Parks as Larry Parks in *Jolson Sings Again,* or Buster Keaton plays all three members of the orchestra, both members of the tap-dance duo, and all seven members of the minstrel line in *The Playhouse.* By blocking out a fraction of the image to shoot a scene, rewinding the film in the camera to precisely the same starting point, and then precisely blocking out the other half (or third, or seventh) to shoot the identical scene again on the identical piece of film, a movie can convincingly present the natural impossibility of a single human being's existing doubly (or triply, or infinitely) in space.

Another visual variable closely connected to the use of lenses is the selection of *exposure,* the amount of light that will pass through the lens to the film. The lens aperture can open very wide (signified by a *low f*-stop number, such as $f/1.4$, $f/1.9$, or $f/2.5$) or very narrowly (signified by a *high f*-stop number, such as $f/16$ or $f/22$), depending on whether the speed of the film, the degree of illumination, and the tone of the scene require a lot or a little light to record the desired image.

The demands of exposure can often determine the lens that must be used (because some lenses are "faster" than others). For *Barry Lyndon,* Stanley Kubrick demanded the manufacture of such fast lenses (lenses permitting such low *f*-stop numbers) that a suitable image could be exposed by candlelight alone. Should the filmmaker want to shoot an outdoor scene at night on a city street, using only available light, he might well need to use a wider (and, hence, faster) lens rather than a longer one—even if he wants to achieve the flattening look of the long lens. Filmmakers must constantly compromise because of their equipment and the instability of shooting conditions; artistic "choices" are frequently not matters of choice at all. Hollywood studio filming avoided these technical compromises because it controlled all the vagaries of shooting conditions. But then it necessitated other kinds of compromises. The new lenses for *Barry Lyndon* reflected the rare director's demand to make the equipment control the conditions, not the other way round.

The demands of exposure also determine the depth of field of any lens, since the wider the aperture (i.e., the lower the *f*-stop number), the shallower the depth of field—and vice versa. If the filmmaker needs an immense depth of field, he must try to "stop the aperture down" (in everyday English, close it up) as far as possible—which might also dictate his using very fast film, a wide-angle lens, and artificial lighting to boost the natural light source. If, conversely, he wants to produce the softer effects of a shallow depth of field, he must try to use as long a lens and to open the aperture up as much as possible—which might also dictate the use of a neutral density filter, the choice of a slower film, and the minimum of artificial lighting.

In addition to influencing the effects of screen depth, a shot can be deliberately under or overexposed to achieve a visual and/or tonal effect. An overexposure washes the image in a glaring overbrightness that obliterates detail and dazzles the eye. Underexposure works conversely, drenching the image in an inky dimness that also obliterates detail with its ultra-blackness. The most familiar use of overexposure is as a subjective device depicting dreams, fantasies, and near-dreams. The recurring dream sequence of *The Shop on Main Street*, in which Tono fantasizes a time when he can escape from political realities by waltzing with the Widow Lautman in the sunlight, is glaringly overexposed in blinding whiteness (and further fantasized by the successive effect of slow motion). Sol Nazerman's recurrent flashbacks to his previous life in Nazi Germany (*The Pawnbroker*) are slightly overexposed (and also use slow motion), to give them a distant, dreamy, faded look of gone-forever pastness. The outdoor, sunny sequences at the beach cottage in Bergman's *Persona* are very slightly overexposed, just enough to give them the slightest suggestion of unnatural harshness and brilliance (especially in contrast to the black clothing of the women).

This contrast of black costume and brilliant sunlight reveals that one of the more subtle and special manipulations of exposure occurs whenever the cinematographer must choose between proper exposure of bright or dark objects or areas within the same shot. A less frequent problem in the studio era (because of its complete control of lighting intensities and variations), today's use of actual locations and consequent dependence on available light often compels the choice between lighting for the bright areas of the shot, or for the dark ones, or for making some compromise between them. So, too, if the shot contains both light and dark objects—say, the black-clad human figures in a brilliant sun- or snow-scape—the choices are either to overexpose the brilliant background severely, or to underexpose the darker human figures severely, or to make some less severe compromise between the two. A consistent choice in *Chinatown* is the slight overexposure of sunny areas in the outdoor shots, emphasized by the shadows in which the protagonist consistently sits and the dazzling cream-colored clothing and cream-colored dust of the Mulwrays and the earth in the sunlight. In general, choosing to overexpose the bright areas and objects produces harsher, blinding effects, choosing to underexpose the dark areas and objects produces moodier, somber effects, and choosing the compromise is an attempt to eradicate the visual problem, rather than to emphasize it for some effect.

The most familiar use of underexposure is for the day-for-night sequences of most studio films, which evoke the feeling of nighttime by admitting so little light that the image not only seems dim but also lacks the daylight characteristic of strong contrasts between sunny and shaded areas. In monochrome filming, the neutral density filter aids the softness of underexposure. For color filming, the underexposure of day-for-night shooting might combine the neutral density filter with a deep-blue one (or a blue dye or tint applied in the lab or printer) that washes the dimly contrasting image with something that parallels the color of moonlight. Because of the artifice of this device (underexposed day-for-night filming is an attempt to depict objective reality, not a subjective fantasy, as is extreme overexposure), day-for-night shooting cannot be used for any nighttime shot that contains direct sources of light that are intended to contrast with and illuminate the darkness. The torchlit nighttime scene at the slave camp in *Spartacus*, the dance in the headlights of *Badlands*, or the cream-colored glow of the wooden house that hides Mrs. Mulwray's sister-daughter in *Chinatown* could have been shot only at night. Day-for-night shooting would extinguish all torches, headlights, and glows—and tint them blue.

The final variable in the interrelationship of lens and film (and the transmission of light between the two) is the *film* material itself. Film can be distinguished, first, by its gauge (or format): 8, super-8, 16, 35, 55, 65, and 70 mm. The only consistent visual principle that is a general consequence of film gauges is that the wider the gauge, the more detailed (sharper, clearer, brighter, livelier) the projected image. Super-8 was developed precisely to produce a sharper photographic image than standard 8; although the film is the same inexpensive width, a frame of super-8 is 40 percent larger (because the space required for its single sprocket hole is smaller). When a 35-mm movie is reduced to a 16-mm print, the result is called a "reduction print." The artistic (kinetic) consequences of this metaphor should not be overlooked—especially since most film courses and film societies show 16-mm prints. As previously noted, many anamorphic lenses produce crisper results with the widest gauges of film.

A second distinguishing characteristic of film is its sensitivity to light. The entire history of film stocks in this century parallels the history of photographic plate in the last one: the constant search to make film faster and faster. The earliest black-and-white stocks for motion-picture filming were very slow; by the mid-1930s they had become many times faster; by the 1960s they had become many times faster still. The first Technicolor film of the early 1930s was as slow as the first primitive black-and-white stocks of three decades earlier; even in the postwar 1940s Technicolor film was four or five times slower than was black-and-white at the time; but by the late 1960s color stocks had been improved to perhaps half the speed of today's fastest black-and-white stocks.

The advantage of a fast film is that it is far more flexible than a slow one; it is always possible to suppress light (to use minimal lighting, or to reduce it with a neutral density filter, or to stop down the lens), but it is often impossible to add it (particularly in certain documentary and cinéma vérité situations). Another advantage of the new, faster films is the increased clarity and depth of the image, permitting much deeper fields of sharp focus than were possible forty years ago. Their disadvantage is the loss of some of the softer visual effects, which can now be achieved only by tricks and distortions such as gauzy filters and rack focus.

The speed of a film is determined by the fineness, density, and size of its "grain"—the light-sensitive silver particles in the film emulsion. So is its degree of contrast, which can vary between an extremely low-contrast film (producing a soft, gray image that reduces the differences between light and dark) to an extremely high-contrast one (producing a hard image in which contrasts between light and dark are so absolute that the result seems more like an abstract pattern than a photograph). These extremes of high and low contrast are generally reserved for special filmic effects; they produce an even more pronounced impression of unnatural otherworldliness than the extremes of over and underexposure.

The final significant characteristic of film is its sensitivity to color. Black-and-white film was originally color-blind. It could not "see" all the colors of the spectrum and automatically "filtered" some of them out. The most popular black-and-white film of the silent era was orthochrome, which was blind to red. Because orthochromatic film would register any red object as a grotesque black, the bow lips of Clara Bow or May McAvoy might well have been kissed with a coat of green lipstick, and that red dress for the big ball would have been any color but red. In addition to its color-blindness, orthochrome was much slower, producing a softer, more silvery kind of image, complementing the soft dreaminess of silent film with its own gentle luminousness. If a modern director wanted to capture the look and visual texture of silent film (rather than merely undercranking ad nauseam), he would need a red filter (plus making the color compensations in make-up, décor, and costume), a slow film (and a slightly low-contrast film at that), and as wide apertures as possible.

Panchromatic film, which could "see" every color of the spectrum and translated it into a varying shade of gray, was developed in the mid-1920s and replaced orthochrome at almost the same time that sound replaced silence. It was originally developed to render colors not into the shades of gray but into the colors themselves—as the basis of a color-additive process. For no one saw any deficiencies in the monochrome renderings of orthochrome. According to legend, Robert Flaherty's *Moana* (1926) first used panchromatic film to black-and-white effect—and it did so by accident. Flaherty originally intended to make the film in color. Because his color cameras had been damaged in transport, he put the new film in his conventional black-and-white cameras. And lo, the wondrous effects of shading and detail when he projected the results.

The eventual discovery of a stable method of color filming was a subtractive (not an additive) color process,[3] requiring three different rolls of film to be exposed at the same time, each of which was "color-blind" to two of the three primary colors. One subtracted all colors but red, the second all but blue, and the third all but green. The process then compensated for and combined the three exposed, subtractive images in the laboratory and printer. This first practical system of color filming, Technicolor, was applied to animation films (for example, Disney's *Trees and Flowers*) as early as 1932 and to a live-action short in 1935 (*La Cucaracha*). Rouben Mamoulian's *Becky Sharp* was the first feature-length movie to use Technicolor (in 1935) and *The Trail of the Lonesome Pine* (1936) was the first to be shot entirely on location. The original Technicolor camera used three lenses, one for each roll of film, a bulky apparatus which did not make shooting any cheaper or easier.

Since the early 1950s, color film has been manufactured in a monopack (the three light-sensitive layers of film have been bonded together and can be shot by a conventional, one-lensed camera). It has been dominated by the Eastmancolor process, which closely resembles the

German Agfacolor process. The German process passed into the public domain in 1945; and so the total conversion to color of the last twenty years is apparently one of the spoils of the Allied victory in World War II. Eastmancolor has been marketed under many fancier names—Metrocolor, Warnercolor, Japan's Tohocolor, Italy's Ferraniacolor—all of them variations of this same film. Technicolor continues to exist as a laboratory with a special process for developing exposed Eastmancolor film, as do its competitors such as DeLuxe and Movielab.

So when one compares the effects of black-and-white film with color film today, one is really comparing fast panchromatic film with fairly fast Eastmancolor monopack. The variants of these two kinds of film in the past twenty-five years have been few and minor, often dominated by economic rather than artistic considerations. The Republic studio, which survived solely by making films cheaply, used Sepia-Tone as its monochrome equivalent during the Second World War and the early postwar years. The black-and-white of Sepia was more a russet-brown-and-beige, producing images that seemed to have been burned, rusted, and then left to rot into orange. The slower, inexpensive film was much less subtle in its ability to render sharp detail. For its color films, Republic first used Cinecolor, a cheap two-color process (Technicolor and Eastmancolor are three-color processes) whose shades and color values tended toward the blandly and milkily pastel. In the early 1950s, Republic switched its color allegiance to Trucolor, another cheap two-color process whose shades and color values (despite its name) were no more true—as grotesquely brazen and garish as the hues of Cinecolor were bloodless. *Johnny Guitar*, 1954, is Republic's most interesting and effective movie in Trucolor; its story and passions are as brazenly garish and grotesque as its spectrum.

Because the dyeing and processing of color film are so important to the accuracy, subtlety, and richness of color cinema, the primary visual variant of color film today is often the work of the laboratory that processes and prints it, rather than any inherent qualities of the film stock itself (other than its speed). The processing laboratory takes responsibility for the color film from the initial receipt of the raw stock to the final reproduction of release prints—maintaining the consistency of dyes, the consistent temperatures of chemical baths, the constant protection against dirt, humidity, and scratching. For this reason, the credits of today's color movies usually cite the laboratory (Color by Technicolor, Color by DeLuxe, Color by Movielab) and make no mention at all of the film's manufacturer. Color by Technicolor no longer means the same thing as it meant thirty years ago, when Technicolor both manufactured and proc-

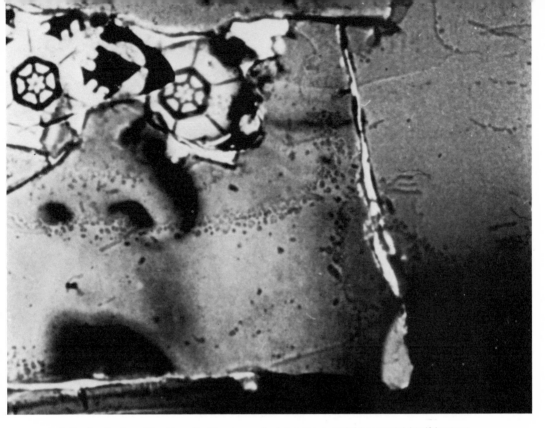

Collaging in *Dog Star Man:* Brakhage manipulates the celluloid material itself by turning a baby's eyes into Christmas bulb-like snowflakes, revealing an interior view of innocence, rather than von Stroheim's exterior view. (Note from page 119 that this is merely one frame in the film's succession.)

essed the film. What with the recent change (and cheapening) in the Technicolor dyeing process, which eliminates many of its most careful procedures and costly chemical dyes, Color by Technicolor may no longer mean anything at all.

A final (and completely different) consequence of the materiality of film is the option of treating it not as film (which records images), but as mere celluloid (which passes through a projector and through which light is projected). The possibility of using film not as photographic material but as a mere band of moving plastic has produced all those experiments of tampering with, of "adulterating," the film material itself. Filmmakers have made scratches in the film emulsion, colored them, and then printed the rhythmically dancing results. They have made collages by scattering bits of glue, paper, pins, nails, whatever, on the celluloid itself and then printed those results. Stan Brakhage scratched directly on the celluloid after recording photographic images on it—either as an attack on the apparent depth of the projected image or as a metaphor for sight itself. (In *Reflections of Black*, he scratches out a blind man's eyes.) Perhaps the most ingenious of these "adulterations" of the film material itself is Brakhage's *Mothlight*, a "film" that was not made of film at all. Brakhage pasted bits of natural objects—seeds, leaves, ferns, flowers, moths' wings—between two pieces of transparent splicing tape—in effect converting splicing tape into film. *Mothlight* is a film only as projected artifact; it was not made as a film or of film. Further, its natural objects—seeds, leaves, and such—are not perceived as seeds and leaves (which they would be if they had been photographed); *Mothlight* ironically converts these natural objects into rhythmically dancing abstract shapes—as if they were blotches and scratches on celluloid.

Those other references to the artificial, celluloid basis of cinema (say, the inclusion of the dots that end a roll of film, or of film leader, or of the light flashes and flares from exposing the celluloid to light when loading or unloading the camera) are also popular in experimental films (most notably, Brakhage's). They function as pointed reminders that the apparent naturalness of cinema is artifice, that its recording material is highly artificial, and that the act of making sequential visual images is as artificial as the making of any other artifact.

Lens and Object

Lens, filter, exposure, and film are the primary visual variables affecting the passage of light between lens and film during the filming of images. In addition, two primary variables affect the capturing of photographic objects by the lens during this filming: the angle of the shot and the activity of the camera during the shot. The camera *angle* is usually divided into three components: its distance, its level, and its perspective. The distance of a shot can obviously range from extremely close (say, a shot of a single eyeball) to extremely far (say, a mountaintop panorama that can see for ten miles). The traditional terms used to describe camera distance are imprecise and relative rather than mathematical: extreme close-up, close-up, medium close, medium, medium far, far shot, extreme far shot. A "medium" shot is medium only in the sense that it isn't very close or very far, however close or far very close or far is.

Clearly, the terms refer to the way the photographic subject will fill (or not fill) the frame. Even in shooting, the term far shot refers exclusively to our perception of the projected image rather than to any literal distance between lens and object during the shooting itself. Obviously, the apparent distance of a shot varies with the focal length of the lens. A close-up with a long lens may well be shot from a distance of fifteen feet from the subject, whereas a close-up with a short lens might well be shot from a distance of three feet. For a short lens, a distance of fifteen feet would produce a medium or medium far shot, not a close-up.

The implication of such vague terms as close-up and far shot is less to define distance than to define the photographic subject of the particular shot. The famous courtroom close-up of Mae Marsh's hands in *Intolerance* was not simply a close view of a pair of nervous and anxious hands; it defined those hands (and the implications of their nervousness) as the essential photographic subject of that shot. At the opposite extreme, the immense shot of Belshazzar's Babylon in the same film was not simply a distant view of a vast area; it defined the vastness and complexity of that ancient civilization as its primary photographic subject, the primary "information" that the shot wanted to convey. When the filmmaker chooses his "distance" he is really choosing his photographic subject—the "information" he wants us to see clearly and well.

Chaplin's mime and Astaire's dancing tend to use "medium" shots because their photographic subject is the motion of their whole bodies in space (and medium shots are vaguely defined as containing the full figure of a single human subject). When Keaton uses long shots, he does so because his photographic subject is the motion of his resilient but tiny frame in response to the vast natural or mechanical universe that surrounds him. Dreyer shoots his *Passion of Joan of Arc* in close-ups because his photographic subject is the human face and the Platonic notion of the way the face mirrors the purity or baseness, feelings or thought, that exist in the soul beneath the surface. To convey the drugged emptiness that overtook Lenny Bruce, Bob Fosse shot the Chicago nightclub sequence in *Lenny* (the "raincoat" act) from a great distance (and without a cut—to further the impression of a man drowning in his own helplessness with no one, not even the filmmaker, to throw him a line). This far shot contrasted with the tighter compositions (and active editing) of the earlier nightclub sequences in San Francisco, when Lenny was vibrantly alive and his act was a hit.

Once the "distance" of the shot has defined its subject (or its subject has defined its "distance"), the director (or cinematographer, or both) can determine the best level (or height) for capturing that subject and conveying its "information." The level of the shot can range from directly overhead (as in one of Busby Berkeley's kaleidoscopic dance patterns) to directly underneath (as in René Clair's male ballerina in *Entr'acte*, who pirouettes on a pane of clear glass). The tendencies of both these extremes, 180 degrees high and 180 degrees low, is to convert the photographic subject into an almost abstract visual pattern, emphasizing formations of people as geometric shapes, not as thinking, feeling beings (precisely the method in Lang's *Metropolis* and Riefenstahl's *Triumph of the Will*). For this reason, most shots that use human features, faces, and feelings as their essential photographic subjects tend to use a more restricted range of angles, between 45 degrees downward and 45 degrees upward.

A high angle shoots downward at its photographic subject, tending to reduce it in importance, power, and dominance. The human figure shot from above would necessarily support a fairly large head in relation to a recedingly smaller body that tends to taper away at its base (an effect that can be steadily increased as the focal length of the lens grows shorter and shorter). The high-angle shots often convey a subjective impression—the feeling that the photographic subject is short or small or weak. Either he feels himself dwarfed by the presence of the figure who is observing him from the camera's point of view, or he seems puny in the "eyes" of that observer, whose superior physical position and mental attitude has been mirrored by the camera's point of view.

Conversely, the low angle shoots upward at its photographic subject, tending to increase its impression of power, importance, and dominance. The human figure shot from below is necessarily built on a broad, strong base which rises (like a mountain) to a peak at the top, implying that the mental structure of a human being (the head at the top) is also a properly supported architectural edifice (an effect that can also be emphasized with the short lens). *Citizen Kane* provides some of the most striking low-angle shots of a ferociously powerful human being, consistently thrusting himself upward over the human beings that he dominates. Like the high-angle shot, the low-angle perspective can either imply that the photographic subject feels himself powerful or has impressed the camera-observer with his powerfulness. As Pudovkin noted (and Pudovkin was perhaps the first theorist to write lengthily on the psychological effects of high and low angles),[4] the low angle can either produce a feeling of genuine human strength and importance or satirically deflate the self-important pretensions of a vain and petty human figure. These effects of highness and lowness necessarily increase and intensify as the camera departs from the norm of eye level and as the wide-angle lens magnifies these shifts from the norm.

Yasujiro Ozu makes a very different use of the low angle, increasing the intimacy of his films by shooting at about the eye level of a human observer sitting on a tatami, the mat on the floor of a Japanese house—which is precisely where people sit in Japanese houses. Such a "special"

High and low angles in *Citizen Kane*. The boy's view of his imposing guardian in a low-angle shot and the guardian's view of the boy's smallness in the reverse high-angle shot. (Note how the boy's white face looms out of the darkness, just as his adult face did for Thatcher in the shot on page 144.) *Courtesy Janus Films*

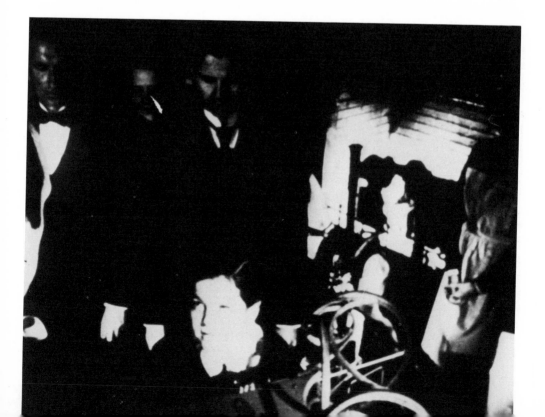

High and low angles in Fritz Lang's *M*. The little man, falsely accused as the child-murderer, feels tiny in the overpowering presence of his menacing accuser.

shot in Ozu's work is merely a Japanese translation of the normal or standard or neutral objective shot in an American or European movie, which is also an eye-level shot—but at the eye level of an observer standing or sitting in a chair (which is what people do in Western houses).

Indeed, this question of camera level is merely another specific application of the more general issue of the camera's perspective or slant on the photographic subject. It is worth discussing separately only because to refer to high and low angles (like the references to close and far shots) is a common way of talking about a shot. The lens must view every subject from some angle or other, and where it sees will determine what we see and how we see it. Rudolf Arnheim is especially good at developing the implications of effective camera angles, but his fine examples do not support his major argument. For Arnheim, camera angle is important because the photographic image reduces three-dimensional vision to a two-dimensional plane; because we cannot see all three dimensions of, say, a cube on the screen, the film artist must choose what view of it we will see. But no living person can see all six sides of a cube at the same time either. Because we are all single beings in space, we are frozen into our single perspective at any specific moment.

It is this parallel between the movie camera and the human condition that makes it such an effective narrator of film stories. If the camera wants to see more than one side of an object within a single shot, it must travel around it (as Kramer's camera travels around the embracing Gregory Peck and Ava Gardner in *On the Beach* or as Scorsese's camera travels around the piano bar in *Alice Doesn't Live Here Anymore*). If the camera wants to reveal more than one point of view toward the same event or being, it must cut to it at some later time (for example, the standard close-up and reverse close-up of any him and her during a love scene; or the multiple perspectives of the opera performance from Jed Leland's point of view in the audience of *Citizen Kane* and the subsequent reverse perspective from the stage and Susan Alexander's point of view). The camera is potentially omniscient in its general being during the course of an entire film (just as it ultimately becomes a god in *Citizen Kane*); the totality of a movie's structural and imagistic successions confers this omniscience upon it. But its vision is limited in the course of any single shot (just as each of the individual human observers is limited by his or her single perspective in *Citizen Kane*).

This limitation can be exploited in such a way that the photographic subject of the shot actually becomes the camera's limited way of seeing it. Arnheim uses two classic Chaplin examples, in which we see Charlie from behind, facing away from the camera, on a ship (*The Immigrant*) and in

The metaphoric implications of occasional high-angle shots in *Citizen Kane*. Welles-Toland depart from their usual low angle to depict quantities of objects from above—newspapers, Kane's possessions. So when the high angle shoots downward at Susan among her reviews, it reduces her to one of Kane's "things." *Courtesy Janus Films*

a study (*The Idle Class*). On the ship, Charlie's back appears to be "heaving" in a rhythmic manner; in the study, it appears to be "shaking" with a quicker rhythm. We infer from the first that Charlie is vomiting from seasickness, and from the second that he is weeping from lovesickness after his wife has left him. Then the surprise. Charlie turns around and we discover that he has (1) caught a fish and (2) is mixing up a cocktail—two opposites of sea and lovesickness. Ernst Lubitsch plays similar games with what he shows and what he suppresses—for example, his fondness for depicting scenes inside rooms by keeping his camera outside the windows or doors of the rooms.

Such devices play deliberately and self-consciously with a fact of cinematic life that most audiences and critics take for granted—every shot necessarily reveals some things and suppresses some other things. In order to discover what an angle truly reveals requires integrating the single shot into the film's imagistic and structural successions.

Yet another of the facts of cinematic life that we take for granted is the paradox that the camera's perspective can be simultaneously subjective and objective. If a high camera angle can imply that the character "feels small" in those surroundings, then the shot subjectively depicts internal feelings and is an objective recording at the same time (for the character who is feeling is also a photographic *object* in the frame). So too, in *Red Desert* Giulia's head is an object in the frame, but so is the blurry, subjective way that head perceives the rest of the world. To depict such internal feelings in a purely subjective way is certainly a cinema possiblity. We might see all the objects in the room looming hugely before the lens, apparently dwarfing or about to crush it (as in one of the porter's subjective flashes in *The Last Laugh*). But to substitute the camera's lens for a character's eye is such a special distortion and violation of narrative objectivity that it is usually reserved for special sequences like the dreams and visions in that German silent film. To make a whole sequence or movie in this purely subjective way (as if the camera were inside someone's head) is more than a trifle cute (for example, *The Lady in the Lake*). On the other hand, Miss Havisham's room in David Lean's *Great Expectations* looks cavernous because it seems cavernous in the eyes of little Pip.

The paradox of point of view in the cinema is that while we look at a figure as a photographic object, we are also often asked to participate subjectively in his or her feelings (feelings that are communicated by other elements of the image, and/or of succession, and/or of the sound track). This narrative condition may indicate a radical difference between cinema and fiction, which easily and frequently buries point of view inside a character's head (for example, the narrative strategies of Faulkner's *The Sound and the Fury* and *As I Lay Dying*). Because words invite us to conjure up images but do not present us with concrete images, as cinema does, the words can as easily come from inside a character's mind as from the mind of an outside observer—without striking us as bizarrely tricky (as any purely subjective cinema shot would).

But the novel can also manipulate the cinema paradox of simultaneous objective and subjective narration. The magnificent game of Jane Austen's narrative strategy in *Emma* is that the narration appears to be objective (it is in the third person), but really represents the subjective assumptions, observations, and projections of Emma Woodhouse. Flannery O'Connor is also a master of simultaneous objectivity and subjectivity—looking at a character on the outside, judging and evaluating his or her actions; exploring the values and feelings of the character from the inside, the way he or she sees the world. Although it is easier for novels to narrate in the first person than for cinema, and although it is more common for cinema to narrate in what appears to be third-person objectivity but is, at the same time, first-person subjectivity, both narrative cinema and narrative fiction share these complexities of point of view.

Such complicated considerations reveal that the issue of camera angle is far more complex than such numerical issues as the focal length of the lens or the speed of the film. To reduce the question of camera angle so that it merely seems to pertain to the camera—which is the implication of terms like close and far, high and low, objective and subjective—is a reduction indeed. The camera's angle determines what the photographic subject *is;* and what that subject is determines the function and effect of the shot in the work's literal, imagistic, and structural successions. Certainly, the lens is a part of the camera, and its relationship to what it photographs will determine what is recorded on film. But this classification for the sake of clarity should never obscure the impossibility of divorcing the angle from which the image is recorded from the content (or "information") of the image itself.

To speak of a camera angle is to imply that the camera's point of view in a shot is usually fixed. And it usually is. But because a shot is a continuous succession of frames, there is nothing to stop the camera itself from moving during that succession. Camera *activity* can be divided into two general kinds of movement: the kind in which the camera moves on a fixed fulcrum, either horizontally (panning) or vertically (tilting), analogous to a person's standing still but moving his head; and the kind in which the entire camera moves in space (called tracking, trucking, dollying, or traveling, all of which are vaguely synonymous), analogous to a person's walking or riding on the ground or through the air.

There are two general reasons for the camera to move. The first is obviously to follow the action of the photographic objects. If that object moves a bit from left to right, the camera can pan to keep our attention on it as the center of compositional interest. If that object moves a lot, the camera can travel, in effect, "walk," with it. If that subject stands up from a chair, the camera can tilt to stay with it as it rises. If it climbs up a long ladder, the camera can climb with it (perhaps by means of a crane or a hydraulic lift).

The second general strategy of camera movement is less obvious—a consequence of the kinetic power of moving images. If visual movement in the cinema excites and delights the eye, that kinetic sensation can be even more exciting when the camera moves along with the recorded movement (for example, the compelling energy of the perpetual traveling shots in Ophuls's *Lola Montès*). Ever since the Griffith era (and perhaps even before that with the railroad show Hale's Tours), filmmakers realized that the moving camera generated its own unique and independent excitement. When it combined that exciting movement with the rapid movement of photographic objects and the breathless suspense and tension of the last-minute rescue, it turned the screws of excitement and enjoyment as tightly as they could go.

Camera movement can also serve other, more special purposes. A pan can follow the mental or emotional movement in a scene (for example, the way a character reacts to another's utterance) rather than just its physical movement. By panning to catch a reaction, the director avoids the disjunction of a cut, linking the two figures firmly in the same physical space, perhaps increasing the tension or intimacy in the shot's "emotional space." (This method is a favorite device of Godard's.) In *Trouble in Paradise,* Lubitsch uses a variation on this kind of pan which develops the gulf between the uncomprehending speakers of two different languages. Lubitsch pans regularly back and forth between a group of chattering Italians and a French hotel guest (played by Edward Everett Horton, speaking English that is supposed to be French), who has been robbed but cannot make himself understood. The physical pan between the groups, who never share space in the same frame, mirrors the linguistic gulf between the different speakers.

Another evocative and striking use of the pan is Renoir's 360-degree panning shot around the entire courtyard in *The Crime of Monsieur Lange.* Renoir's shot produces suspense (in that it deserts the central characters of the action at a key and climactic moment), surprise (in that we discover the crime in the course of it), an awareness of thematic relationships (in that it reveals the wholeness yet violability of the courtyard world of the movie), and the movie's delicately ironic flavor (in that it performs this astonishing 360-degree maneuver with such ease, grace, and effortlessness that it seems quite oblivious to its own beauty and its own significance). When a camera movement does so much for a movie, we are no longer simply discussing camera movements.

The Japanese use a unique style of panning to catch a reaction that I have seen rarely in Western films (most notably Godard's), but frequently in Kurosawa, Mizoguchi, and Ichikawa. I would call the device a push pan. Rather than panning very smoothly or very violently from speaker to reacter (the two common Western styles), the Japanese seem to push (or bump) the camera over to the next figure, moving it quite jerkily and stopping it with surprising abruptness. Whereas the smoothness or rush of the Western pan tries either to obliterate or underline our consciousness of the camera's moving back and forth, the Japanese style mildly and softly underlines the movement (a kind of colon, rather than a comma or an exclamation point).

The violent panning effect in Western films is called the swish pan, the panning of the camera so swiftly that the world seems to swish past it, producing only a streaky blur (and another reminder of the difference between lens-film and eyes-brain as perceptual systems). The swish pan is primarily a transitional and punctuational device; for example, it punctuates the disparate vignettes of the mounting breakfast-table antagonism between Kane and Emily in *Citizen Kane*. In that short but telling dissolution of a marriage, the swish pan serves, at the same time, as a disjunctive device (separating the isolated moments of the chronicle), a unifying device (tying the vignettes together as a briefly digressive account of a single process), and a tonal device (letting us know that the causes of the marriage's collapse are being exposed casually, lightly, in swift and broad strokes, so as not to divert us from the central study of Kane himself). As a cinema punctuation device, the swish pan might perhaps be considered a unit in a film's structural succession (parallel to the wipe or lap dissolve), although it is produced by camera movement, not the printer.

Special effects of tilting seem to be less common, inhibited by the limited potential of human vertical movement in a single shot. When a shot contains extremes of this kind of movement (say, Lola's climb to the top of her ladder in *Lola Montès*, or Julie's climbing the same kind of ladder in *Day for Night*, or Harold Lloyd's climbing a tree and then falling from it in *The Kid Brother*), the camera is forced to travel (on some kind of crane or vertical dolly) rather than tilt. Perhaps two of the most spectacular tilt shots in movies are the identical 180-degree tilts in Dreyer's *Passion of Joan of Arc* and Chukhrai's *Ballad of a Soldier*. Both shots are from a very high angle; both follow a line of trooping soldiers. As they march past the camera, they also pass beneath it, and the camera tilts continuously to follow their departure, finishing its half circle "on its back," with the horizon and the earth startlingly, beautifully, awesomely upside down (and with a clear implication about their makers' views of armies and warfare).

The traveling shot, in addition to following the action or generating excitement with its restive motion, can play a key narrative (and narrator's) role. A very great number of movies begin with a traveling shot that seems to zero in on something and/or end with a traveling shot that seems to pull back and take its leave of the people and events it has followed. There are two common beginnings to movies: inside out (plunging us *in medias res*) and its opposite, outside in. Movies that plunge us *in medias res* almost inevitably begin with fairly close or medium shots. They immediately immerse the viewer in the world and experience of the movie, often confusing us deliberately before we get our bearings, allowing us to feel a part of the movie's world by "discovering it" as we are experiencing it (*The Pawnbroker, Bonnie and Clyde,*

City Lights, Stagecoach, Vertigo, His Girl Friday, To Be or Not to Be, Lenny, Easy Living, 8½, Pather Panchali, Loves of a Blonde, Intimate Lighting, Wild Strawberries, Persona). Such movies, with this narrative structure of moving from inside to outside, almost never begin with traveling shots.

But the other kind, the structure that begins on the outside and at a distance from the characters and then begins to bore its way closer to the center, very frequently does. Such an opening shot becomes a metaphor for the narrative strategy of the whole movie, which transports us out of our own worlds and into the surrogate world on screen (the swooping down into Manhattan of *West Side Story;* the traveling argument that opens *Nights of Cabiria,* complemented by the final traveling shot on the road of the same film; the traveling shots of revelers in *Blow-Up,* complemented by the ultimate pullback from the revelers in the final shot of the same film; the camera prowling through the railway station in *Shanghai Express* and along the coils of cable in *Rules of the Game;* the moving camera's descent into the pit with the garbage in Kurosawa's *Lower Depths;* and that familiar traveling toward Xanadu and Kane in *Citizen Kane*).

Movies with this outside-in structure that do not begin with traveling shots tend to begin with very long panoramas (*The Seventh Seal; The Man Who Shot Liberty Valance; Rashomon; Early Spring; Thieves Like Us; Throne of Blood,* and many others). *Psycho* combines its long shot (of the entire city of Phoenix) with a zoom (into the specific and sleazy hotel room). *Day for Night* uses the two beginnings of inside out and outside in at the same time—quite ironically and deliberately. On the one hand, the movie plunges us immediately into the world of the movie studio, although we are not at all aware that it is a movie studio rather than "life," and it takes us a while to get our bearings and discover that fact. On the other, we travel around an apparent Parisian street, steadily searching out and moving toward the significant people and event (that climactic slap before the director calls "Cut!") in this movie's movie-within-the-movie. The film's opening traveling shot contains the same tension between true/false and natural/artificial that propels the entire film—except that we are completely unaware of its metaphoric appropriateness as we watch it. When a camera movement can play such important metaphoric and structural roles in a movie, we have once again deserted the province of the image itself for a consideration of its relevance to the film's structural succession as a whole.

Film and Lab

Both after the film has been exposed and after it has been edited it is subjected to the developing and printing processes that are commonly lumped together as "lab work." Developing the film is the first step, immersing the exposed raw footage in chemical baths so as to produce the original negative or (if it is a reversal film) positive. The primary visual effects of developing are its rendering the clarity and sharpness of monochrome film and the accuracy and richness of color film. But the visual and special effects of printing are more complex and numerous. The optical printer is a machine that exposes a virginal roll of film by "projecting" the previously exposed, developed, and often edited footage onto it.* While making such a print, the optical printer can also interpose visual effects on the strip of celluloid that did not exist in the original image. All the transitional devices (fades, dissolves, and wipes) are among these visual effects (which then function as units in the movie's structural succession).

There are, however, any number of visual effects that can result from the printing (and occasionally developing) of the film. Color tinting of the image can be achieved by the printer (although it can also be accomplished by immersing the exposed film in a color dye). Dyeing was the common method of tinting monochrome film in the silent era—to produce blue, orange, green, red, or yellow "washes" that toned the projected image. It is not so precisely contollable with color film, which would tend to use color dyeing for crude or garish effects (as does the dream sequence in Corman's *The House of Usher*).

All forms of superimposition are optical effects (since such transitional devices as dissolves are specific applications of superimposition). The primary effects of superimposition are as one of those overtly subjective devices (connoting drunkenness, dizziness, or madness—as in *The Last Laugh*), as a supernatural device (as in the vampire's dissolution into the morning air in *Nosferatu* or in the mysteriously haunting burial scene of Jean Epstein's *The Fall of the House of Usher*), or as a surreal visual pattern (as in Cavalcanti's *Rien que les heures* or Man Ray's *Emak Bakia*). As the examples indicate, the 1920s was the classic age of superimposition, when creative filmmakers sought the means to make the purely visual image as expressive as possible. Experimental filmmakers

---

* Two other kinds of printers—the contact printer and the step printer—also exist for making work prints and release prints. The optical printer is capable of affecting the visual values of the image itself.

The uses of superimposition. In Jean Epstein's *The Fall of the House of Usher,* the superimposed candles and leaves over the mourning Usher's face create his melancholy reaction to his beloved's death. But in *Citizen Kane,* the superimposed newspaper, stage setting, and worklight summarize Susan's frantic and excruciating opera career. *Courtesy Janus Films*

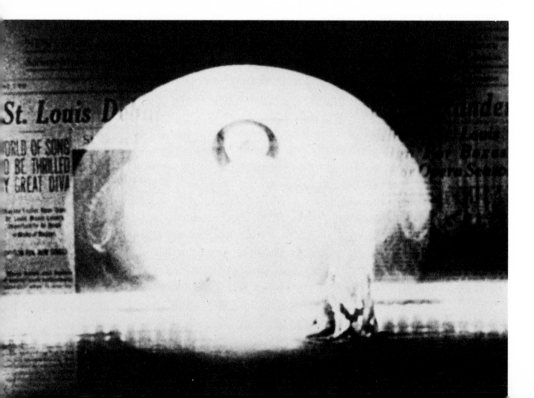

like Stan Brakhage and Michael Snow remain far more committed to superimposition today than narrative moviemakers, for one of the assumptions of certain experimental films is that the optical printer can compensate for the suppressed effects of montage. Further, the artist can create several layers of meaning in a single image simultaneously (as many as four layers in Brakhage's *Dog Star Man*).

A parallel way of altering the look of the image so that it seems otherworldly is more a directorial decision than an optical effect (although it proceeds from the chemical treatment of the film material itself). The filmmaker can decide to insert a section of negative film into the final print, reversing the black-white values of monochrome film or the color values of color film. The use of negative usually implies that the natural experience recorded on film has entered a negative or reversed region of anti-life, like Alice stepping into the other side of her looking glass. Murnau uses negative film for the journey of the phantom coach in *Nosferatu*, which carries the protagonist from the domain of the natural to the vampire's castle (and back again). *The Fly* also uses negative during the process of converting a human being into an insect—another transposition from one mode of being to another. As opposed to these supernatural effects, Stan Brakhage's *Flesh of Morning* uses negative film as a means of intensifying the sexual climax of masturbation—of developing the way that such an experience transports the rational human being into an isolated region of pure and personal sensuality. Michael Snow inserts a strip of negative color film into *Wavelength* as another way of revealing how different that same loft can look.

Another way to alter the look and effect of the exposed footage when developing it is to "push" it—to compensate for a possibly under or over-exposed image by bringing out or reducing a film's grain with greater or less immersion in the chemical baths. Although the usual reason for pushing footage is to eradicate the problems of insufficient illumination or human error when it was filmed, pushing introduces interesting visual effects of its own. One can usually push a fast (i.e., fine-grain) film one stop without producing severe visual distortions (i.e., develop the film as if the lens were open one stop wider during the original exposure). But as you push film more and more, the visual image gets softer, fuzzier, and grainier. I have seen a student film, shot at night with very fast film and available light, that had been pushed three stops; the image had the velvety softness of a "stopping by woods on a snowy evening"—although it was not snowing that particular evening.

Whereas an overexposure washes out the image with light, a push spots the image with dancing grain. The reason newsreel cinematography often looks so grainy is that the cameraman must do the best he can under difficult shooting conditions with very fast film and available light, compensating for any imperfections by pushing the footage in the lab. One can duplicate this "authentic" look of newsreel footage to deliberate effect in narrative movies (for example, to produce the feeling of spontaneity, "truth," and documented reality in *The Battle of Algiers*) by shooting and then pushing the film under the same conditions. When used this way in movies, the pushing of film parallels lens flare and the hand-held camera in creating the impression of authenticity by incorporating deliberate "mistakes" into the artistic plan of the movie's style. Because newsreel or *cinéma vérité* photography are among our means of documenting reality, a grainy image in a movie masquerades as a piece of documented reality.

Two operations of the printer do not so much produce a special visual effect as modify the original photographic format of the film so that it can be projected in a new format. The first is the making of a reduction print, reducing 35-mm film to 16 mm for showings in classrooms or on television. In reducing a film's width, the reduction almost inevitably reduces the potential size of the image that can be projected without a significant loss of clarity and resolution. Conversely, some experimental or documentary films are originally shot in 16 mm and then blown up to 35 mm or even 70 mm for showings in commercial theaters (if they should be fortunate enough to get commercial bookings). 8-mm films can also be blown up to 16 mm, an occasional practice with experimental films for showing in classrooms and film societies. Such enlargement prints quite frequently betray their 16-mm origins when projected in 35 mm with a greater graininess and far less crispness than a film shot originally in 35 mm. But *The Concert for Bangladesh* was blown up from 16 mm to 70 mm with little loss of crispness and gain of grain.

A parallel operation of the printer affects not the visual characteristics of the image but the visual effect of the literal succession of frames. The repeating of individual frames by the printer can be used not only for the striking arrest of successive motion (as in the "freeze frame"), but to convert the successive motion of a silent film into an equally fluid succession when combined with a sound track. By repeating every other frame, the printer compensates for the 50 percent difference in the sound and silent projection speeds, eliminating the need to sacrifice the visual "music" and rhythms of the image for the sake of the music on the new sound track.

American television requires repeating every fourth frame of film, for it scans at thirty images per second (European television scans at twenty-five, close enough to film's twenty-four so that no conversion is necessary). This particular successive "effect" of the printer is not to change the look of the image so that it appears strange, but so that it appears "normal"; like any effect of literal succession, it plays on the differences between recording and projecting successive images—except it "plays on them" by trying to erase, not emphasize, the differences. If you see a silent film with a sound track, and the film looks like a parody of silent film (i.e., ultra-fast and herky-jerky), that is a certain sign that the producer did not use the method of repeating frames. Conversely, the printer can also make a normal-speed film look like a herky-jerky silent one by skipping or repeating frames—another synthetic effect of literal succession produced by printing rather than shooting.

A final effect of the printer that is certainly perceived as a special effect of the visual image is to incorporate several different and discrete images into the same frame—commonly referred to today as a split screen. Most of these split-screen effects are descendants of the multiscreen films (especially Francis Thompson's *To Be Alive* for Johnson's Wax) at the New York World's Fair of 1964–65. Multiscreen movie experiments have been consistently popular at world's fairs, ever since Léon Gaumont's circular-screen process at the Paris Exposition of 1900. Indeed, Edison's first motion-picture machine, the Kinetoscope, was unveiled to the amazement of the public at a world's fair—the Chicago Exposition of 1893.

In *To Be Alive,* Thompson used his triple screen in several ways. He could extend a single image over the entire width of the three screens, producing the same sweeping and peripheral visual effects as Cinerama. But the use of black dividers between the three screens avoided the Cinerama problem of the jiggling and bothersome joining lines between the three images. Whereas Cinerama tried to pretend that it was a single image (although we could clearly see it was three), Thompson admitted that his unity had three clear parts—at a very slight sacrifice of verisimilitude. Once having admitted that his unity was three, Thompson could use the three screens in several other ways: to show different views and angles of the same process; to repeat the same image on two or all three screens for emphasis; to show different evolutionary steps in the same process; to give the camera a kind of multiplicity in the same "shot," freeing it from the single viewing perspective that usually imprisons it in a conventional shot.

It was only a matter of technology to convert a triple-screen process into a single frame with three (or more) images at once. Richard Fleischer's *The Boston Strangler* (1968) was one of the first films to take advantage of the possibility, dividing its huge Panavision rectangle into various smaller ones to give different narrative and psychological perspectives into the same human event. The trickiness of the split screen is somewhat in narrative disfavor today, and it has passed into the hands of the experimentalists (Bruce Baillie, Scott Bartlett), the documentarists (*Woodstock, Mad Dogs and Englishmen*), and the televisionists. The reduction of the split screen to fit the tiny television screen seems to weaken both the awesome kinetic power and the intriguing perceptual power of the device, reducing it to a piece of merely decorative design (for example, the opening titles of the *Mannix* series).*

These split-screen possibilities, of course, seem to call my definition of the shot into question (a projected succession of unedited frames). A single split-screen "shot" (say, four different rectangles within the main frame) would contain four different "mini-shots." There could be edited successions of images in each of the four mini-frames, while the master frame kept its same relationship to all of them without any editing of that master frame itself. Rather than reject the definition of shot, it seems more useful to view the technique as manipulating shots-within-a-shot, and the master "shot" itself is parallel to a "shot" in an animated film, as determined by the background cel.

Sports telecasting has also appropriated the split-screen device, and a recent baseball telecast used a five-image split screen (the batter and the runners on first, second, and third in four symmetrical rectangles, with the pitcher in a circular hole in the center). But baseball telecasting has been using split screens (albeit less fancy ones) for over two decades; usually the speedy runner on first, who was a threat to steal, appeared to be scooped or cut out of the lower-right-hand corner of the screen. In baseball telecasting, the original device created dramatic tension out of the duel between pitcher and base runner—to supplement the tense duel between pitcher and batter. There are those who feel that baseball telecasting needs all the dramatic tension it can get. Perhaps for this reason, telecasts of football—a more active and dramatic sport—apply the trickiest split screens to purely analytical purposes (the "instant replay"). That tricky five-way split in baseball seemed so fractured and fancy that

* These split-screen effects are nothing new, by the way. They were extremely common in the first decade of this century, before Griffith's development of cutting. The early movies believed that the only way to show two actions occurring simultaneously in time was to depict them within the same framed space. *The Life of an American Fireman* (1903) uses a split-screen, so do several Max Linder comedies of 1908, so does René Clair's *Les Deux timides* (1928). From these few examples, we can be sure that the device was used by thousands of films. Today's split screen enjoys the advantage of size; the huge screen allows each of the splits to be almost as large as a regular screen, eliminating the "cuteness" of the shrinking device. Television obviously has the "cuteness" now.

it reduced the dramatic tension of watching "live" (i.e., unpredictable) action to the cold, after-the-fact analysis of football's instant replay.

Sports telecasting also uses a less fancy principle of split screen to interesting effect with its little inserts of, say, the clock (to reveal how much time remains) or the coach's face (to reveal his feelings and concentration). These inserts increase our information and, as a result, the dramatic tension of the sporting event (particularly its climax). They almost inevitably occupy a very small portion of the frame, leaving its major business to dominate our attention.

But the split screen's gain in visual interest and information from a multiplicity of perspectives also results in its loss of the concentrated dramatic power inherent in a single image. The device has certain technological (if not visual) affinities with 3-D, another tricky process that sacrifices concentration for multiplicity and visual stimulation. Like the split screen, 3-D projects more than a single image within a single frame (but projected "on top of" one another, not discretely as in the split screen). Very much like 3-D, the split screen seems to be doomed in narrative moviemaking, for its overt trickiness increasingly fails to justify its limited effects, its growing familiarity, and the inevitable predictability of its choices.

THE TONING OF THE IMAGE

Whereas the filming of images classified the *direct* operations of light upon film, the ways of affecting the direct transmission of light through lens or printer to celluloid, the toning of images includes all operations of light upon the surfaces of those objects captured by lens and film. That film can record an image at all results from the indirect refraction of light off the solid surfaces of photographic objects; the way light strikes and illuminates those surfaces controls the way those objects will strike and illuminate us. The toning of images differs from the content of images in that it refers not to the objects themselves, but to the way their surfaces are shaped, toned, defined, and developed by light, which is itself not an object and seems "invisible," except that it is the source of visibility for those objects that can be seen in the image. The toning of the image has three primary variables: the direction of the light, the intensity of the light, and the shade(s) or color(s) that the light produces.

The source of a scene's illumination must come from some direction or other, and the *direction* that the director (or cinematographer) selects will determine which surfaces receive the greatest illumination and will cast the strongest shadows on which other surfaces. The most common lighting direction for movies is the high angle from about 45-degrees above, for this angle-direction is the kindest to the human face and features. Lighting from above tends to sharpen the features and slim the facial structure. Hence, virtually all live theater today uses overhead lighting and has dispensed with footlights altogether—except for special grotesque or burlesque effects. Lighting from above also throws its shadows downward, off the face and toward the floor, where they are less noticeable and distracting.

Low-angle lighting produces a more special kind of effect—usually of the grotesque, bizarre, or horrific—since it casts shadows on the human face that can rarely be seen in nature. Neither our natural nor our artificial illumination comes from below, with the exceptions of campfires, sandy beaches, and snowscapes. Low lighting tends to fleshen and fatten the human face, casting the shadow of the chin toward the nose, the shadow of the nose toward the eyes, and the shadows of the eye sockets toward the forehead. Low lighting also throws its shadows of the human figures onto the surfaces of the walls behind the humans, where the shadows can tower grotesquely above the figures who produced them (as they often do in Eisenstein's *Ivan the Terrible*). Side lighting turns the human face into a halfmoon, often for moody, pensive, or internalized effects (as in Bergman's shot of Death as Confessor in *The Seventh Seal*). Back lighting converts both people and objects into shadows themselves, surrounded and defined by diaphanous streaks and shafts of light (as in the projection-room sequence of *Citizen Kane* or several nightclub sequences of *Lenny*).

Indeed, *Lenny* can serve as almost a primer for the effects of lighting direction. In an early nightclub sequence, Valerie Perrine's striptease receives lighting directly from above and below at the same time. The opposite sources of light convert her body into a sensual series of layers— a top and bottom layer of gleaming white flesh, separated by a gray layer of fleshy sediment between. Lenny's nightclub performances use several different principles of lighting direction—and each shift of lighting conveys the comic's vitality and success at each stage of his career. Bob Fosse uses back lighting to frame Lenny's head as a silhouette in the blazing spotlights (indicating his mystical power over his audience and converting him into a messiah with nimbus); he uses smoky, vital overhead lighting for the San Francisco nightclub (where Lenny plays at the top of his game); he uses harsh, even, institutional-style overhead lighting for the courtroom scenes (where Lenny's "act" is less of a hit); he uses a narrow overhead light surrounded by blackness in the Chicago nightclub (where both Lenny's act and his life "bomb out"). The "candid" interview sequences that frame the movie's chronicle of the comedian (with Lenny's wife and his agent) use side lighting as their dominant direction, evoking the spontaneity and naturalness of documentary interviews, which can be filmed only with available light (and where the only light available streams in through a window).

One of the discoveries about film toning in the "Griffith era" was that lighting direction both controlled a film's tone and convinced an audience that it was watching fictionalized "life," not fakey fiction. A striking characteristic of early films (perhaps of every pre-1910 film) was that outdoor sequences often looked convincingly natural and real (and were capable of great beauty), while indoor films and sequences inevitably looked flat, empty, and ugly. The indoor and outdoor sequences of Porter's *Life of an American Fireman, The Great Train Robbery,* and *Rescued from an Eagle's Nest* or Griffith's *A Corner in Wheat* seem so stylistically schizophrenic that it is difficult to believe that both were shot by the same camera and eye. One reason for this indoor two-dimensionality was quite literal: early film sets were two-dimensional, painted theatrical flats (even the name is significant), not the three-dimensional architectural edifices they are today. But even when the sets became more architectural (as they did in even the weaker Griffith films of 1910 and 1911), the indoor sequences continued to feel two-dimensional.

The reason is that their illumination remained two-dimensional, as unlike authentic indoor lighting as painted flats are unlike functional walls, doors, and windows. Early film lighting did not use electricity; indoor scenes were shot outdoors, using sunlight (with a sheet of muslin to soften its shadows). There are many unintentionally amusing moments in these early films when a tablecloth or dress starts flapping from a violent gust of wind that could never exist inside a human dwelling. Often the pioneer actors would have their hands full keeping the set and props from blowing away.

Authentic indoor lighting falls in streaks and pools—from windows, lamps, candles, fireplaces. Griffith's *The Drunkard's Reformation* (1909) used what, at the time, was an astounding device by lighting its final scene with a single low-angle light (impersonating a fireplace's glow). The lighting effect not only made the room feel like a room, and not only produced a soft, cozy feeling; it also fit precisely into the film's dramatic and allegorical structure (the prodigal husband returning to the comfort of hearth and home). From such a discovery it was clear that all films would need to use the direction of lighting to make a room feel like a room, and to make people inside the room feel like people inside a room.

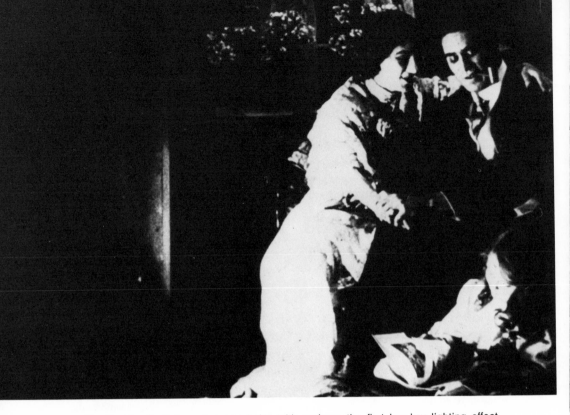

The Drunkard's Reformation concludes with perhaps the first low-key lighting effect in cinema history. The profligate has returned to the warmth and security of hearth and home.

They would also need to control the *intensity* of the light. As with the effects of camera angle, the effects of lighting angle (or direction) are capable of a very wide range of possibilities—from extremely grotesque and striking to extremely subtle and barely perceptible. The primary way of emphasizing or softening the effect of a lighting direction is in controlling the mixture of key and fill lighting. The key light is the dominant direction of a shot's primary lighting; the fill light (as the name implies) is the supplementary lighting that fills in the potential gaps and erases the grotesqueries of the key light. The typical studio-era lighting of a shot inside a room that is supposed to feel like a bright, cheery, authentic room would use high-angle key lighting for the actors, special key lighting for pools and shafts of illumination around the sources of light (lamps, windows), and plenty of fill lighting to erase the gaps and keep the shadows (of the actors, of the boom, of the camera) off the walls.

Our eyes do not perceive gaps between bright and shady areas of rooms; nor do we cast extremely noticeable shadows on our walls. This use of lighting to produce the even blend and unity that our eye effects automatically and naturally is yet another of the reminders of the difference between lens and eye, film and brain. This "bright" kind of movie lighting is called high-key lighting, presumably because it appears "high" and bright and even and registers a high number on an exposure meter—and approximately the same number in all areas of the shot. But it might more accurately be called high-fill lighting.

The opposite kind of lighting is called low-key lighting, presumably because the lighting seems "low" and moody and registers a low number on an exposure meter—or very sharp contrasts between high and low numbers in different areas of the shot. But it is actually lighting with a powerful (but often isolated) key light and very little fill lighting (if any). The vagueness of such terms is a reminder that high- and low-key lighting are general terms employed by technicians in the industry and are no more precise or concrete than the vague terms for camera distance and angle (far shot, low angle). The very fact that these terms are so vague implies the tacit realization by technicians that film devices and effects cannot be reduced to precise and mathematical formulas. High- and low-key lighting refer to approximations of tone and feeling.

Most of the striking lighting effects in cinema history (and all of those mentioned above: *The Drunkard's Reformation, Citizen Kane, The Seventh Seal, Lenny*) are examples and variations of low-key lighting—as would be any effect in which the lighting appears to be very intense in a particular direction, very concentrated in its focus, and surrounded by pools or shadows of seeming blackness. Such an effect is another example of the way the cinema deserts literal reality to produce a metaphoric atmosphere that feels more real and natural than nature. Obviously, the human eye does not perceive a human figure in front of a fireplace as a bright speck in a black void; nor does it perceive human beings as solid and inky silhouettes that are framed and animated by shafts of light behind them (as in *Citizen Kane* or *Lenny*). The eye does not perceive such absolute separations of dark and light, but blends them together into a unified and gradually shaded whole.

The filmed shot of a single face by a fireside produces the feeling, atmosphere, and impression of the quiet, reflective event, not the literal or natural appearance of it. It is another cinema device that is paradoxically objective and subjective at the same time. The exposure meter is an indispensable tool of toning because it "sees" the light exactly as film does—mechanically—not as the eye and brain do, making "corrections" for insufficiencies and oversufficiencies automatically. For this same reason, the light-sensitive exposure "eye," a handy tool of some "home movie" cameras (which adjusts the exposure automatically to suit the amount of available light), is a useless tool for narrative movies (for it

Low-key lighting in *Citizen Kane*. Kane steps into the shadows to sign his "Declaration of Principles"—implying perhaps that the "I" of those principles is only a phantom. It would have been as easy to light Kane's face as Leland's and Bernstein's. *Courtesy Janus Films*

obliterates the variations and contrasts in atmospheric lighting that an image must use to evoke the feeling of an experience).

The final operation of light in the toning of the image is the way it saturates the objects themselves to produce their *shade* or *color*. The master of monochrome shading was probably Josef von Sternberg, whose films can be seen in terms of attempts to shade degrees of blackness (*Shanghai Express*), degrees of whiteness (*The Scarlet Empress*), and the clash of black against white (*The Blonde Venus*). Among other effective and affective examples of monochrome shading, I might cite the dazzling white richness of the walls and furniture of the Imperial "Suit" (i.e., suite) in Leisen's *Easy Living*, the white-on-white of the Paris hotel suite as opposed to the dark-wood-against-white-walls of the Constantinople hotel suite in Lubitsch's *Ninotchka*, the degrees of whiteness and light-grayness in the final, circular, circus-ring "dance" of Fellini's 8½, the stark contrast of black figures, white paths, and gray shadows and trees of the formal garden in Resnais's *Last Year at Marienbad,* the clash of the white brides-to-be and the single black-clad Keaton in the church sequence of *Seven Chances,* or the variations of parched white and white-gray in the sand, mountains, and sky of Death Valley in von Stroheim's *Greed.*

The functions of color (and its relation to light) have already been discussed, but might be summarized briefly here. Color can serve a purely kinetic purpose (producing direct feelings and sensations that shape our emotional responses to a scene, event, person, or object); it can serve a purely metaphoric purpose (producing more indirect and conceptual responses to a scene, person, event, or object conditioned by our associations of emotion with color—white as purity, green as fertility, purple and black as death, red as passion); or it can serve as a purely intellectual or symbolic *leitmotif* (the use of red in Tati's *Playtime,* Bergman's *Cries and Whispers,* Preminger's *The River of No Return,* and Scorsese's *Taxi Driver,* flesh-pink in Antonioni's *Red Desert,* beige and black in Peckinpah's *The Wild Bunch,* ivory-cream in Polanski's *China-*

The integration of lighting and camera angle in *Citizen Kane.* The high angle implies Kane's dwarfing Susan both mentally and physically, as he casts an ominous shadow across her face (and soul). *Courtesy Janus Films*

town, green and lavender in Fellini's *Juliet of the Spirits*). The most effective color movies, however, use color in all three of these ways simultaneously.

Truffaut's *The Story of Adele H.,* for example, uses color both so subtly as to go almost entirely unnoticed and so carefully and crucially that the entire movie depends on it. There are six dominant color schemes in the film—each of which corresponds to a specific geographic or emotional region. For the Nova Scotia sequences Truffaut bathes his images with the drab, dull, somber and neutral—the muted deep browns, dark grays, and pale beiges of wood paneling and wool clothing. The muted colors mirror the muted quality of life in this cold northern region as well as the muted, weak quality of its light.

The most colorful object in that climate is Adele herself. She first appears in the darkness, a dazzling peacock-blue ribbon attached to her hat; the ribbon, which she wears periodically throughout the Nova Scotia sequences, is consistently the brightest object in the frame. Her most familiar piece of clothing is her silky russet-maroon dress, muted enough to harmonize with her neutral surroundings but still more richly colored than the drab walls, clothing, and people that surround her. When Lieutenant Pinson visits for their first reunion, she changes into a pale-blue dress, pale but still colorfully blue enough to match the blueness of her eyes and contrast with the ripe redness of her lips. At this moment of joy, she is not only the most colorful object in the frame; she also displays more color than she ever will again.

In striking contrast are the color and light of the Barbados sequences. Truffaut bathes the image in striking primary colors—reds, golds, yellows, blues that, like the people and the flowers, are vibrantly alive in the light of an intense sun. Amazingly enough, Adele's russet dress, that sinewy, colorful maroon in Canada, now looks muddy brown—drab, dull, and neutral—in this new light. The dress is dirty and tattered, of course, a sign of her mental degeneration. And it is strikingly out of place—in style, texture, weight, and color—in these tropical surroundings (as is Adele). But the change of light and color environment make the same dress look not the same at all (just as Adele is not the same at all). In contrast, Pinson's navy-blue uniform, so drab-looking in the pale northern light, seems positively brilliant in Barbados; the gold trim, which had been so coldly muted, now sparkles brilliantly in the full and brilliant light.

The one striking color sequence in Canada is the hypnotism scene, dominated by the same overripe red as Adele's lips in the first scene with

Pinson. The richness of the color mirrors the passion and romance of the moment in Adele's view—her last hope to seize Pinson's affection. That red later recurs as the door of Judge Johnston's house, the one striking note in a gray, dull object where Adele will destroy Pinson's plans of marriage. In contrast to this red is the muted darkness of the graveyard scene, bathed in a cold, slightly blue light. Truffaut emphasizes the scene's neutrality with the blackness of the night, the grayness of the tombstones, the black of Adele's tuxedo disguise, and the now lifeless navy of Pinson's uniform. The relationship between Adele and Pinson is as dead as the setting, as dead as the noncolor that engulfs them.

The Guernsey sequence is dominated by green and greenery—not the brilliant flowers and yellow earth of Barbados nor the gray-brown furze-like vegetation of pale Canada, but the rich, lush green produced by a moderate climate and plenty of rain. And Truffaut reserves his final color-toning for the recurring dream sequences and the photographic stills that conclude the film. Both the vision and the stills seem to use a monochrome close to Sepia-Tone. Just as Truffaut used monochrome for the dream sequences of *Day for Night*, he made Adele's brief visions of Leopoldine, superimposed over the dreamer's tortured face, appear drained of color—emphasizing the strangeness and otherworldliness of the nightmare. When the stills at the end reiterate the same brownish shade, both stills and dream seem set in historical brackets, pushed into the past, in the same way that Sepia is part of the faded look of "pastness" of old movies and old photographs. With such careful control, Truffaut succeeds in making color informative and evocative, geographic and mental, natural and symbolic, overt and subliminal, internal and external, all at the same time.

Three other ways of affecting the color shading and toning of objects are with laboratory dyes and with colored filters (as discussed above) and with light that is itself colored. Richard Brooks used pools of red and other-colored light to convey sensuality in the opening sequence of his *The Brothers Karamazov*. Roger Corman used a pale rose-colored light in *The House of Usher* to convey the corrupting sickliness of the Usher family (the Ushers were consistently linked to the shades of red) and pale blue or blue-green light to depict the disruptive forces that enter their house (blue was consistently linked to the fiancé from Boston and the climactic lightning storm). Even apparently artless movies often take the trouble to use color in an artful way.

THE CONTENT OF THE IMAGE

Although the operations of light on film and on objects control our perception of the image and produce our ability to see it, an image also "contains" the forms of physical objects themselves. The content of an image is literally the two-dimensional reproduction of physical objects or formal patterns within the frame, the surfaces of solid matter or drawn forms that the camera records on film. This content can be divided into three classes, based on three questions: What are the objects? Where are the objects? and What are the objects doing? These three classes of objects, their composition, and their action interweave complexly, leading to difficult theoretical issues.

For example, a scholarly paper recently claimed that Jacques Tati's *Playtime* was "about the contrast of horizontals and verticals with arcs and curves."[5] Now, prevailing critical opinion is probably that *Playtime* is "about" the contrast of old and new, modernity and tradition, Europe and America, men and machines, or some such abstraction. The two conflicting interpretations begin to merge, however, if you see *Playtime* as being "about" the contrast of freedom and constraint, suppleness and rigidity—a dichotomy broad enough to include both the spatial and the social interpretations. There seems little dispute that some kind of contrast and dichotomy is at the center of what *Playtime* is "about," but in what sense is an image "about" something? Which is to say, what is the content of an image? And are the images and the movie necessarily "about" the same things? Or might an image be "about" things which then lead to more general inferences about what the movie is "about"?

One of the specific images of *Playtime* sticks in my mind, both as a means to test the validity of these different interpretations of the movie's "aboutness" and to develop the three kinds of content in an image itself. These three different kinds of content are responsible for the different views of what this movie is "about."

Toward the end of the movie, Tati creates a quiet, early-morning scene; it is the "morning after" the nightclub, just before the American tourists leave Paris for home. Tati shows a mixed group of Parisians and tourists taking their morning coffee in a slick, modern café. A delivery man enters the café, pushing open its plate-glass door and leaving it ajar. As the glass door swings open, we suddenly see a transparent reflection shining on the glass in the morning sunlight. It is the cathedral of Sacre Coeur. Now, what is the content of such a shot?

First, although the setting is a café, it is not the charming Old World

Parisian sidewalk café of the travel posters (or of Minnelli's *An American in Paris*), but an ultramodern café of glass, cement, metal, and Formica, such as can be seen in any modern city in any part of the world. Indeed, the café's name is "Drugstore." This disappearance of oldness and cultural distinctiveness, the influence of the leveling international force of creeping modernity, is one of the consistent *leitmotifs* of the movie: the international trade exposition of modern office furniture and equipment; the travel posters that depict the identical architecture regardless of the name of the city; the modern, just-built nightclub that the tourists visit. (No charming, atmospheric Moulin Rouge, this one. But then the old, charming Moulin Rouge in Montmartre is now merely the shell of a new, modern nightclub.) The architecture of the new Paris looks like any modern architecture anywhere.

Second, the door is made of glass, that hard, artificial, bodyless building material that is as international as modernity itself. Glass and glass reflections are also consistent *leitmotifs* of the movie: the glass door that breaks and does not exist at the new nightclub (except that none of the patrons ever notices that it is missing); reflections on a glass window that is being cleaned and that make the bus miraculously appear to dance or fly; the shots from inside the bus of the city through glass windows, as if Paris were under glass; the plate-glass windows that dominate the architecture of the new buildings.

And third, the cathedral is Sacre Coeur—that old, rambling, domed pearl of the Paris skyline. Further, it is old Sacre Coeur reflected in new glass. It is a juxtaposition of old and new (like the travel poster on the wall of the café, which juxtaposes a shot of modern architecture with one reminder of the "old" and unique culture—a red double-decker bus in front of a skyscraper in the poster titled LONDON). The very fact that the movie brings a group of tourists from the New World to see the charm of the Old World, which has, in turn, been swallowed by the styles, manners, and methods of the New World, is ironically related to this juxtaposition of old and new. The new doesn't obliterate the old, but no one seems to notice or care about the old anymore. In fact, no one seems to notice the new either, nor the juxtaposition of old and new.

There are three undeniable answers (at least) to what are the *objects* in the shot, three undeniable "whats": modern café, glass, Sacre Coeur. And the resonances of what these objects are, what connotations they produce in and of themselves and in the culture of France and the rest of the modern Western world, and how they parallel or contrast with other objects in this movie—these questions cannot be overlooked in any attempt to describe the content of this particular shot.

But there are other questions that cannot be overlooked, other elements that are equally and undeniably a part of the shot's content. The café has a long, horizontal bar, at which a long, horizontal line of people stand to drink and chatter. The horizontal of the bar stretches back toward the rear of the frame, where it leads the eye to the travel poster on the wall, a sharp rectangular object with strong vertical and horizontal edges. The glass door is also a sharp rectangle, and the juxtaposition of Sacre Coeur and glass door is identical in shape (as well as spirit) to the juxtaposition of double-decker bus and modern skyscraper in the rectangular travel poster. All the glass windows and doors in the movie (of buildings, of the bus, of the nightclub) are equally sharp rectangles, and indeed, modern architecture itself is built of these straight lines—as opposed to the curves and arches of older architectural principles. Tati's affection for the warmth and comfort of irregular lines and soft curves is clear in his depiction of the ramshackle Old Quarter in *Mon Oncle*.

Like that *Vieux Quartier,* Sacre Coeur is an irregular edifice—a building of spires and domes, of curves and roundness, of a bulbous and inefficient eccentricity. It is a product of that older, arch-and-dome architectural theory, the architectural theory that built the Paris that tourists come to visit in the first place. Its circularity contrasts sharply with the hard regularity of the glass door in which it is reflected. And Sacre Coeur is white, not transparent, as is glass, just as the double-decker bus is red against the neutral gray of modern architecture in the London poster. This juxtaposition of curves and lines, roundness and rectangularity, visibility and invisibility, color and colorlessness, is yet another consistent motif of the movie—for example, the shots of arc-shaped street lights that soar aloft, as seen through the "invisible" rectangular windows of the bus. To note the importance of these lines and sharp angles, juxtaposed with freer, curving shapes, is to realize that the content of an image includes its *composition*—where the objects are and how the objects are shaped, both in relation to one another and in relation to the shape of the screen rectangle itself.

But a third element in the content of this shot must include the fact that Sacre Coeur appears on the glass door as a result of its being pushed open. A human being performs a simple, everyday act (opening a door) that unexpectedly produces a magical result. Whether Sacre Coeur is really reflected on the glass or whether Tati has superimposed it there in the lab is irrelevant; the result is magical in either event. The ordinary opening of windows and doors produces similar magical results throughout the movie: the doorman opens his invisible door, which the customers accept as visible, at the nightclub; the magically silent door at the office exposition makes no noise whatsoever; the bus seems to fly magically through the clouds as a result of its moving reflection in the tilted windows.

Further, no one in the café notices the sparkling apparition of Sacre Coeur in the glass door; they simply go about their business. Nor does anyone notice any of the other apparitions in the film; not even M. Hulot notes any ironies. But then M. Hulot is always oblivious to the ironies with which Tati surrounds him. Tati simply presents them for our eyes, without underscoring them with any reactions by the movie's participants. The only underscoring is that no one ever notices anything. (A thematic implication? That magic still exists in human experience, even as the new swallows the old, if anyone would take the time to notice it? Perhaps. After all, the cause of all this magic is the cinema, which is a mere machine.) What happens to the objects in the shot, what the people do with them or do not do with them, is as important an element in a shot's content as any other.

So what is the image (and the whole film) "about"? About all these things, obviously—the contrast of old and new, of straight line and circle, of action performed and result unnoticed. But because all critics cannot discuss all things in every shot (the urge for perfect completeness in cinema analysis is no more attainable than any other urge toward perfection), different critics select either what strikes them most or what strikes them as most important. The "literary" (or humanist, or thematic, or narrative) critics tend to be most interested in the photographic objects: what they signify in the abstract, in the culture, and in relation to the other objects in the film. The structuralist (or formalist) critics are most interested in "formal analysis": the compositional arrangement of objects in the frame in relation to one another, to the fixed limits of the frame itself, and to the compositional system that dominates the other shots of the same film. A third kind of critic (less numerous, so that no term exists to describe a particular "school") might be interested in Tati's comic style, pace, and tone, an analysis of the languid rhythm and understated comic method that makes Tati's comedy "work" (that gives those who "buy" it their conviction in the vitality and humor of the shot, rather than the impression that Tati is trying hard to be funny without succeeding). This critic would be more interested in exactly how the inanimate and animate objects in the shot interact, what each does with and to the other, when, and how.

Photographic objects (the "whats") can be divided into two broad classes: animate whats and inanimate whats. Although there is a tendency to distinguish between people and material objects when discussing, say, comic technique (for example, Chaplin's gift of manipulating objects so as to make them seem alive), both animate beings and inanimate things are parallel photographic objects in the camera's eye. It is in this sense that Cavell meant that in the cinema human beings are not favored over anything else in nature.[6]

Like the drama, narrative cinema (a movie) has no choice but to try to reveal internal states—of mind and feeling—by means of external surfaces alone. The cinema is even more dependent on those surfaces, for words—which dominate the drama—are probably a closer link with internal psychological forces than are bodies and motions. (However, one of the consistent implications of modernist drama is that words are also surfaces, often inconsistent with the feelings beneath them or inadequate to express them, as in Chekhov, Pirandello, Pinter, and Beckett.) The silent cinema was exclusively dependent on the manipulation of physical surfaces. And if cinema theory still continues to emphasize the purely visual power of communicative surfaces some fifty years after the demise of the silent film, it is because the communicative demand on these surfaces remains the same in principle, even when supplemented and extended by words, music, and noise.

Because human beings are merely animate photographic objects for the camera, the human objects that have dominated the movies throughout their history have been either stars (for the major subjects) or types (for the minor ones), both of which are reductions of human beings to surface objects. The surfaces of such beings communicate their values and temperaments instantly, and the best and most successful stars and types have had the most communicative, the most distinct, and the most interesting surfaces (Garbo, Dietrich, Bogart, Gabin, Gable, Cooper, Mifune, and the like, or Edward Everett Horton, Franklin Pangborn, Eric Blore, Percy Kilbride, Majorie Main, and their like). The debates about the differences between stage and screen acting tend to take such forms as: stage actors act, screen actors *be;* stage actors are active, screen actors passive; stage actors are three-dimensional, screen actors are types.[7] Underlying all such distinctions is the fact that stage actors are living beings impersonating other living beings while screen actors are photographic objects. As Stanley Cavell pointed out, screen actors should not be called actors at all; the term "star," something to be gazed at, is a much more accurate description of their being.[8] Even in 1915 Hugo Münsterberg noted that "the really decisive distance from bodily reality . . . is created by the substitution of the actor's picture for the actor himself."[9]

Inanimate objects have had an equally illustrious career in the history of movies, and simply to mention one of them is to recall instantly the name of the film in which it "starred": a Murphy bed; a Confederate flag and a Union cannon; an alarm clock; a boot; a movie projector; the *Texas* and the *General;* a steamboat; a porter's greatcoat; a baby carriage; a water bucket; music boxes; a geranium; a glass of milk; a child's sled; a cigarette lighter; a string of pearls.* Drawn figures are a variant kind of inanimate object that the cinema brings to life—either figures in the form of animate beings (Bugs Bunny, Mickey Mouse) or pure abstractions (as in Len Lye or Oskar Fischinger). Although Len Lye's figures are drawn directly on the film and are not photographic objects, when projected they behave like photographic objects.

Among the objects of a shot are all those apparently insignificant and ordinary things that (as the semiologists develop) supply crucial information with symbolic meanings that refer to either traditional "codes" of cinema, general "codes" of the culture, or specific "codes" of the individual filmmaker. Among those objects that refer to traditional codes of cinema meaning are the black and white hats of Westerns, the black Easterner suit and tie of the same kind of film, the checkered tablecloth on the breakfast table (which, as Panofsky remarked, signifies the happy but humble home that is about to be tested by adversity), and the flipping of a coin in a gangster film. Among the kinds of objects that might refer to general cultural codes in a shot would be whether an American husband puts on a coat and tie to go to work or a work shirt and hard hat, whether his wife goes off to work or stays home to tend kids and kitchen, and whether their son wears jeans and a T-shirt or a uniform when he leaves for school. And among the objects in personal directorial codes would be a pot of soup or stew on a stove in a John Ford Western, a woman (particularly Marlene Dietrich) wearing men's clothing in a Josef von Sternberg movie, a man (particularly Cary Grant) wearing women's clothing in a Howard Hawks comedy, ornate offices and board rooms and all the other architecture and apparatus of high finance in a Capra movie, pipes of Pan (or some reasonable facsimile) in a Renoir or Chaplin movie, and so forth.

Another distinction between photographic objects might be between parts and wholes—whether the entire animate or inanimate object fills the frame or just some isolated part of it. Such a distinction takes us once again to the point that the "distance" of a shot (close-up, long shot) has nothing to do with distance and everything to do with the content of the shot itself. To depict Mae Marsh's nervous anguish in the courtroom

---

* How well did you do on the quiz? *One A.M., The Birth of a Nation, The Pawnshop, The Gold Rush, Sherlock Jr., The General, The Navigator, The Last Laugh, Potemkin, Mother, Rules of the Game, Grand Illusion, Suspicion, Citizen Kane, Strangers on a Train, Morocco.*

scene of *Intolerance,* Griffith isolates a part of the whole to display the most efficient and effective physical surface—the clenched hands she nervously twitches while she waits for the judge to pronounce guilt and pass sentence. To depict the emotional gulf between husband and wife in the process of signing their divorce papers, Ingmar Bergman (in "The Illiterates" sequence of *Scenes from a Marriage*) shoots the full bodies of both people, seated on two chairs, a large gulf of space between their bodies, which seem to hunch toward one another but are separated by the gulf, surrounded by the institutional gray carpets, overwhite walls, and horizontal bookshelves of the husband's office. The use of such devices makes the surfaces "speak."

But the effectiveness of the Bergman shot is produced not only by who or what the objects are and how much of them he depicts, but also by their spatial and angular relationship to one another: the implications of the shot's composition. The two bodies (and chairs) occupy absolutely symmetrical positions within the frame. The two symmetrical verticals are separated and defined by the dominant horizontals of floor, ceiling, books, shelves, and the screen rectangle itself. Their bodies occupy identical and symmetrical positions in space—a slight angularity as their backs lean toward one another tensely. The symmetrical and "empty" composition of the frame contains its own information and supports (or perhaps even carries) the shot's ability to make surfaces lead us to essences.

But the parenthetic tension in that last sentence indicates the potential danger of a pure devotion to compositional analysis. Although the barren, symmetrical composition of the shot clearly implies the emptiness of the figures and the emotional gulf between them, that information also comes to us from several other sources at the same time. The lighting of this image is harsh, white, and cold, the kind of fluorescent lighting one would expect in an office, but a terribly harsh ray to shine on the questions of love, affection, need, and longing nonetheless. Then there are elements of the moment's contextual relationship to the movie's structural succession: that this apparently "perfect pair" of "happily married" people at the film's beginning gave an interview to a magazine about the sources of their marriage's success; that they have since gone through a scene of confession, a period of separation, and are now on the verge of a legal act of termination (such legal acts being the wife's occupation); that they have just copulated on the gray rug of this very barren office (a desperate attempt to reach one another? to arrest the inevitability of the legal separation? to write *finis* to the marriage with a grand finale?).

Then there is the role of the single shot in the movie's imagistic succession of shots. It is the first and only distant two-shot in the scene. All Bergman's previous shots in "The Illiterates" have been tight two-shots or close-ups of single faces; the shots have been so tight that it has not been at all clear exactly what this room was or was like—how large, how shaped, how designed. We have not been in this room before. Suddenly, after all this tightness, Bergman reveals the whole—two bodies, the walls, shelves, floor. And he reveals it not by pulling back (in a track or zoom) but in a straight (harsh) cut. He uses a short lens, which makes the room seem surprisingly large, the people surprisingly small within it (whereas in the previous tight shots they seemed to dwarf the room as they dwarfed the frame), and keeps all the objects in sharp, harsh focus. And the moment is silent—no talk, no noise, nothing.

Finally, the shot is static. There is no movement of the objects at all (as contrasted with the frenzied and tense movement in the previous shots of the sequence). Since the *activity* of the objects in a shot is a part of its content, the act of doing nothing is also an activity—especially in cinema in which something is almost always doing something. The key distinctions in terms of what the objects do in a shot are movement and stasis, broad and subtle, fast and slow. Movement can be extremely subtle and slight (an eyelid blinking, a smile, a narrowing of the eyes, or even a slight muscular tension that begins to narrow them); or it can be the more rapid and noticeable kinds of human movement, such as walking, running, gesturing, pointing, shaking the head, and so forth.

Inanimate objects are obviously capable of motion, too (automobiles, custard pies, speeding trains, and the like). Perhaps an entire history of cinema could be written around the movement (both inside and outside) of the train: *L'Arrivée d'un train en gare, Black Diamond Express, The Great Train Robbery, The Lonedale Operator, Intolerance, The Pilgrim, The Iron Horse, The General, Turksib, Shanghai Express, The Road to Life, Twentieth Century, La Bête humaine, The Lady Vanishes, Night Mail, Union Pacific, Sullivan's Travels, Monsieur Verdoux, Strangers on a Train, High Noon, The Organizer, The Wild Bunch, Murder on the Orient Express, The Sting.* And, as mentioned earlier, the activity of photographic objects in motion makes demands on the camera, which must be similarly active and in motion to capture them.

The three variables of a shot's content (objects, composition, and action) are interrelated and inseparable. Take, for example, a single shot from *The Wild Bunch*—the one in which Pike rides off slowly on his horse, completely alone, back toward the camera, after previously having fallen down trying to mount because of the pain in his wounded leg. Pike's fall had aroused the scornful laughter and caustic comments of his

Bunch—that he's too old, that he can't cut it anymore. Without speaking, Pike makes another and supreme effort, swinging his leg awkwardly over the pommel and hoisting himself into the saddle; without saying a word (not even his usual "Let's go!"), he rides the horse slowly toward screen right.

Peckinpah then cuts to a shot of Pike's receding back on top of the horse, the horse moving away from the camera but seemingly not moving at all (long lens), the dark outline of man and horse looking like a single black blot against an evenly and pitilessly white-beige sky. The effect of the shot is a quiet moment of loneliness, pain, and anguish for Pike, separated from the men who laughed at him, alone with his pain, bearing his own cross and his own doubts. How does Peckinpah achieve this internal feeling (Pike's and ours—the two are one.)?

First, there are strikingly few objects in the shot. The image is startlingly simple and bare. There is man and horse (the two of which melt into one), contrasted with the harsh, white surroundings. There are, in effect, two objects (figure, background) which contrast and clash violently in color, size, shape, and mass. Nothing more.

Then, the composition aids this bareness and contrast by putting the single man-horse in the dead center of the huge Panavision frame, surrounded by whiteness on three sides, a seemingly isolated island of darkness in a white sea, floating on air or riding in a void because there is no earth in the shot to anchor it. The wide Panavision screen cuts off the horse just below midleg, so both it and its rider seem to be cast adrift and alone in empty space. This kind of wide-screen composition deliberately violates the dominant shape of the frame: a single vertical figure seems cut off at the bottom in the midst of a vast horizontal expanse, with nothing at all to fill either side. Despite its theoretical "wrongness," this is exactly the right way to shoot and convey this emotional moment.

Then, the movement of the horse is very slow (emphasized by the long lens); the reason that man and horse seem like one is that they move as one—in the same rhythm, with the same motion, at the same pace. And there is no other movement of any kind in the shot at all (no birds, no "leaves rippling in the wind"). The single other thing to move is a subtle and slight zooming of the lens, seemingly boring into Pike's back, further emphasizing his isolation.

There are, of course, other "signs" to intensify the objects, composition, and action in the content of this shot. From the structural succession, we know about Pike in general, his feelings as leader of the Bunch, his feelings for the Bunch, both their respect for him and their jealousy of his position; we also know the immediate fact that he has just fallen while trying to mount, accompanied by their scorn. Then there is the harsh color contrast between the dark rider-horse and the bright-light sky. Then there is the prolongation of the shot in the film's literal succession of frames; we dwell on Pike's back for a considerable amount of time, allowing the feeling of the event to sink in. As it sinks in to Pike (with the "sinking" movement of the zoom lens), it sinks in to us. This kind of emotional transferral takes time. Then there is the fact that the shot is strangely quiet—the only sound being the melancholy music of mournful strings—in marked contrast to the hostile noise that preceded it.

Such a shot is a reminder that although, for the purposes of discussion, it is possible to isolate the variables of succession, image, and sound, and, further, of filming, toning, and content of the image, those variables rarely function in isolation. This classification of elements of the visual image has demonstrated the number of variables that each shot must manipulate and control if it is to manipulate and control our responses to it. Because the cinema is totally dependent on kinesis for its effect, what we see and hear is what we feel and know.

8/(Recorded) Sound

"I see a voice."

A Midsummer Night's Dream, V, 1

The movies have never been silent. There were pianos in nickelodeons before there were movies (i.e., feature-length narratives). The pit musicians accompanied the first film showings in America's variety theaters before the turn of the century. The piano was as essential to the early nickelodeons as the projector. Even as early as 1915, when Hugo Münsterberg wrote the first book-length theoretical study of *The Photoplay,* the piano and the allefex ("all effects"—a sound-effects machine) were already taken for granted as a part of the cinema experience. The accompaniment of music and sound effects even preceded the discovery and application of the principles of editing (of imagistic succession) during the early Griffith era of 1908–12—principles which are said to mark the invention of the *art* of cinema itself. So sound has been a part of that art for longer than the visual principles that defined the art.

Before the movies talked, the audience simply thought of "silent" movies as movies, or films, or motion pictures, or photoplays—not as *silent* films. And the term "silent film" has been drenched in imprecise evaluative associations from its first contrasts with its opposite, the "sound film." For an industry marketing its new wares, "silent film" was pejorative—that dull, old, outmoded thing that you folks don't want to pay good money to see anymore. For the critics and theorists of the late twenties and early thirties, the term was laudatory—that wonderful, imaginative, creative thing that was so much more inventive than the vulgar and lifeless new gimmick They intend to foist on us now. Perhaps "silent film" and "sound film" are poor descriptive terms because they never really served a descriptive purpose.

Throughout the "silent era," there was an urge to wed picture and sound precisely. Edison's original film dream had been to combine his new kinetoscope with his old phonograph. W. K. L. Dickson, Edison's film foreman, claims to have invented a sound camera and projector (the kinetophonograph) as early as 1889.[1] The French cinema inventors— Demeny, Joly—sought to combine word and picture in the late nineties and the early years of this century. Between 1908 and 1912 in America, live actors, narrators, and singers frequently performed behind or beside screen during the film showing, an attempt to add the human voice to the mimed picture. The Edison company made a vaguely synchronized musical film of *Mother Goose Tales* in 1912.

The urge that produced these experiments and performances seemed to slumber in the twelve golden years of "silent film" that followed *The Birth of a Nation*—perhaps because the visual material itself had become so complex and compelling, because the accompanying music for movies was more carefully and complexly scored, and because a suddenly powerful industry wished to stabilize its procedures and investments. But the urge awoke, talked, and conquered in the late twenties. Although its influence on Hollywood's conversion to synchronized sound has only recently been realized, one of the major goads to develop a synchronized-sound film was obviously radio—whose commercial expansion and acceptance were contemporaries of the sound track.[2] If visual images could be recorded mechanically, and if sounds could be recorded mechanically, why could they not be recorded mechanically together?

The advantages of the synchronized-sound track were, like those of most technological advances in film machines and materials, greater flexibility and precision. Sound could be wedded permanently to the precise visual image or divorced from it altogether, whereas the old piano music and improvised sound effects were capable of only a vague courtship and accidental separation. The fifty years of synchronized-sound films have convincingly refuted the initial fears of the theorists without, however, refuting their general assumption that the visual element must dominate the motion picture. This paradox (valid premise, invalid deduction) merits further consideration.

Significantly, none of the early theorists objected to the musical underscoring of images (just as few experimental filmmakers or puristic theorists today object to the use of music in cinema). Although Münster-berg (and others) felt uncomfortable with specific sound effects (gunshots, bells, birds, thunder, wind, and so forth), he accepted music as an appropriate and valuable complement to the visual images precisely because it was a kind of *under*scoring: a means of intensifying and toning effects already inherent in the images themselves, rather than producing some self-contained effect or added information. Erwin Panofsky's principle of "co-expressibility" makes a theoretical dogma out of the same assumption—that the dialogue should provide *no more* information than the images themselves.[3] It was synchronized speech that alarmed the theorists then (and still alarms the purists today). First, why? Second, how has cinema managed to preserve its visual power while assimilating dialogue (and the other effects of sound)? The answer to the two questions is identical and is a consequence of the relative specificity of image, word, noise, and music.

In their ability to represent reality, image and music are at the two poles of concreteness and abstraction. One of the appeals of music is its vague approximation to general states of human mood and feeling, but the vagueness of this connection guarantees a kind of general bathing of human responses in a sea of musical feeling without any concrete referents to reality in the bath itself. Much more specific information comes from the concreteness of visual images, which evoke more specific responses and recognitions. Such specific information might be supported or emphasized by the general tendencies of the music. The principle would be parallel to the notion of harmony in music; the specific images play the dominant role of melody while the musical underscoring fills in the background chords.

To some extent, the "mixed arts" of opera and ballet combine the same opposite effects of concreteness (words or physical gestures) and vagueness (the intensifying effects of music)—a fact that makes clear Arnheim's finding these two compound arts acceptable and appropriate.[4] The problem with words and noises is that they both use sound more specifically than music. Although he does not voice his objections in such terms, Arnheim's real concern is that the *equal specificity* of images and words is incompatible, conflicting, and either redundant or contradictory. One would not have harmony (as in the uniting of concrete picture and vague music), but either unison (which is boring) or cacophony (which is ugly).

But the Arnheim predictions fail to envision the possibility of another form of musical construction—counterpoint—in which several melodic lines maintain their discrete individuality and yet play in juxtaposition with one another, organized according to principles of dominance and subordination. Words and images are not necessarily equally specific. Although the word "chair" is a more specific symbol of an object in reality than a C-major chord, it is far less tangible than a specific picture of a specific chair. The word "chair" conjures up different shapes, colors, types, and associations for the individual speaker or listener (i.e., high-backed chair, upholstered chair, wooden chair, beach chair, rocking chair, armchair—each of which also has its own personal associations). The chair that we see depicted in a shot is that specific chair and no other. Whereas language is a symbolic system that requires translation from the symbol (the word or the sound of the word) into the concrete object it symbolizes, the pictorial image presents us with not a symbol for a thing, but "the thing itself."

Of course, an image doesn't quite give us "the thing itself," but Stanley Cavell develops that we have *no word* in English to describe the relationship of a photograph and the thing that it is a photograph of.[5] It obviously falls somewhere between being a symbol of the object (for it is the object, not a symbol) and the object itself (for it isn't the object, but a photograph of it). As Cavell demonstrates, calling it an "icon" doesn't solve the problem either. This linguistic inexplicability accounts for the mystery of photographs and their greater impact on our senses than words. One of the key differences between words and images as semiotic systems is that words require both "translation" into their denotative, literal meanings and assimilation for their "poetic," connotative effects, while filmed images do not require "translation" for their literal meanings, but only assimilation for their "poetic" effects.

The difference in the immediate, kinetic impact of the two semiotic systems guarantees that visual images cannot easily yield their dominant and primary position to words. Although it is common to discuss the way that early talkies sacrificed their visual expressiveness in order to record dialogue, such a fact in no way contradicts the primacy of the image, but tends to support it—and even in those very talkies. In *The Jazz Singer, Broadway Melody,* and *The Lights of New York* (indeed, even in much better 1929 talkies like *Applause, Hallelujah,* and *The Virginian*), the visual images were often so strikingly ugly, remarkably static, and both compositionally and dramatically inept that they overwhelmed the feeble power of the dialogue. The talk (under those visual circumstances) could not have succeeded in moving us with all the words in Webster.

Similarly, I think the real discomfort of "canned theater"—of recording a theater performance on film without bothering to suit the play to cinema—is not that words displace images, but that the static images very successfully resist the attempts of all the words to displace them, imposing their lugubrious and leaden ugliness on all the winged words, weighing them down and refusing to let them soar. I think this is precisely what Bazin felt and meant when he distinguished between the "décor" of the cinema and of the stage as a pure sounding board for words.[6] Conversely, those critical references to 1930s films in which we "merely" watch the conversing faces and figures of Harlow, Gable,

Garbo, Hepburn, or Dietrich severely underrate the visual power of those "mere" faces and figures (those stunning photographic objects of the image).

Further, sight is the primary human sense, our most important biological resource for responding to the world outside us. Although my St. Bernard is far more responsive to barking dogs on the sound track than to pictures of them (and she would really love Smell-O-Vision), the primacy of the image is one of the consequences of our being human. Finally, the work of cinema manipulates two systems of visual stimulation (a spatial and a temporal one), but only a single system of sound stimulation. The cards are stacked and the game is over; Hamlet's soliloquy (p. 24 above) cannot hold the screen with the dazzlingly "trippy" space ride of 2001. Despite the fears of the theorists, the warnings of the purists, and the vulgar clumsinesses of 1928–29 Hollywood, the visual image could not be deposed. By 1931 even the most ordinary movies had discovered that their task was the "scoring" of dialogue (and noise) with images, just as their previous task had been the scoring of music with images.

Although visual images almost inevitably dominate the work of cinema, the contribution of the sound track cannot be ignored—as it is in so many film theories and movie reviews. Behind this tacit neglect of sound in films lies the theoretical conviction that the recording of music is not uniquely cinematic (for phonograph disk and radio can both transmit "canned" music) and that the recording of dialogue is even less uniquely cinematic (since dialogue is essentially theatrical and recorded dialogue is the province of radio drama). Without venturing another go-round on the issue of the "uniquely cinematic," let me quickly confess that sound is not a visual quality of cinema. But let me mention that cinema is the only art (with the exception, of course, of television, its wayward child) that can juxtapose visual images that are completely free from the restrictions of time and space with sounds that are equally free from those restrictions. Further, the integration of sound and images is subject to as broad a range of varying degrees as is the integration of kinesis and mimesis; there can be visual images with no sounds at all (as in Dog Star Man), visual imagery in which the sound track plays a secondary and supporting role, or, when the images are scored so as to permit it, visual images in which sound serves as the primary source of our information or pleasure in a shot, scene, or sequence. Several films (for example, the opening sequence of Hollis Frampton's Zorn's Lemma) use a completely black and blank frame, with only the sound track providing any information whatever.

The three variables of the sound track are music, words, and noise (all those other effects of sound, which are not organized according to either musical or verbal patterns).

MUSIC

Music is the oldest kind of sound in cinema, and the general principles of its use have not changed much in seventy years. Music in cinema can be divided into two major classes: (1) background music of the type an audience might not specifically notice (the oldest and most familiar form, often called "movie music," descending from the piano in the nickelodeon); and (2) more distinctive music, designed to call attention to itself (a type that became possible only with the conversion to synchronized sound).

The most stereotypic "movie music" is an amorphous blob of emotion-tinged sound that exists not for its own sake (as does a usual musical composition), but for the sake of that which it supports. It is program music in which the "program" obliterates most other musical considerations completely (as opposed to a Tchaikovsky or Stravinsky ballet or a Strauss tone poem). It is movie "Muzak," which is considered most effective when the audience feels it is there without noticing that it is there. Despite the thousands of scores of this kind that have been composed for films, despite the fact that hundreds have been recorded for listening at home, perhaps less than a dozen can stand repeated listening as self-contained works.* The most successful composers of "movie music"— Franz Waxman, Max Steiner, Miklos Rozsa, Nino Rota, Bernard Herrmann, Georges Auric, Georges Delerue, Alfred Newman, Dmitri Tiomkin, Erich Wolfgang Korngold, John Williams—have been less successful at serious musical composition (and almost all of them have tried). Listening to this "movie music" in isolation from the images feels like taking a tepid emotional bath, with no particular beginning or end, no particular development, expansion, or variation. The music just rolls and flows along.

The clichés of "movie music" are familiar. For love scenes there is the

---

* I find that I can regularly listen to Prokofiev's *Lieutenant Kije* and *Alexander Nevsky*, Walton's *Henry V*, Vaughan Williams's Symphony no. 7 (*Scott of the Antarctic*), Antheil's *Ballet Mécanique*, and that's about it. Even these works had to be distilled and structured into suites and symphonies by their composers. Although the same is true of much ballet music, it is both possible and pleasant to listen to the complete *Firebird, Swan Lake,* or *Daphnis and Chloe.*

rancid violinic mush that masquerades as the worst of Tchaikovsky (and in some films, like *The Jazz Singer,* actually is the worst of Tchaikovsky). There is the ominous rhythmic thrumming of basses to build suspense, as the movie's hero and audience move steadily and suspensefully toward the danger that threatens to engulf and terrify them. There is the bouncy, playful, bright movement of brass for the comical and happy scenes. There is the crashing sweep of the full orchestra for violent storms and fights; there is the breathless gallop of the full orchestra for the climactic chase, or rescue, or race on horseback. There is even nondescript, bouncy, vamp-till-ready "traveling music" for those bridgelike sequences of movement or change or progression in which nothing is happening yet, but soon will. In the teens and twenties of this century, you could buy collections of appropriate piano tunes for underscoring the various film moods. The synchronized-sound film kept the "moods," but expanded the instrumentation and the precision of the synchronization.

The amazing thing about these clichés is that, as predictable as they are, they often succeed at imparting exactly the right mood for a scene or emotional effect. And with surprising effectiveness. What could be more clichéd than the scream of violins during the knifing scenes of *Psycho?* Hitchcock (and Herrmann) substitute the screams of violins for high-pitched human shrieks. How corny, how obvious—how terrifying. (Of course, Hitchcock always delights in proving that clichés work.) The screaming violins in *Psycho* work because Hitchcock's manipulation of editing (in the shower scene), of the high camera angle (in the stairway scene), and of low-key lighting (in the basement scene) so disorient the viewer that it is impossible to say exactly what kind of terrifying sound we are hearing at all. Only upon a second viewing did I hear those grating screams as violins. In the initial experience they seemed like screams from my own imagination (neither the victim nor the attacker is actually screaming in the sequences), my own release of the tension that Hitchcock's plot (structural succession), editing (imagistic succession), and composition had developed. The screaming strings were more terrifying than natural human shrieks precisely because they were such strained, unexpected, and strange-sounding eruptions, which seemed to come more from my fear than from that of any of the victims.

Or in the same film, there is that predictably pulsing, rhythmic vamp (which echoes the opening motif of Khachaturian's Violin Concerto) which accompanies the windshield wipers as Marion drives in the rainstorm toward the ominous Bates Motel, where she will meet her death (and the screaming violins). The rhythms of the throbbing music accompany the metronomic swish of the wipers, as we gaze out the windshield into the murky and engulfing darkness, occasionally pierced by the wet glare of headlights or the blazing neon of a roadside restaurant or motel. The driving rhythm (both visual and musical), the inky darkness, and the punctuating glare give the sequence a feeling of driving through an abstract netherworld of dangerous uncertainty—the rhythmic music alone tightening the screws of uncertainty and suspense.

Such clichés work when the movie's systems of succession and image provide the visual interest and emotional intensity to make them work. When our visual and emotional engagement is intense enough, even ludicrous clichés that are musically much less interesting than Bernard Herrmann's work for rather than against a movie's effects. For example, the wretched scores of *The Informer* and *Rashomon* still intensify rather than impair the power of the two movies and cannot even be noticed unless you make a special effort to listen to them. The brazen dum-dum-de-dum exclamation points in Max Steiner's score for *The Informer* and the ridiculous pastiche of Ravel's *Bolero* in Kurosawa's sexual confrontation between bandit and bride in *Rashomon* cannot keep me (or most others) from experiencing the power of those very moments. Not only did both these movies win Academy Awards, but Max Steiner won an Oscar for his score of *The Informer*. Such examples of "successful movie music" underline the fact that its success has little to do with the music itself and much to do with the succession of movement, image, and events that we can see on the screen.

The affective emotional elements of "movie music" are its rhythm, tempo, volume, and orchestration—everything to do with its "color" and nothing to do with its musical form. "Movie music" is coloring—like the use of colored tints for emotional toning in monochrome "silent films." In this sense, music contributes to the toning of images (and the toning of the effects of structural succession); it is an ally of the effects of lighting. The music's rhythm is one source of its color—either insistently repetitive and regular (suggesting tension and suspense, as in *Psycho*), or skittish and capricious (suggesting playfulness, as in the drunken sections of *City Lights*), or stirringly steady and militaristic (as in the "Guadalcanal March" of Richard Rodgers's score for the television series *Victory at Sea*), or languid and waltzy (as in the easy gliding through space of *2001*), or quietly unobtrusive and deliberately unrhythmic (for scenes that need a musical tone but want the freedom of working without a constraining rhythm).

Tempo combines with rhythm to further the intensity or leisureliness of a scene, frequently combining with the action in an *accelerando* or *decelerando*, to hasten or retard the impact and intensity of that action.

Volume is the third source of color, remaining so quiet as to be almost imperceptible or rising to great heights when the action or emotion requires it. As with tempo, volume is capable of infinite yet subtle gradations (the *crescendo* or *decrescendo*), which can occur so unobtrusively as to increase the effect of a scene without calling attention to itself at all.

Finally, orchestration and instrumentation are further ways of controlling musical color—the brashness of brass, the liquidity of bowed strings, the resonant thumping or clicking of plucked strings, the percussive beat of drums, the casualness of a tinkling piano, the immense power of the full symphonic orchestra, the fleeting informality of the single instrument. Miklos Rozsa specialized in scoring biblical and Roman epics (for example, *Ben Hur*) because of his abilities with the blaring cacophony of brass; Max Steiner specialized in intense (melo)dramas (*The Informer, King Kong*) because of the grating insistence of his strings and the crash of his emotional exclamation points; Dmitri Tiomkin specialized in Westerns and balladlike films (*High Noon, The High and the Mighty, Giant*) because of his ability with a balladlike melodic line underscored by soft and leisurely strings; Bernard Herrmann specialized in bizarre and aberrant human psychology (*Citizen Kane, The Magnificent Ambersons, Vertigo, Psycho, Taxi Driver*) because of the dark and mysterious texture of his strings and the uncomfortable dissonance of his orchestrations. John Williams (*The Reivers, Jaws, Family Plot*) develops a folklike atmosphere by contrasting the percussive use of strings (piano, banjo, harpsichord, plucked strings) with a more liquid use of the other stringed instruments underneath.

Given the proper musical shading to color an effective succession of images and events, the actual melodic content and musical form of "movie music" can be anything at all. Those scores that seem more distinguished and interesting than others (Prokofiev's, Walton's, Hermann's, Rota's, Jean Constantin's for *The 400 Blows,* John Williams's for *The Reivers,* Leonard Bernstein's for *On the Waterfront,* David Raksin's for *Laura*) are more colorful, more melodic, more distinctive, or more carefully structured than the images absolutely required. The parallel with lighting is again an apt one. Although there were few major Hollywood films from major studios that were not well lit (whose lighting angles and levels were not absolutely correct at sculpting the scenes and texturing our emotional responses), there were few as exquisitely lit as *Shanghai Express* and *The Scarlet Empress,* or *The Informer* and *The Grapes of Wrath,* or *Citizen Kane, Wuthering Heights,* and *The Best Years of Our Lives.*

Like film lighting, "movie music" is environmental. The individual moments and devices of "movie music" are perhaps less noticeable and less distinctive than are the moments or devices of film succession or imagery. There are physical reasons for this difference. First and second, the relative kinetic responsiveness of eye and ear and the cinema's double system of visual stimulation but single system of aural stimulation (as developed earlier). Third, the ear is able to turn any regularized series of sounds into part of its environment and, consequently, tune it out. In this century, people have learned to talk, think, and sleep through ticking clocks, rumbling trains and subways, humming air conditioners, and recorded music of any kind. The psychological and physiological basis of Muzak and similar background-music systems is that the ear converts this bland and syrupy musical pap into a vaguely pleasant setting for eating, talking, shopping, or sitting in restaurants, stores, and the dentist's office. Even the person who is certain that Muzak is an invention of the devil and notices it wincingly upon entering a restaurant has usually tuned it out by the time the waitress brings the salad (or the martinis).

And, fourth, the sound track is continuous (and indivisible), while the images are a successive synthesis of discrete units. As opposed to visual imagery in the cinema, the sound band on celluloid is not composed of distinct units, but is perfectly continuous. The fact that film's apparent visual continuousness is an optical illusion makes those images even more hypnotic, just flickeringly different enough from our visual perception of spatial and temporal continuity in nature to attract our attention even more. I know of no studies of the disorienting effects of watching moving, successive images, of the hypnotic power that might arise from this slight disorientation, primarily because film theorists have concentrated almost exclusively on the way that moving images simulate life, not dissimulate it.

But studies of subliminal indoctrination through the use of moving pictures (for example, flashing the words "eat popcorn" or "Coca-Cola" on a single frame of film during the movie) showed that the audience somehow got the fleeting message (the proof was in the eating and drinking, for the sales of popcorn and Coca-Cola subsequently rose in the theater lobby).[7] This kind of subliminal suggestiveness makes cinema an even more dangerous and powerful sort of propaganda than has generally been envisioned. The political propaganda in *Triumph of the Will, Potemkin,* or *State of Siege* is quite conscious and is, therefore, capable of being examined. But how does one examine the invisible? If a viewer can perceive (however unconsciously and subliminally) some kind of discrete meaning in a $\frac{1}{24}$-second piece of film, it is probably true that we do not perceive a successive strip of filmed action as an absolutely continuous and natural whole.*

Even so, there is clearly a difference between a filmed object or action (it is a *photograph* of the thing or act) and a recorded musical sound. For it *is* the sound itself.[8] There is no ontological difference between hearing a violin in a concert hall and hearing it on a sound track in a movie theater. Granted, there may be a difference in the purity, clarity, and resonance of the sound (the fidelity of the reproduction), but there is no difference in what it is we are hearing. We hear the sound (more or less pure, clear, or resonant) of a violin. "That's a violin." But there is a major difference between watching grandma walk across a room and watching a synthetic moving photograph of grandma apparently walking across that room. "That's *a picture of* grandma." Because the sound track is continuous (as is sound in nature) and because the music we hear on a sound track is not different in kind (only perhaps in degree) from "live" music, "movie music" is capable of melting into an environment of vague emotional resonances.

To give one detailed and concrete example, let me try an infrequent kind of cinema analysis. Let me examine Herbert Stothart's scoring of George Cukor's *Camille*—a movie that is extremely typical of the studio attitude toward cinema music, but that, because of its gifted director and high level of production taste, is extremely careful and judicious in its manipulation of musical effects. There are two kinds of music in the movie, both of which function primarily as typical, background "movie music": about half the music is "motivated" (it is produced by a visually established source such as an orchestra at the theater or a piano at a party); the other half is "unmotivated," a pure addition of the movie's orchestrater that comes from nowhere at all. Together these two kinds of music fill up over an hour of the film's total one hundred minutes (meaning that only thirty to forty minutes of the film are without any background music at all).

Virtually all the music in the movie is some form of waltz (to give the flavor of Paris in 1847) and virtually all of it is scored for prominent violins (for this is a love story). There are only two melodic themes for the entire hour of music, two primary waltzes—a Paris waltz (attached to Marguerite's life as a frivolous "Woman of Paris") and a country waltz

---

* This fact of cinema perception—and its difference from our perception of nature—also supports the claim of those who, like Gregory Markopoulos, argue that the single frame, and not the shot, is the smallest significant unit of cinema meaning. The problem, however, is that although you can perhaps perceive and intuit some "meaning" in a fleeting frame, you cannot discover that "meaning" without stopping the successive flow of film to study the single frame.

(attached to her pure life of love in the country; unfortunately, it unintentionally uses the same musical phrase as the popular song "Makin' Whoopee!"). All the music in the movie (whether motivated or unmotivated) is a variation on one of these two themes—running them into one another, disguising them by prolonging, de-emphasizing, or breaking the ¾ rhythm, or transposing the musical progressions into the minor key. Such disguises of musical coloring keep the audience from realizing that all the movie's music is melodically the same, yet give the movie's action and emotional texture a subtle unity at the same time.

A strikingly consistent practice of the movie, however, is that the scenes without any background music at all are inevitably the "prosaic" ones—the comic scenes with Olympe and Prudence, the affectionate scenes between Marguerite and Nanine or Gaston, the painful "Let him go" scene between M. Duval and Marguerite, and the scenes between Marguerite and Baron de Varville, who is her keeper, not her lover. Musical underscoring (especially the unmotivated music) is reserved exclusively for the scenes of passion—the scenes between Armand and Marguerite, or the moments of reaction by either of them after a painful, prosy scene (for example, the music swells under Marguerite's tears only after M. Duval takes his leave). This musical separation between the scenes of reason and passion is both very obvious (should someone listen carefully to the score to chart its ebb and flow) and completely unobtrusive (for the audience experiencing the movie). Its subtle separation of moments of reason and passion is precisely parallel to the difference between the aria and the recitative in opera or, even more closely, to Shakespeare's "subliminal" distinction between scenes in prose and scenes in verse in his comedies—prose for the low comic scenes, prose for talking with servants and sometimes friends, verse for talking with royalty and sometimes parents, verse for passion and love.

Given this general principle, the movie does some interesting things with the tension between using and not using music. The first love scene between Marguerite and Armand takes place in her bedroom, after her first major coughing spell. One of her party guests has started to play the piano (hence motivating the music), but it is less than accidental that the pianist plunges into a suitable waltz immediately after the lovers' first kiss. The audience, however, does not notice the coincidence, which merely feels as if the music has arisen from the passionate kiss itself and has been produced by that passion, not by a party guest.

A contrary use of music operates in the very next scene as Marguerite sits at that same piano, alone, playing a waltz, indicating that both Armand and his kiss are on her mind. After a few bars, she is visibly startled by the entrance of Varville (for she awaits Armand); she breaks off the music as soon as she sees him. But by the end of the scene, Varville has sat down at the piano to play a difficult polonaise that Marguerite now feels too distraught to execute. As he plays the tortuous notes, Marguerite begins to laugh with pain and desperation (for Varville has destroyed the rendezvous with Armand). As her desperation rises, so does the insistence and volume of the piano. The stridently desperate music increases the impression of her own desperation and loss, just as, only a few moments earlier, its graceful passion increased the impression of her love and longing.

The second love scene between Marguerite and Armand takes place in *his* bedroom; she wants to know if he is really leaving both her and Paris, and the scene begins comically (with Prudence) and tensely (when Marguerite enters), because of her uncertainty about him. There is no music during this prosy beginning. After a fade, we see Armand with his head in Marguerite's lap; he will not leave her. The tensions have faded, their love has blossomed, and, of course, the violins have joined the encounter.

The next two scenes provide an interesting musical contrast and tension between two styles of life and two levels of emotional sincerity. The first is the scene in which Marguerite informs Varville that she is off to the country for her "health," asking him for a final gift—the forty thousand francs she needs to pay her bills. The scene is without instrumental music, dominated entirely by the vocal "music" of Varville's crisp, nasal rasp as he delivers his poisonously nasty words. Without the silence on the musical track, Varville's crispness could never cut into our minds like a vocal knife. After a fade, the track (and the imagery) change completely. The music is bubbly bright and the images are of the sunlit coach that carries the lovers through trees, fields, and meadows to their country retreat. The two juxtaposed scenes and the opposite principles of musical scoring convey such thematic and dramatic oppositions as love rather than lust, affection rather than cash, surrender rather than strategy, nature rather than affectation, and light rather than darkness.

Another interesting contrast of scenes with and without music are the two arguments that mar Marguerite's and Armand's country idyll. The first is not serious, over a copy of *Manon Lescaut* that he had lent her and a conversation that he subsequently overhears. The violins play sweetly under the argument, undercutting its force, revealing that this rift between the two is superficial. By the end of the scene the two run off lovingly across the fields and over a brook; as they run the music swells (as if it is their passion itself, swelling to its fullness) for the fade-out.

The second argument, the one in which Marguerite fulfills the request of Armand's father, is not a superficial one. As Marguerite wounds Armand by feigning as much callous haughtiness, money-hungriness, and rampant sensuality as she can, there is no music underneath to weaken, soften, or sweeten its painful brutality. The music swells up only after Marguerite takes her leave to see Varville. As Armand watches her cross the field that separates (both literally and figuratively) their house of love from Varville's house of plenty, the violins mirror his internal pain and loss.

Perhaps the only music in the movie that does not underscore this general internalized contrast of passion and reason is the more external-ized, tempestuous, troubled swirl of angry violins that accompanies the flight of the bees. Some bees have escaped their hive, an apparently comical country incident; their flight, however, is accompanied by the kind of anxious "movie music" that usually signifies the onset of a storm. Indeed, the swarm of bees looks like a dense black cloud. The ominous-ness of the storm music is justified, of course, because immediately after this musical ominousness the coach drives up with Armand's father who starts the terrible emotional storm that destroys Marguerite. Perhaps this apparently externalized stormy music is actually a sign of Marguerite's premonition, her internal fear that this absolute happiness cannot really last.

Music accompanies the climactic death scene, of course, taking its cue from Marguerite's fear that Armand is not coming back to her. Her command, "Send for the priest," also summons the violins, which persist underneath the scene of prayers and sobbing. But when Nanine tells Marguerite that Armand has come, she brightens up immediately—and the music stops. A prosy interlude follows, as Marguerite, all girly and fidgety, wants to pretty herself up for the last meeting. The music returns only when Nanine gives Marguerite her final bouquet of camellias from Armand, and the two lovers embrace. During Armand's speech of his hopes for their future, the music is significant for what it does *not* do. As Armand voices the hope to return to the country, the music does not swell; its volume remains constant. Whereas a *crescendo* would support his optimism that the lovers have a future life together, the constancy of the volume subtly undercuts those hopes, implying that, like Marguerite's body, their passion has no more strength. As Armand continues to talk, Marguerite's head falls—and the violins strike a pronounced (but far from exaggerated) minor chord. The chord is so subtle that Armand goes on talking (and so do the violins), neither realizing that she cannot hear them. Only when Armand looks down to see that her eyes are closed and that she is dead do the violins change their tone to a series of minor and cold progressions that echo his realization of her death. As he holds her in his arms, the music swells to the final fade-out.

Underlying the scoring of *Camille* is the assumption that music can serve very effectively as an external sign of internal states. The abstract relationship of music to human emotions allows it to serve subtly yet clearly in cinema as a sign of those emotions. For a character to proclaim, "I love you, I love you, I love you," as Don Lockwood does to Lina Lamont in *Singin' in the Rain,* would fail to convince anyone that he really loves. The information is clear enough; it simply cannot carry our conviction. The result of Lockwood's proclamation was the audience's jeers and laughter. But to show in soft focus a still and starry-eyed face, underscored by the glide of violins, is much more likely to convince an audience that he loves her, he loves her, he loves her. So "movie music" not only is a way for the director or producer to "soup up" a film's moods for an audience; it actually communicates the internalized states of feeling and thought of the characters themselves. How much more effective for the music to change from major to minor when Armand sees that Marguerite is dead than for him to exclaim, "My God, she's dead!" We know she's dead (partially because of the previous minor chord), and he wouldn't need to inform himself. Used in such a way, music plays a central role in the movie's structural succession.

Fashions of film music change, and the old-style "movie music," like so many of Hollywood's old-style devices, is out of favor today. The least careful studio movies simply refused to be silent, stringing musical backgrounds together whenever there was no dialogue (and usually underneath it when there was), seemingly fearful that if the music ever stopped the audience would lose both interest and the continuity. When watching one of these less artfully scored movies (particularly of the mid-1930s), I frequently awake out of a musical doze (as I often do in Muzak-infested restaurants) to notice: "Has that been going on all this time?" European movies were less devoted to this kind of musical conditioning from the beginning of synchronized sound, and one of the striking characteristics of an early Renoir sound film (say, of *Boudu* or *Toni*) is its complete musical silence, except for those sequences when musical accompaniment was strictly motivated or served some special purpose. This difference in musical underscoring may well have been disconcerting for American audiences of the thirties who perceived that these European movies were somehow different from the home-grown product, disturbingly different in their style and tone, but did not know why. As with so many of the "new" American movie fashions that emerged in the late 1960s and early '70s, their ancestors were European rather than American.

The other class of film music is that kind which does not masquerade as invisible but exists specifically to be noticed in all its specialness and uniqueness. In the studios, this was the type of music that was considered appropriate to musicals, in which the music was important and special because the musical numbers were important and special. Synchronized sound created the singie-and-dancie as well as the talkie, and for the first three years of the "sound era" it was almost unthinkable to make a movie without musical numbers. The precision that synchronized sound provided in the wedding of music and picture allowed that wedding to become increasingly imaginative and complex.

Ernst Lubitsch could choreograph a duet between a soprano and a chugging locomotive, using the rhythms of the music and the rhythmic devices of cutting as the means of developing this bizarrely innovative "song-and-dance" (*Monte Carlo*). Rouben Mamoulian could choreograph the musical sounds of Paris awaking from its slumbers or could trace the surprising journey of an informally whistled love ditty all the way from the streets of Paris to the heroine's castle in the country (*Love Me Tonight*); Busby Berkeley could create choreographed extravaganzas of bizarre camera angles, cutting, and kaleidoscopic patterns on shining surfaces with a seeming infinity of smilingly beautiful ladies and their violins, pianos, and pennants, as they danced on glass, on pyramids, on staircases, under water, in parks, Pullman cars, hotel corridors, nightclubs, and nowhere in particular; Fred Astaire (and Hermes Pan) could conceive dances in which Fred performs with his own reflections and shadows, in fun houses or in fogs, with coat racks or on ceilings; Gene Kelly could dance in the land of daydreams, of French Impressionism, or in the rain.

Siegfried Kracauer has a good deal of trouble understanding why such frothy and "unnatural" fun should be so persistent throughout the history of the synchronized-sound movie. His confusion is not surprising, since musical numbers have little concern with redeeming, much less depicting, physical reality. After admitting that

> it is hard to understand why musicals should prove attractive as films. Their unrealistic settings and self-contained songs would seem to be germane to the stage rather than the screen . . .

Kracauer then finds two reasons that seem easy for him to understand:[9]

> First, musicals invariably capitalize on everyday incidents to launch their diverse production standards.

Now, this is true of such Astaire numbers as "Isn't It a Lovely Day" from *Top Hat* or the ceiling dance in *Royal Wedding*, and of such Kelly numbers as "Our Love Is Here to Stay" from *An American in Paris* or "Good Mornin'" from *Singin' in the Rain*. But what everyday incident triggered "Bojangles of Harlem" or "Gotta Dance" or "Pettin' in the Park" or "The Lullaby of Broadway" or "I'm Young and Healthy" or . . . or . . . or? And is the "launch" a sufficiently credible impetus to the immensely intricate and magnificent "vessel" that follows? The "launch" is a formulaic convenience, and Kracauer may be the only one who ever took one seriously; certainly no scriptwriter or studio executive or song-and-dance man ever did. Further, these "launches" in movies are no more credible than nor different from the identical kind of "launch" on the stage, the "everyday incidents" that produce the inevitable song cue.

> Second, musicals reflect tensions at the core of the cinema—tensions arising from the always possible conflict between the realistic and formative tendency.

The only time I notice such tensions between realism and stylization in a musical number is when the number doesn't work for me—such as the "realist" dances of *West Side Story*.

Kracauer's summary of the issue unwittingly makes more sense than his argument:

> In sum, the musical *playfully* affirms cinematic values in the dimension of *sheer divertissement* [italics mine].

What Kracauer cannot say (because of his theory of film and reality) is that imagination needs no apology, complex rhythmic, visual, and physical sensitivity need no apology, and musical numbers on film represent some of the most imaginative and complex integrations of music, décor, costume, color, physical movement, camera participation, cutting, energy, and grace that have ever been accomplished. Such musical numbers are appropriate to cinema ("cinematic") because, like dance, music, painting, and photography, cinema has a powerful kinetic, sensuous appeal, and the musical number combines *all four* of these sensual appeals with the inherent kinetic power of successive movement and successive images.

Although such musical numbers have always seemed appropriate to musicals (which Kracauer, and others, believe "lack the serious-mindedness of regular films"), they have become increasingly prominent in "serious-minded" films as well. Without developing a detailed argument about this prejudice against musicals, let me note that although a movie like *Camille* takes itself more seriously than a musical, and that an MGM executive probably took it more seriously than one of his musicals, I doubt that many "serious-minded" people would take *Camille* as more "serious-minded" than, say, *Singin' in the Rain*.

So many of the classic, "serious-minded" movies contain musical numbers of one kind or another: *Citizen Kane, Fort Apache, Nights of Cabiria, Casablanca, Modern Times, Morocco, The Blonde Venus,* and almost every film of Renoir's. With all the attention paid to Renoir's exquisite visual imagery and the complex philosophical conflict between art and nature in his films, it is surprising that so little has been paid to his musicality: the French and German songs in *Grand Illusion* (which underscore the similarities in these supposedly warring and antagonistic cultures and even carry whole sections of the action—such as the escape of Maréchal and Rosenthal and their reunion on the road); the "Blue Danube" waltz in *Boudu Saved from Drowning* (which underscores the bourgeois gentility that threatens to engulf the tramp and contrasts with his own anarchic singing at the beginning of the movie); the Spanish folk songs in *Toni* (which underscore the vital life of the Spanish immigrants); the sitar music in *The River,* the minuets in *The Golden Coach,* and the buoyant popular music of Montmartre in *French Cancan* (all of which convey both the values and the vitalities of the cultures the movies depict); the Saint-Saëns "Danse Macabre" in *Rules of the Game* (which underscores the fact that the whole movie is a *danse macabre*). Renoir even built a whole movie, *The Marseillaise,* around a song.

With its musical interludes the cinema accepts a traditional dramatic assumption (especially of the English and Italian dramatic traditions): that the theatrical experience gains an added dimension of both entertainment and commentary by interrupting dialogue scenes for an occasional musical moment. (Songs are especially important in Shakespeare, Jonson, Wycherley, and, hence, of their principal descendant, Bertolt Brecht.) Among the effective postwar uses of musical interludes in "serious" cinema are Kurosawa's compellingly rhythmic song-and-dance of the card players in *The Lower Depths* (a song-and-dance that is metaphoric of the rhythms and energy of life itself), the satirical use of syrupy popular tunes ("Try a Little Tenderness" and "We'll Meet Again") in Kubrick's *Dr. Strangelove* or the comic "perversions" of Beethoven and other composers in his *A Clockwork Orange,* the idyllic moment of spontaneous and easy joy with "Raindrops Keep Fallin' on My Head" of George Roy Hill's *Butch Cassidy and the Sundance Kid,* the rock-and-roll songs that Wolfman plays in George Lucas's *American Graffiti,* the contrast between pop songs of the 1930s and '40s ("You'll Never Know," "Where or When") with rock music of the '70s ("Daniel") in Martin Scorsese's *Alice Doesn't Live Here Anymore* (a contrast of music that parallels the movie's central contrast between the "old" and "new" values of a meaningful life), or the affecting use of Mexican folk songs in Sam Peckinpah's *The Wild Bunch.*

Like the uses of background "movie music," this more prominent kind of music has an undeniable tonal and textural function—to color our responses to a scene and our relationships with the movie's characters and events. But the very prominence of such music gives it a stronger grasp on our perceptions and reactions; by forcing us to listen to it (rather than hiding itself as a subtle "objective correlative" of internal emotion as in *Camille*), it also forces us to make connections between its information and the information of the movie as a whole. As a result, such music (as can be seen from these examples) plays a much greater and more explicit structural role (rather than the implicit role of conveying character and motivation, as it does in *Camille*) in a movie than the mere coloring of "movie music."

For example, the Mexican folk songs in *The Wild Bunch* serve as a kind of unconscious motivation for Pike and the others, accounting for their decision to destroy the enemies of these very people. The longest musical interlude comes as Pike and the Bunch ride out of the desolate little village where Angel has just learned that Mapache killed his father. Peckinpah's camera remains riveted to the faces and bodies of the departing riders and their mounts, as the Mexican song bids its gentle and rich farewell. At the end of the film, after the slaughter of Mapache and the others at Agua Verde, these very Mexican people enter to take possession of the guns and the land that are rightfully theirs. In a sense, their repossession of that town is the flowering of the seed that was planted by the earlier song. That the Bunch is capable of responding to the song is emblematic of the fact that they are capable of responding to the genuine needs of worthy people. Despite the fact that they are bandits, their response to the song reveals their personal codes of honor and morality.

The view that music in the cinema need not be characterless "movie music" has led many directors to use established musical forms that become more prominent precisely because they have character: folk music (in *The Wild Bunch, Toni,* or Jancsó's films), rock music (in *Easy Rider, Midnight Cowboy, American Graffiti,* and so on and on and on), classical music (in *Rules of the Game, The Lovers, Death in Venice, A Clockwork Orange,* and the Indian classical music in Satyajit Ray's films), and jazz (in *The James Dean Story, Anatomy of a Murder, The Man with the Golden Arm, No Sun in Venice, Murmur of the Heart,* and many others). In some of these movies, their music is arguably the most interesting and affecting element.

This prominent music can either be clearly motivated (the Mexicans sing, the teen-agers listen to Wolfman on their car radios, Alice sings in a bar) or erupt with brazen disregard for any motivation at all (the Kubrick music, "Raindrops"). If the defiantly illogical music works at all (and it seems to work better in Kubrick than almost anywhere else), it is because it is part of the stylistic texture of the whole movie, part of the same point of view that controls the director's handling of camera, cutting, characters, and structure as a whole. Unlike background "movie music," this noticeable music does not sneak itself in (usually triggered by an event of the plot, like a kiss, which covers its tracks) and sneak itself out (covered either by an action or by the climactic swelling to the fade-out, serving as an emotional punctuation mark). It brazenly announces its entrance and exit, setting that sequence apart from the preceding and succeeding prosy moments of the movie. (In both Shakespeare and "movie music," the mood shifts from prose into passion surreptitiously, without announcing the shift or warning the audience.)

Film music, then, serves as emotional coloring, as a means of adding a stylistic texture, as a means of propelling the structural succession literally, metaphorically, psychologically, or rhythmically, and (even in "serious-minded" films) as a pleasing kinetic appeal to be enjoyed for its own sake.

WORDS

Words in the cinema provide information from two sources: their sounds and their meanings. The human voice is a musical instrument and, whatever their meanings, words come to our ears during a film projection in the same way that music does—as sound. Unlike words in a purely literary work (a novel, or reading a play or poem), words in the cinema (as in the theater) come to us through vocal filters, which give them specific sounds, stresses, tones, and pitches. These sounds can be divided into two primary types: the sounds of the speakers and the sounds inherent in the words themselves.

In the discussion of *Camille*'s music, I mentioned that the scene of conflict between Marguerite and Varville over the forty thousand francs used no background music: first, because the scene was an argumentative display of reason; and, second, because the real "music" of the scene was in the rasping nasality of Varville's voice. In effect, this scene becomes a musical duet for two vocal instruments: Henry Daniell's affected, supercilious, and nasal crispness, which plays in counterpoint against Garbo's mellifluous, throaty, and heavily accented richness. This clash of "music," however, is more than a mere sound effect. It is the essential difference between these two characters as human beings. Varville is manipulative, cunning, a man of pure surfaces; he treats other human beings as objects that he can buy, use, and dispense with when consumed. Marguerite masquerades as a similar being, but beneath her courtesan's covetous surface is the ability to feel and love and give. Just as her voice is warmer, richer, deeper, more mysterious than Varville's harsh rasp, so is her soul. Hence, the clash of musical voices in the scene is also a clash of souls, and each voice leads directly to the soul (or lack of same) that produces it.

Perhaps not every scene in every movie contains such a clear-cut clash of vocal music that leads directly to the central thematic and structural issues of the movie; but the apparent ordinariness of this *Camille* dialogue scene ought to be a caution against dismissing the vocal sounds of any dialogue scene. However "literary" verbal communication may seem to be, no word ever comes to us as a *word* in the cinema (as an amalgamation of type on a page); it comes to us as a kinetic, sensual stimulus. The whooping, grunting, cackling hoots of Tojamaro in his version of the incident in *Rashomon* define the way this creature sees himself as a powerful sexual animal; in other versions of the tale he loses this predatory power, partially because the others do not hear his voice in the same way. In the same movie, the Bride's voice is mellow and sweet in her self-serving version of the incident; in the Woodcutter's version, however, that sugary voice becomes shrill and cackling.

When Ingrid Bergman asks Sam to "play it" in *Casablanca*, there is a light and fond lilt in her request, a sound of softness and longing and nostalgia for something lost. When Bogart growls, "Play it, Sam," there is coarse gravel in his throat (but then the gravelly Bogart voice was his consistent camouflage to protect the vulnerable soul it masked). W. C. Fields also used his voice as camouflage; like his fancy euphemisms and fancy costumes, an apparently complacent and honey-combed voice makes a fine adornment for artfully crooked or nasty intentions. Marcel Herrand's nasal, pinched, tight-throated voice in *The Children of Paradise* reveals the barren futility of his murderous and meaningless life—and this in a movie whose central concern is the contrast between spoken and silent acting. Hepburn and Tracy made such an admirable movie pair (as did Jean Arthur and Gary Cooper or James Stewart) because they "sang" such effective duets—her crackling, snappish bite in contrast to his quiet, shambling drawl.

In addition to the musicality of pure human voices, the recording process can add its own effective impurities with a series of "musical" distortions and emphases. The voices can be transmitted with exagger-

ated softness or loudness—just as lighting can dampen or harshen the
tone of a scene. The voices can be strained through distorting echoes and
repetitions, which transpose the aural stimuli into the subjective key,
mirroring the internal perceptions of one of the listeners (just as distorting lenses can transpose reality's visual stimuli into the key of subjective
experience). Repetition and echoing distortion (such as the echoing
reverberations of the repeated word "knife" in Hitchcock's *Blackmail*) are
two ways of altering the sounds (and, hence, information) of recorded
words. Significantly, the movie cliché for depicting the human mind's
blacking out or waking up is a sound-and-picture effect: as the lens blurs
into or out of clear focus, the sounds of conversation blur into or out of
clear comprehensibility. Microphone and playback devices can control
our information and responses, just as lens and printer can.

With all the attention that has been paid to the Welles-Toland photographic style of *Citizen Kane*, it is surprising that so little has been paid
to the movie's careful scoring for the human voice, perhaps as imaginative a verbal track as any in movie history. Welles's apprenticeship in
radio convinced him of the evocative powers of the human voice, and his
movie uses those powers magnificently. There is the hollowly echoing
rasp of "Rosebud" on Kane's dying lips; the booming-basso parody of the
voice-of-God narrator of Louis de Rochemont's *March of Time* in "News
on the March"; the muffled incomprehensibility of the voices in the projection-room sequence; the mausoleum-like tinniness of the echoing
voices in Thatcher's library-crypt; the effects of age in the maturing
voices of Thatcher, Leland, Bernstein, and Kane; the nasal reediness of
Susan's speaking (not to mention singing) voice; the honeyed sweetness
of Emily's voice at the beginning of the breakfast-table montage, a voice
that turns sour and then silent as that sequence progresses; the contrast
between Kane's amplified and unamplified voices at the political rally;
the flattened emptiness of Susan's and Kane's voices in their gargantuan
"living" room at Xanadu; the muffled echoes of the reporters' voices in
the basement warehouse that shelters all Kane's "goods"; and so many
more. The vocal sounds of many of these sequences are at least as communicative as the specific words that the sounds form (hence my discomfort with the Thompson-Rawlston "tension" on pp. 70–76).

As with the manipulation of words in purely literary forms, there are
also sounds inherent in the specific vowels and consonants that cinema
speech uses. The effects of alliteration, assonance, consonance, onomatopoeia, liquidity, "softness," "crispness," and so forth, are as possible for
the sounds of cinema speech as for any other. One major difference
between their use in movies and in literature, however, is that we literally

hear these effects. When reading poetry, the "sound" effects of vowels and consonants are frequently visual effects; we see them while reading and translate them mentally into aural effects. We do not literally hear them (unless we attend a poetry reading or unless we are so attracted by the "sounds" we "see" on the page that we read them aloud to ourselves). In cinema speech, these sound effects inherent in language are necessarily heard as sound effects.

When we turn from the communicative power of words as sounds to the communicative power of their denotative and connotative meanings, we enter a region where many film theorists refuse to tread. Perhaps it would be interesting to consider the consequences of eliminating articulate and synchronized speech from the cinema altogether. First, it would seem both arbitrary and strange to permit the sensual appeals of all sounds in the cinema except the one that is the most common in human experience. To allow music and noise in the cinema but not speech would necessarily convert the cinema into a more conventionalized and stylized art (like ballet). This kind of stylization was indeed the *donnée* of "silent film," which audiences accepted as a symbolic or metaphoric depiction of actual human experience because articulate speech had been removed by convention (again, like the ballet).[10] In the "silent film," however, speech was absent of necessity, not by convention; the audience accepted the art only *as if* speech had been removed by conventional agreement between themselves and the artist. Only in the synchronized-sound film is this kind of removal of speech truly conventional (because to use or not use speech is an equally possible prerogative). Most of the experimental, lyric films (as well as certain innovative movies like Chaplin's first sound films or the Jacques Tati comedies) exercise the option of eliminating or restricting articulate, synchronized speech. The filmmaker who exercises this option, however, deliberately removes his work from depicting familiar social reality in which an audience can have conviction, creating a work that can be taken only as a stylized metaphor for that reality.

And so if you are to make a work of cinema that purports to depict the realistic personal and social lives such as human beings do live, it is necessary to use the realistic and social speech such as human beings do use. The realistic depiction of actual human experience has been one of the interests of cinema from its beginning, and without speech the "silent film" was forced to resort to such substitutes as metaphoric gestures, or manipulating the "plastic material,"[11] or facial smiles, smirks, and grimaces, or, worst of all, to printed title cards to convey the kinds of verbal communication that human beings attempt. It is not surprising that the realist critics (such as Bazin) see speech as an advancement for the cinema's inherent realistic tendency, not a degradation (which is the view of the antirealists: Arnheim, Eisenstein, Youngblood). If cinema is to be granted the possibility of depicting realistic human social behavior, it must be granted the possibility of using articulate speech.

This articulate cinema speech is typically divided into two categories: dialogue (in which the photographed objects seek to communicate with one another) and narration (in which a voice, frequently disembodied, seeks to communicate directly with us). Those theorists who most strongly object to speech in the cinema feel far more comfortable with narration than with dialogue (as if Orson Welles's parody of the voice of God were not warning enough!). Their reason, it seems to me, is a false application of the Rule of Economy in art. Narration is preferable because the voice can be (and almost inevitably is) divorced from its source, allowing the film to capture images that may be related to the words, but are not necessarily identical to the information of the words themselves. Picture and speech can work in harmony or counterpoint, but need not work in unison. However, to show a human face while its mouth moves and words come out is a redundancy; it represents the *identical information* in sound and picture. Redundancy is one of the cardinal sins of art. Q.E.D. Class dismissed.

This argument has been accepted for so long (since Eisenstein's manifestoes of 1929) that even the realist theorists have shied away from it. I would simply like to ask how it is theoretically possible for an image of a human face and an articulate sound to be in any sense *the same*. How can a word and a face provide identical information? (Unless there is new wisdom in Bottom's "I see a voice.") One of the central concerns of Godard's *La Chinoise* was to keep his camera ruthlessly riveted to the faces of his endlessly speaking speakers. The very ruthlessness of this attention (despite its frequently painful tediousness) constructed a drama between the words that seemed to be uttered with fierce sincerity and the faces that seemed to express fierce sincerity. But were they? Was there a lie anywhere to be seen? A doubt? An indecision? The result of this sustained, two-hour mystery was uncertain; the mystery of the potential tension between face and word was never resolved—perhaps because life never resolves these kinds of mysteries for any of us, except as we resolve them for ourselves.

The Godard film reveals an inherent trait of filmed dialogue. The information we receive from picture and word can never be "the same." The picture reveals surfaces (for it photographs objects); the words are concrete manifestations of thoughts and feelings (more "internalized," as I mentioned, but more suspicious for that very reason). There have been, to be sure, millions of dull movie shots of inexpressive faces speaking ineffective words. But if a scene of synchronized dialogue feels dull, static, and lifeless, it might not be because the words and picture are working redundantly—because of an "uncinematic" use of the medium. It might be because the image is weak (the particular face or faces, and the setting that surrounds it or them, and the way of recording it or them) and/or that the words are banal, boring, clumsy, awkward, inappropriate, or stupid. You can examine the strength and quality of the elements of the image and dialogue, not merely assume a general principle about using dialogue in a visual medium. Must the content of the image inevitably be weak if that content is a speaking face? Look again at the faces of Garbo, Gable, Monroe, Davis, Dietrich, Hepburn, and so on.* To make a general argument based on the worst uses of filmed dialogue is both unfair and invalid—like the arguments against montage based on the most excessive, least expressive uses of the technique.

So often those who discuss dialogue in movies seem to assume that, unlike acting or lighting or composition or narrative structure, filmed dialogue is incapable of varying qualities of better and worse in itself, as well as a varying degree of appropriateness in relation to the movie's other informational systems of succession and image. The implication of Panofsky's "principle of coexpressibility" is that dialogue's effectiveness can only be in relation to the accompanying visual imagery and not to any inherent power of its own. But the "principle of coexpressibility" is clearly, simply, and obviously false. Even in movies that are dazzlingly visual—such as *Citizen Kane* or *The Blonde Venus*—the dialogue provides *more* information than is contained in the images themselves. (Try watching one of these movies without the sound track sometime and see how much you discover about it.)

The general tendency of effective cinema dialogue shares, first, one trait with a similar tendency of theater dialogue in the twentieth century, and, second, a general assumption about all forms of verbal communication that has dominated this century's linguistic thinking. One of the major trends of theater dialogue (its origins can be traced to Strindberg and Chekhov) is its assumption that the text is not always capable of communicating the complicated emotional and psychological material in the "subtext," the mass of vague feelings and perceptions that lie beneath the verbal surface and cannot be summarized easily (if at all) in concrete, precise, economical words. There is a gap between the verbal sur-

---

* I suspect that most of the antidialogue theorists do not see the powerful visual imagery of these stars' faces as photographic objects. But then there are other critics and theorists who do not see the visual power of dancing lines, squares, circles, and blotches.

face and the emotional undercurrents beneath that surface—either because the character is not completely in touch with those undercurrents, or because the vague undercurrents defy verbalization, or because the character senses the undercurrents but for some reason or other suppresses their overt expression in the company of others. Significantly, perhaps the foremost contemporary English practitioner of the Chekhovian assumptions of verbal inadequacy is Harold Pinter, who also writes film scripts, and whose approach to film dialogue is identical with his approach to stage dialogue.

The movie character who explicitly proclaims, "I am sad," or "I am angry," certainly seems to be passing along some clear and unequivocal information. The question is whether such an explicit proclamation can ever carry an audience's conviction that the character indeed feels sad or angry. And so the unequivocal information becomes quite equivocal because we believe that sad or angry people do or say sad or angry things, rather than issue emotional bulletins. (We would more likely accept such a bald proclamation of sadness as satirical, as a sign that the character suffers from hypochondriacal melancholia—which is precisely the way we respond to Masha in Chekhov's *The Sea Gull.*)

To return to that Marguerite-Varville scene, Marguerite never proclaims that she is lying for the purpose of extorting money from her keeper to pay her bills, so she can then run off to the country with her lover. She talks flutteringly and offhandedly about her need for a trivial forty thousand francs; she claims that she needs to go away solely for her health; she makes light of the entire extortion process—as if she were not manipulating the man in a callous and hypocritical way (justified, of course, in the movie morality by the virtuous end of her devious means and his generally vicious and devious being). He takes the extortion (which he recognizes as extortion) lightly also—as if the money did not mean anything to him (and it doesn't). The only indication that he feels the encounter as less than light is that irritation in his nasal voice and the startling slap he gives Marguerite to end the scene (even as he gives her the money). It is his ego, not his wallet, that is his prize possession, and he will not give her the proceeds of the one without also giving her a token of the other. The dialogue in the scene scrupulously avoids touching directly upon any genuine emotional concerns of either of the characters.

The cinema seems a much more suitable medium for manipulating dialogue of this sort than the theater—simply because the cinema is able to provide so much more information from other sources. Pinter's early plays were far more radical and innovative than his screenplays have been because they applied the principles of filmed dialogue to the stage, where they had never been quite so thoroughly applied before. By keeping the characters' internal feelings so smothered and their surface dialogue so spare and oblique, Pinter succeeded in baffling most of his early audiences and critics, who were sure that something significant and important was going on, but were not sure what. Marguerite's strategy in *Camille* is perfectly clear (because we have seen so much of her before, and because we can hear when she forces a laugh or a word that she doesn't mean, and because the lighting and camera angle and cutting control our awareness of precisely what she is doing). The close-up exploits the semiotic capabilities of the human face in a way that the theater cannot. The strategy of the characters in Pinter's early plays was not at all clear because the stage suppresses any information that we cannot see or hear clearly or loudly (and because Pinter deliberately emphasized this suppression by plunging us into the pure presentness of seeing events and persons on a stage without supplying the conventional exposition).

To articulate feelings into speech is a strategic decision—not only the artist's decision in determining the best strategy for depicting characters and shaping scenes, but also the individual human being's decision about what hidden thought he wishes to bring out of hiding, for whom, and to what end. In ordinary human social intercourse (I'm talking about life now, not just "art," although this attitude in life shapes the way an artist will build a scene, if it is to carry our conviction that we are watching fictionalized life), a verbal utterance is significant not only in what is said but in that it is said. One of the special provinces of movies is the close and realistic examination of such kinds of ordinary social intercourse. Because of their confinement to a universe of "objective" surfaces of photographic objects, the movies have become especially adept at preserving the integrity of those surfaces as barriers as well as providing the means of peering beneath them. Filmed dialogue is another of those surfaces, and it often reveals the feelings that lie beneath less by referring to them directly than by avoiding them specifically, or by a pause, or by a torrent of words in which the torrential sound is more significant than any specific word in the torrent, or by some other oblique means. The vague obliqueness of "movie music" is precisely what makes it such a useful "objective correlative," a means of providing internal information externally without betraying the way that people genuinely feel things and genuinely communicate those feelings.

The familiar maxim of movie dialogue—that less is more—is true, but not for the familiar reason. "Lessness" is functional not in a quantitative sense but in a qualitative one (for example, the torrent of words in which there is a lot of sound but little specific meaning). The reason is not that there should be *less* dialogue and *more* picture in cinema (the usual Panofskian formulation), but that there should be less explicit references to internal feelings and more elusive and oblique talk because that is precisely the kind of real speech that dominates our social affairs (particularly the process of getting to know a "stranger"—as in falling in love—one of the central narrative concerns of movies). The casual superficiality of movie talk is not a consequence of the visual demands of the medium, but of the intensely realistic possibilities of the medium.

Perhaps for this reason I frequently find the beginnings of certain Hollywood movies much more successful and vital than their endings. I refer especially to "conversion" movies (like *Camille, Nothing Sacred, Dark Victory,* and *Ninotchka*), in which the main character (inevitably female) is "bad" at the beginning (or "hard," which, in the movie morality, amounts to the same thing for a woman) and becomes "good" at the end by falling sincerely in love. Whereas I find their "badness" absolutely delightful and credible in the movies' early sections, I frequently find the conversions sentimental and obligatory—at least partially because the spirited, offhand, flip chatter of the "bad girl" has converted to "I'm so happy" and "I love you so much" and "Where would I be now without you?" (They'd be back in the first section of the movie, just where I'd have them. I realize, of course, that such a view is laced with my own assumptions about human behavior and personality, but I am now discussing *my* sense of conviction.) In such "conversion" movies, the characters seem to fall in love with each other's faces, treating the sharp and surface words as strategic camouflage. Although there may be a Platonic conception underlying this Hollywood attraction to the surface (of seeing the soul in the face and eyes), the Hollywood morality seems much more to support the notion that people are more capable of communicating as physical objects than as thinking beings.

It is the rare Hollywood movie that can bring about the conversion to love without converting the characters into dead heads and mush mouths (because in these rare movies, the lively heads and mouths were what attracted the lovers to one another in the first place). For this reason I so much admire Hawks's *Bringing Up Baby, Twentieth Century, His Girl Friday,* or *I Was a Male War Bride,* or Lubitsch's *Trouble in Paradise* and *The Marriage Circle,* or Cukor's *Pat and Mike* and *Adam's Rib,* or Sturges's *The Palm Beach Story* and *The Lady Eve:* because they are capable of converting human emotions without creating characters who lose their character and conversations that lose their life. I also think that one of the reasons that these "screwball" movies are enjoying a renaissance of audience appreciation today (especially Hawks) is that their psychology is so surprisingly contemporary. The other choice (of converting internal emotions by converting the character's way of life and talk) is much less frequently successful for me. Perhaps Capra is its master, and I feel he truly succeeded with the method only twice—in *It Happened One Night* and *Mr. Deeds Goes to Town*.

This discussion of the strategies of filmed dialogue is radically different from the usual methods—all of them based on Kracauer's categorization of cinema speech into Synchronous and Asynchronous, Parallelism and Counterpoint.* My quarrel with the Kracauer formulation is, first, that it implies that words do not have or ought not to have any specific communicative power in and of themselves. Why should music be communicative as both sound and "meaning," but not words? Second, it is a system based entirely on the effects of integrating words and picture (a double system), rather than integrating words with the informational systems of succession as well as of image (a triple system).

NOISE

By noise I mean all those less organized and patterned cinema sounds than music or words—more specific than music (since twittering birds, ringing bells, thumping hearts, and banging doors all have clear and concrete referents), less specific than speech. These sounds can serve three functions: for realistic atmosphere and texture, for emotional atmosphere and toning, and for conveying essential narrative and structural information. The first function of noise—as an expected realistic accompaniment—is a consequence of the cinema's conversion to synchronized sound. If a character walks along a seashore, we expect to hear the sound of waves. If we do not, we immediately suspect an intentional artistic reason for the suppression of a "motivated" sound that we can actually see being made (the character is dreaming of walking on a beach, or is actually walking, but so locked into thought that she cannot hear the waves). If a character walks through a crowded city without the noises of traffic, we again assume that she is walking in some sort of subjective daze or other. Imagine the effect of a character's walking through a thick forest, surrounded by the sounds of the forest as well as by its branches, only suddenly to hear the sounds vanish into silence (as Jiří Weiss did in

* To simplify, Kracauer's categories distinguish between whether the source of the sound is visible or not and whether the picture supplies information that parallels the sound or differs from it (*Theory of Film*, pp. 102–32).

his *Golden Fern* or as Jack Clayton did in *The Innocents*). The effect would be unearthly—precisely their intention.

These earthly noises are essential elements in convincing an audience that it is watching "real" events on our familiar, natural earth. Before synchronized sound, of course, one did not identify the absence of waves, traffic, or forest birds with unearthly or subjective effects, for the accompanying music translated the absent sounds into their metaphoric equivalents. To some extent, the same principle governs those increasingly obligatory traveling scenes in automobiles when the sounds of motor and highway disappear to be replaced by a "rolling along" rock song on the sound track ("Mrs. Robinson" in *The Graduate* or "Daniel" in *Alice Doesn't Live Here Anymore* or dozens of others). The substitution of traveling music for traveling noises immediately converts the sequence into a subjective emotional interlude—the gliding-along feeling for both character and audience of traveling at high speeds over long distances. But imagine the feeling of one of these automobile sequences if it were absolutely silent (for example, the traffic-jam nightmare that opens 8½).

Clearly, one of the most astonishing effects of the sound cinema is silence. Until there was a sound film there was no truly silent film, for whenever there was an absolute silence during a "silent film," the audience assumed that the pianist had either dozed off or stepped out for a smoke. Absolute and powerful silence is an astonishing contrast that is possible only in a medium in which the usual moments of nonsilence exist to define it and in which the use of pure silence becomes a deliberate, conscious, and controllable special effect. Although such silence often serves a narrative effect (informing us: this is a dream, a reverie, a hallucination), its most powerful effect is as tonal intensification—underscoring the loneliness, emptiness, tension, or terror of a particular moment (the silence of the separated couple in the shot from "The Illiterates" sequence in *Scenes from a Marriage*, the silence in the opening scene of *The Eclipse* as two empty lovers realize how empty their relationship truly is, the silence of the dreamlike scene before the mirror in Bergman's *Persona*). In these scenes, silence becomes a kind of "negative music," intensifying the presence not of some powerful "positive" emotion (love, joy, melancholy, fear), but of a "negative" one (uncertainty, loneliness, emptiness).

Other, noisier noises also serve "musically" for tonal underscoring. The ticking of a clock during the suspenseful wait for some dangerous threat can be as successful at turning the emotional screws as the insistent pressure of "suspense music." Another sound that functions similarly is the rhythmic thumping of the human heart, which Peckinpah uses subjectively at two key moments of *The Wild Bunch* (just before the first bank robbery and the quiet holdup of the army train). The director made no attempt to indicate whose heart (if anyone's) was beating so expectantly in these preludes to a violent action. Perhaps it was the "group heart," their communal tension and energy building to the task they were about to perform; more probably it was intended as a mirror and stimulus for our own hearts, building us up to the orgiastic climaxes of violence that were promised (and kept). Repetitive and rhythmic noises are especially good for these kinds of "musical" effects (ticking clocks, pounding hearts, rousing drumbeats, rolling train wheels) since, like music, they maintain a regular, rhythmic pattern which can be subtly increased in volume, tempo, and intensity without our awareness. They serve as metronomes for our emotions.

Most of the noises that serve key narrative functions serve as striking tonal and emotional accompaniment at the same time. A sound that moves the plot is usually an extremely moving and evocative noise in its own right. One of the most famous of these noises is the screaming train of Hitchcock's *The 39 Steps*, in which the director substitutes a shrieking train whistle for the anticipated scream of the cleaning lady who finds a woman's corpse. The shift of scream to whistle is not only more disturbing and unsettling than an ordinary human scream, but it also firmly links the murder with the train to Scotland, on which the presumed murderer is fleeing. (Hitchcock executed precisely the same substitution of train whistle for human scream in two earlier sound movies—*Blackmail*, 1929; *Number Seventeen*, 1932—each time demonstrating an increasing sureness and effectiveness in the handling of the device. It was as if the director were rehearsing for the eventual effect that became a classic.)

Screaming train whistles serve the narrative comically in Preston Sturges's *The Lady Eve*, in which the director substitutes the howl of a train whistle for each of the bride's "confessions" about her past lovers to her new husband. In this sequence, the scream of a train represents several different kinds of howls at the same time; the predatory howl of the wife, exercising her power over the stilted emotions of her sheepish husband; the wounded howl of the husband at each painful discovery; and the cynical and gleeful howl of the director, who hoots at the moral assumptions that underly sexual clichés and stereotypes in our culture.

Among the other evocative sounds that have served narrative functions I might mention the tapping of the blind man in Ford's *The Informer* (a tapping that suggests not only the pursuit of Gypo's comrades, but the remorseless pangs of guilt in his own soul) or the beginning of the long-awaited Comanche attack in his *Stagecoach* (which erupts with the hiss and thud of an offscreen arrow hitting home). Or in *Alice*

Doesn't Live Here Anymore, there are the muffled sobs of Alice, alone inside her car, fearing that Tommy and her life are lost forever. The sound is muffled because the windows of the car are tightly closed, and Scorsese's camera remains outside the car, viewing her through the shiny and reflecting glass of its windshield. The implication of the muffled and imprisoned sound is that Alice's life is similarly muffled and imprisoned—and she has suddenly arrived at this realization herself.

There is the hooting parrot that screams his derision after Susan walks out on Kane, the mounting anxiety of racket hitting tennis ball rhythmically in *Strangers on a Train,* the clatter of a typewriter reducing human problems to bureaucratic forms in both *The 400 Blows* and *Masculine/ Feminine,* or the sound of a duplicating machine that concludes our experience of the process of turning a young person into a permanent bureaucrat in *The Sound of Trumpets.* The opening section of Chaplin's *City Lights* is such a brilliant burlesque of public oratory because a musical instrument (the saxophone) plays chaotic musical non-patterns that are mere noises, and these noises are symbolic substitutes for pompous and banal human speech. The music-as-noise-as-speech climaxes with an ironic eruption into pure music—"The Star-Spangled Banner."

Just as noise and silence can work in juxtaposition, noise can also alternate with music and dialogue. One of the characteristics that distinguishes the senses of sight and sound is that sounds can be mixed, overlaid on top of one another, without violating familiar reality as two superimposed images do. In recognition of this fact, the final process of making a sound track is called the "mix." So one additional element that makes the violinic screams in *Psycho* so disturbing (the violinic screams are another example of music-as-noise-as-speech) is that the screams follow immediately after the natural sound of a streaming shower and are interwoven with that lulling sound. The familiar, rhythmic sound of streaming, swishing water tricks us into a kind of dozing acceptance of the moment's ordinariness (juxtaposed, however, with the pornographic slyness of watching a naked woman shower and with the disturbing unnaturalness that Hitchcock's imagistic and structural successions have built into the moment visually and emotionally). Only after this lulling sound do the disturbing premonitions erupt when the grotesque shadow rips open the shower curtain and the violins begin their assault.

Such examples of effective sound scoring indicate yet again that filmed sounds never work in isolation but in some form of integration with the cinema's visual components, just as its visual evocations of individual images work in connection with the evocations and information of the cinema's systems of succession.

9/Integration

These last chapters may have seemed somewhat paradoxical. After initially disputing the claims and applicability of cinema semiology, I have devoted the last four chapters to categorizing the semiotic elements of cinema. But then I originally claimed that there was no cinema language; rather, there were several cinema languages. And these last chapters developed each of them: the "language" of time (succession), the "language" of space (image), and the "language" of sound. Each of these broad categories embraces several species of information, so that many of them (particularly the three systems of cinema succession) might be considered separate "languages" in themselves. Classifying the cinema's communicative elements is an extremely complicated task, and the following chart will summarize that complexity.

SUCCESSION

Literal

Duration of shot

Synthetic Effects
stop-action
animation
pixillation
"slow motion"
"accelerated motion"
freeze-frame

Minimal Film

"Phi" Effect and Flashes of Frames

Imagistic

Visual
light-dark
form or shape
direction
proliferation
variation

Rhythmic
steady
accelerando
rallentando
(motion within shot)
(extended length of shot)

Structural
"general intention"

IMAGE

Filming

Lens and Film
Lens
"normal"-long-shot
zoom
"hand-held"
rack focus
anamorphosis
anamorphic correction
lens flare halation

Filter
colored or neutral
scrims
"haze"
mattes

Exposure
overexposure
underexposure
choice for emphasis or compromise

Film
gauge
speed
color sensitivity
contrast
"adulteration" of celluloid

Lens and Object
Camera "Angle"
"distance" (close, medium, far)

SOUND

Music

Background
Tonal Effects
rhythm
volume
tempo
orchestration

External Sign of Internal Emotion

Special
musical "numbers"
tonal effect
style and texture
implied action or event
pleasure

Words

Sounds
voices
distortions
consonants-vowels

Meanings
Dialogue
obliqueness
"sub-text"
strategy

Narration

SUCCESSION

Literal

fade or burn
dissolve
wipe
iris

Structural

People and Events (Narrative)
personality produces events
events affect personality
interdependence of personality
and event

Kinesis

Musical
theme-variation
accelerando
rallentando
counterpoint
intensification
expansion
repetition

Visual
proliferation
decimation
contrast
parallel
direction

Musical-visual combination

Expository, Logical, and Rhetorical

IMAGE

Filming

"level" (high, low, eye)
perspective (slant, emphasis, attitude)

Camera activity
panning-tilting
moving (tracking, traveling)

Film and Lab
transitional devices
color tinting
superimposition
negative film
pushing
reduction-blowup
repeated or deleted frames
split screen

Toning

Lighting Direction
high
low
side
back

Lighting Intensity
high-key
low-key
artificial-natural

Shade or Color
Monochrome shading

SOUND

Music

Noise

Natural Accompaniment
"motivated"
silence

Tonal Underscoring
silence
rhythmic "metronomes"
"unmotivated"

Narrative Functions
silence
substitution
offscreen

"Mix" of Music, Words, Noise

cause-effect
comparison-contrast
deduction
induction
process
procedure

Evolution of Private Symbolic System

Color
kinesis
metaphor
leitmotif
filtered
colored light

Content

Object
animate-inanimate
few-many
part-whole
face-body
semiotic symbols in codes of film
or culture

Composition
shape of objects
relation of objects to one another
relation of objects to frame
relation of compositions to other
frames

Activity
movement-stasis
subtle-pronounced
fast-slow

From this huge number of affective cinema elements several complexities and consequences arise. The first is that the filmmaker does not manipulate each of these numerous and complex elements individually; his use of any one of them changes and affects its impact on the others, which then affect its power and meaning in turn. The systems of literal, imagistic, and structural succession interact with and influence one another, as do the systems of the filming, toning, and content of images, as do music, words, and noise. And then each of these major systems interacts with and influences the union with the others. The emotional effect of the single shot in *The Wild Bunch* (of Pike's receding back) might be attributed to its integrating the following elements:

SUCCESSION

Literal: temporal extension and prolonging of successive movement in the
  single shot
Imagistic: visual and rhythmic contrasts with preceding shot(s)
Structural: role of the shot in understanding Pike and the Bunch

IMAGE

Filming: slow use of the zoom lens from a very short focal length to a
  much longer one, closer to Pike's "center"
  exposure emphasizes contrast of dark central subject and light surroundings
  Panavision lens and huge resulting frame
  color film
  "far shot" at "eye level" from directly behind
  motionless camera (except for zoom)
Toning: bright sunlight
  harsh color contrast of black and beige
Content: man and horse as single object, cut off at bottom
  central object suspended in the vast midst of huge frame
  slowness of receding motion

SOUND

Music: melancholy strings
Words: none
Noise: none; silence (contrasted with earlier noise of laughter)

Now, Peckinpah certainly never sat down with a chart of cinema elements to tick each of these off, one by one, making sure he had included and integrated the ones he wanted. The particular integration of this single shot was completely intuitive. It simply felt "right" to him—right for this moment, this feeling, this point of the narrative, this mood, this development of character, this human experience, this audience experience. If the shot has been built properly—if its elements have been selected and integrated properly—it can feel as "right" to "the viewer" as it did to the director. "The viewer" can have conviction in the moment, both knowing (understanding) what the moment means and *knowing* (feeling) what the moment means.

But even if the moment feels "right" to the director and to most (or to a great many) viewers, some viewers might have no conviction in it because of "extracinematic" reasons that are not in the projected image itself: the viewer hates cowboy pictures; or is unsympathetic to egotistic characters; or deplores the violent life style of the Bunch; or detests bank robbers; or does not believe that human beings feel things of this kind or in this way; or had a very bad dinner or too many martinis; and so forth. Such "extracinematic" variables underscore the fact that to refer to "the viewer" is a theoretical convenience—a way of separating what is projected on the screen from how each of us differs in perceiving and receiving that projection. There is an obvious difference between "the viewer" as a single hypothetical entity and the millions of viewers who actually view a movie. But this notion of a communal "viewer" seems justified by the fact that despite individual differences of taste and perception, there is also a great communality of opinion about a great many movies. The precise integration of the many cinema elements is the source of this communality of conviction (or lack of it) in every moment of every work of cinema.

Second, this huge number of cinematic elements guarantees that no shot in cinema can ever be absolutely identical to any other shot. When Godard parodies Lumière's *Arrival of a Train* (in *Les Carabiniers*) or Woody Allen parodies Eisenstein's battle wagon from *October* (in *Love and Death*), there are certainly enough elements in the shot for us to recognize the source of the parody: in the Godard shot—its content (train entering station), composition (train on left, platform on right), and camera angle (eye level); in the Allen shot—its content (wagon pushed by straining soldiers), composition (physical tension of the human figures), and low camera angle.

But both shots are demonstrably not "the same" as the originals that inspired them. Godard's used a faster lens and faster panchromatic film, both of which produce a crispness of detail and sharpness of depth that do not exist in the original. Allen's used color film (not monochrome, as did the original) and coupled it with Prokofiev music (which Eisenstein used in other films, but not in *October*). The slightest alteration of one of the cinema elements alters the effect of the integrated compound that we perceive, for the cinema's effect and affect stem entirely from the kinetic elements we can see and hear. And this absolute originality of the cinema shot supports the assertion that every shot in the cinema is an original trope—a means of yoking together elements that have never been combined in that identical way before.

It also proves to be the rock on which the most ambitious claims of cinema semiology founder. The semiologist has certainly made us more sensitive to the cinema as a system of "signs" (and has made the word "sign" a permanent part of the cinema's critical vocabulary). But we now can isolate so many and so many kinds of these signs and can see their information so complexly affected by their different integrations that it is clearly impossible to "encode" them (to distribute the "signs" into any fixed and permanent systems of "codes"). In cinema, both the individual elements (the shots, or "morphemes") and their systems of integration are infinitely variable.

For this reason, many semiologists (for example, Umberto Eco) have abandoned their interest in the cinema's aesthetic issues to concentrate on its cultural or sociological ones. Eco is more interested in the way a movie is saturated with cultural symbols and expectations; these cultural and social signs in movies are so completely natural to others in the same culture that they go unnoticed, seeming both "invisible" and "automatic." But in a biblical epic of ancient Rome, the actor who turns his thumb toward the ground means "Kill the losing gladiator." In a neorealist Italian movie, that same gesture means "Fill my glass with more wine." In an American movie, however, that same gesture means "The thing I am seeing or hearing or discussing stinks." This kind of semiotic discussion is undeniably useful at making us sensitive to the fact that movies are unintelligible without our awareness of these cultural gestures and assumptions. Movies arise from cultural habits and attitudes, and no one who watches a movie can fully understand it if he is ignorant or innocent about those attitudes. But to increase our cultural sensitivity is not an attempt to compile an alphabet, a dictionary, or a grammar of cinema effects and affect. It is perhaps one more reminder that the cinema has a rhetoric without a grammar.

Third, despite this "infinite variety" in manipulating and integrating the cinema's many elements, certain principles and patterns of integration have tended to recur since Griffith expanded and developed the tools of cinema rhetoric over six decades ago. In examining the history of the "silent" cinema, André Bazin distinguished between those directors who "put their faith in the image and those who put their faith in reality."[1] He meant that some moviemakers, particularly the Soviet montagists and German expressionists, emphasized the artificial, manipulative possibilities of the recording and projecting processes—the Russians with their editing of the film strips and the Germans with their painting, decorating, and lighting of the image. Conversely, other moviemakers (like von Stroheim, Chaplin, Flaherty, Renoir) made all consciousness of cinema artifice disappear so that we seemed to see nature itself. Although I have always felt that Bazin had put his finger on some legitimate dichotomy or other, I never felt that the one he stated was the one he found. For example, there is plenty of nature in *Potemkin* (the sea, masses of people, the ships in the fog) and plenty of artifice in von Stroheim (say, von Steuben's spotlit head in *Blind Husbands*) and Renoir (say, the parody of Bacchic drama at the beginning of *Boudu*). Bazin himself goes through critical contortions to include Dreyer's *Joan of Arc* as a work of nature (despite its artificial, expressionist settings and architecture and its self-consciously "close-up" camera style). He calls the movie a "documentary of faces" (which it is—but which makes it no less artificial).

The real dichotomy that Bazin had discovered was between those who put their faith in succession (the Russians) and those who put their faith in the image (the Germans and Americans); further, between those who put their faith in the toning of images (the Germans) and those who put their faith in the filming and content of images (von Stroheim, Chaplin, Dreyer, Renoir, and the like). The musical and intellectual effects of imagistic succession were the dominant emotional and informational forces in the Soviet "silent" cinema. For the sake of that dominant system, the Soviets deliberately curtailed or subordinated the communicative powers of the other cinema systems. For Eisenstein to make his three stone lions leap to life (in *Potemkin*) or his coffee glasses dance to life (in *October*), he had to subordinate (indeed, eliminate) all other communicative elements from those specific images. Their filming was either from slightly below (the lions) or directly above (the cups); their toning was brightly functional; their images deliberately eliminated all content other than the central photographic object.

Of course, one of the reasons that I (and most others) find Eisenstein richer than Pudovkin is not only that his methods of montage (of imagistic succession) are more interesting, more subtle, more dynamic, and more musical than Pudovkin's. Eisenstein's subordinate systems of the image were also much richer (especially the content of his images in terms of both their activity and their composition). True, many of Eisenstein's images necessarily strip their content of all but the simplest and

The different integrative compounds of *Potemkin.* The three consecutive shots of stone lions (simple objects, static composition) contrast with three conse-

cutive shots on the Odessa Steps (complex activity, complex compositional patterns, complex objects in varied speeds and directions of motion).

most important objects (in particular, all those montage sequences that attempt to bring inanimate objects "to life"). But many other Eisenstein images (for example, all those scenes on the Odessa Steps) are jammed with complex activities, camera strategies, and compositional tensions. This complexity itself was an instinctual integrative decision on his part, his awareness of the difference between the satirical device of bringing the dead to life (but emphasizing the deadness) as opposed to the dynamic effect of depicting the chaotic, seething fragments of human passion during the most extreme of emotional moments. Eisenstein's integration of succession and image is very different in the stone lion sequence of *Potemkin* from that in the Odessa Steps sequence of the same movie.

When Pudovkin pulls one of this tricky montage sequences (for example, the beginning of the slaughter in *Mother*),[2] the compositional tension and dynamic activity within each shot of the sequence tends to be weaker and less complex than in Eisenstein's sequences of energetic and chaotic action. But an even more significant difference between their integrative principles is that Pudovkin's non-montage sequences (the ones in which he uses fairly extended shots of human interaction) subordinate imagistic succession entirely to the filming and content of the image. Pudovkin relies much more heavily on film acting, on the evocations of both the human face and the "plastic material" (the concrete objects in the shot) and on camera angle—all of which are elements of the image, not of succession. In such scenes, Pudovkin's integrative compound, despite his Marxist intentions, is not very distant from that of his American cousins, such as D. W. Griffith, or Henry King's *Tol'able David* (no surprise since Pudovkin acknowledged his debt to both).

To describe this difference between their integrative principles, Eisenstein called his montage style "collision," Pudovkin's "linkage." Eisenstein realized that his own specific images (not just his editing methods) were more jostling, more dynamic, more vibrant than Pudovkin's. Pudovkin's usual metaphor for an individual image was a static one; he likened each shot to a brick. Eisenstein, however, likened a shot to electrical charges, atomic particles, and biological cells. These different integrative principles produce different responses in us, the viewers. The Eisenstein compound produces an experience that seems tense, nervous, dissonant, taut, whereas the Pudovkin compound produces an experience that (except for the special montage sequences, which function as punctuating interrupters) seems more languid, leisurely, and calm. The Eisenstein integration converts the experiencing of his work into a primarily musical-visual-sensual adventure, while the more temperate Pudovkin integration of succession and image strikes a balance between musical passages and narrative demands.

The integrative tendency of the classic German movies of the 1920s was precisely opposite. We value the German cinema today for its interesting architecture and décor, for its moodily evocative lighting, and for its impressive use of the moving camera—three devices which manipulate the content, the toning, and the filming of the image respectively. Visual atmosphere and the texture of the individual image, rather than the rhythms and "music" of succession, were the dominant kinetic appeals of these German movies. To develop these atmospheres required a reliance on prolonging the literal succession of frames rather than on the rhythmic effects of frequently successive shots.

This integrative principle also accounts for the German cinema's great success with sound filming in the early years of the talkies. The atmosphere and texture of the extended image could easily support and sustain the addition of dialogue. But the pervasive and inherent rhythms, music, and meanings of Soviet montage (the overpowering effects of imagistic succession) clashed with words, which have their own rhythms, music, and meanings. Eisenstein considered synchronized dialogue a theoretical error, an "uncinematic" use of the medium—and of course he was right if you define the essence of the medium as imagistic succession. Synchronized music caused Eisenstein no problem, for its rhythms and tones could work in harmony or counterpoint with the "musical" succession of his images. Words, however, added a new system of information that could not be integrated with the systems of succession except by their surrendering some of their own communicative power. But such a surrender is no different in kind from Eisenstein's forcing some of his individual images to surrender their potential power so that they could serve the communicative power of succession.

The integrative principle of the talkies discarded both the "language" and the "music" of imagistic succession (except for special nontalk sequences) in favor of the language and music of sounds, supported by the dominant imagery of the human body and face. The use of both black-and-white and the "Golden Frame" aided the intense concentration on words and faces of these talkies—an extremely concentrated (rather than scattered) integrative principle. The individual Eisenstein image is often so rich, so oversaturated (in shape, mass, line, texture, activity) that the demands of imagistic succession do not allow us the opportunity to perceive and absorb its richness on first (or even second) viewing. Often, more goes on in an Eisenstein image that we can absorb at one time.

Rather than oversaturating the eye and imagination in this way, the talkies trimmed away the excess and peripheral in favor of a concentrated purity. Although many found the Soviet method artistically superior (precisely because it was so much more complex, scattered, and rich), this contrast between the scattered and the concentrated is also a difference between, say, Shakespeare and Racine or symphonies and sonatas. Comparative and evaluative conclusions about such opposites are neither obvious nor easy.

A rarely discussed integrative change that the talkies wrought was the conversion of cinema space from outdoor to indoor imagery. Not only did the dominant visual environments move indoors (where talk could be recorded more easily); the passions and conflicts that the cinema examined also moved indoors. The vast forests, plains, and mountains of "silent films" tended to be supplanted by parlors, night clubs, and offices. The wild frenzy of physical comedy, which needed the immense outdoor spaces as a backdrop for its frantic motion, became domesticated; the drawing room has always been the proper physical setting for the more verbal and mental sorts of domestic comedy. This shift was one of the obvious reasons for the demise of Buster Keaton in his early talkies; Keaton's epic and elemental comedy could only take place outdoors. Harold Lloyd, who, despite his famous thrill sequences, had always been a more domestic and domesticated comic being, suffered less in his early talkies. And although Chaplin was rarely dependent on natural imagery (*The Gold Rush* is the obvious exception), his conversion to synchronized talk (*The Great Dictator, Monsieur Verdoux,* and *Limelight*) also moved him into the parlor.

In noncomic movies, the gangster rivalled and perhaps replaced the cowboy, for the gangster was a denizen of the city and his violent life took him indoors to night clubs, back rooms, and speakeasies. Perhaps one reason that Fritz Lang, Ernst Lubitsch, and Josef von Sternberg made such spectacularly visual early talkies was that they had specialized in indoor imagery (and the indoor emotions) in the "silents."

For their scenes without talk, the talkies frequently integrated the cinema's elements as richly and complexly as anything in Eisenstein, either by moving outdoors or by exploiting the immensity of cavernously bizarre indoor settings. The wedding sequence of von Sternberg's *The Scarlet Empress* is one obvious example, a spectacularly oversaturated synthesis of rich and complexly composed images (immense numbers of people; vast interior spaces; objects on conflicting vertical and horizontal planes; flags, icons, statues, and humans), of a complex imagistic succession (cutting rhythmically to the many different distances, heights, and angles; cutting from vast panoramas to painfully tight close-ups of Catherine's veiled face), and of monumental musical sound.

Equally complex is the outdoor "Beyond the Blue Horizon" number from Lubitsch's *Monte Carlo*. Lubitsch synthesizes a steadily accelerating song (whose lyrics and melody imply expansion, hope, growth, and improvement) with an imagistic succession that precisely mirrors its accelerating musical rhythms and with individual images that underscore this progressively expanding and accelerating visual music and musical visual. The wheels turn in rhythm, precisely mirroring the rhythmical forward movement of the song's melody, rhythm, and lyrics. The smokestack belches puffs of smoke at the same time that the musical sounds toot or puff, turning the smokestack into a percussive instrument that punctuates the steady, rolling musical beat and the circularly turning wheels. The train's locomotive tensely fills about two-thirds of the frame, thrusting perpetually forward, threatening to reach the right-hand edge. But Lubitsch's moving camera never allows the locomotive to reach that edge, and so it continues to thrust forward toward its goal without reaching it. The locomotive appears to be on a sort of surging treadmill, wanting to break away but not succeeding, tensely remaining stationary and moving forward at the same time. And its movement from left to right mirrors our cultural view of progress—since we read from left to right.

Such dazzling integrations of the three cinema systems indicate that talkies certainly could have been as complexly and richly "scattered" as the greatest "silent" movies; they deliberately decided against this choice in favor of another kind of integration. And the identical choice still dominates movies today. No matter how tricky, assaultive, colorful, wide, and stereophonic movies have become, their integrative mixtures of the three cinema systems remain very different compounds in their talking and nontalking sections. One obvious example is the differing integrative compounds of the dialogue sections of *2001* (using a wide, fixed frame and the extended take) and its dazzlingly dizzying space ride.

Or consider the differences between the musical numbers and the dialogue scenes of Robert Altman's *Nashville*. The musical sequences use complex systems of cutting (to mirror the rhythms of the music and the attitudes of both singer and audience); and they consistently disorient the eye with unexpected camera angles, "distances," and compositions. But the lengthier dialogue sections tend to use the fixed frame and the extended take—say, the young assassin's telephone call to his mother from the boardinghouse. The young man stands far-screen right talking on the phone, while his boardinghouse bedroom fills left and center screen, complete with the comically gawky-skinny-sexy Shelley Duval, who intends to spend some time there with him. The fixed frame and the extended take allow our ear to absorb the words and our eye to explore the surroundings at the same time.

Of course, one of Altman's pioneering devices—his "overlapping dialogue"—is to treat words as musical passages. Altman's camera and microphone frequently leap from group to group, sticking with each conversation only long enough to catch its gist and its musical tone, but not long enough to hear it all. We get visual-musical passages of conversational middles without the beginnings and ends, which are merely implied. This integrative principle indeed combines dialogue with a rapid and rhythmic imagistic succession (which neither Eisenstein nor prewar Hollywood thought possible or desirable). Although Altman proves that the integration is both possible and interesting, he also exposes the limits of the kind of verbal sense such an integration can make. It gives "blips" of attitudes, ideas, vocal tones, and character insights, not full depictions. Such an integration of words and succession produces two other integrative consequences that are consistent Altman tendencies: his movies often study large social groupings of parallel or contrasting human types and choices; and they frequently diminish or eliminate the need for or the impact of star presences and star performances.

The integrative principles of the American talkie have been challenged or expanded in ways other than by creating exciting, rhythmic oases of imagistic succession in a desert of dialogue and concentrated visual imagery. One is the change noted by Bazin: the development of a richer, deeper, more scattered image that prolongs the literal succession of frames and subordinates the imagistic succession of shots.[3] This method allows the eye to take in the more scattered and enriching visual details of a single shot without distracting the ear from the dialogue by bombarding us with a conflicting succession of visual meanings. This method of deep-focus photography, first manipulated consistently and consciously by Renoir in the early and mid-1930s, then taken up by Wyler, Welles, and others in the late 1930s–early '40s (often dominated by Gregg Toland's camera, which composed in depth), finally ruled supreme with the conversion to the wide screen in the 1950s. The integrative principle dominates that very telephone-bedroom shot in *Nashville*. Despite the stasis of the frame and the prolonged literal succession, the shot is neither single nor static. There is a deliberate counterpoint in the shot between the two women on the boy's mind (mother in the foreground on the phone, sex object in the rearground near his bed), and the shot encourages (indeed, demands) the viewer's comparing the ironic juxtaposition of these two visual planes and these two kinds of male-female relationships.

But the very parenthetic tension in that last sentence raises a question about a Bazinian claim that has never been properly tested.[4] Bazin's view (echoed by both Charles Barr and Victor Perkins) is that the scattered compositional principle of the shot-in-depth allows the viewer to exercise more freedom, to exercise free will in ascertaining the significant elements of the shot. Bazin identifies his "conviction" in a shot with his ability to assimilate its "meaning," its significant elements, for himself. The simple and concentrated shot (as in either Eisenstein's montage or the American talkie) picks out meaning for the viewer, leaving no freedom to deduce it for ourselves.* Behind such a view are a number of moral and political assumptions. Bazin clearly sees our interpreting the scattered image as an exercise in both political democracy and Christian free will, as opposed to our enslavement by the tyrannical propaganda of the unambiguous image. But is Bazin's claim even true? Is there any more choice in a scattered image than in a concentrated one, if the images have been properly constructed? Can't art itself be defined as the elimination of choice, chance, and freedom?

In *Nashville* what freedom have we in that boarding house shot to overlook the juxtaposition of two "women" in the frame (the one present visually, the other only by implication)? Well, we have the freedom to miss it. But then we have that same freedom in any shot. For example, in the Thatcher sequence of *Citizen Kane* there is a highly respected and effective shot-in-depth: the Kane parents discuss Charles's future with Thatcher while the young boy plays in the snow outside the house. The boy's play is both audible and visible through an open window; he plays in the snow, perhaps a hundred yards from the lens, but that joyful playing occupies dead center of the frame, bracketed by the adult faces in the foreground. What freedom have we to ignore the tension between foreground and rearground? To fail to realize that little Charles is a total outsider to this discussion, and yet his future, which will remove him from the snow and the play, will result from this discussion? And that his future is the subject of the movie?

In *Potemkin's* concentrated images of three stone lions we certainly do less interpretive work with each image. But then each image lasts only a second or less (eleven, ten, and seventeen frames respectively).

---

* In order for Bazin (and others) to strip freedom of choice from the Eisenstein image, they must posit his simple "stone lion" images as typical, rather than the complex compositional patterns of the images on the Odessa Steps. This choice is neither accurate nor fair.

Citizen Kane: the shot in depth. As Thatcher discusses Charles' future with his parents, the boy's play is visible through a distant window. In Kane's adulthood, the same shot ironically recurs: Leland and Bernstein discuss Kane's integrity and commitment while his reflection dances in a window. *Courtesy Janus Films*

We have a great deal of interpretative freedom, however, in determining what the succession of these three juxtaposed images means (or implies). So much freedom, in fact, that no two critics agree exactly about what these rising lions symbolize (although they all agree that some kind of rising force or other is implied). In responding to this interpretive freedom with *Potemkin*'s lions, Victor Perkins suggests that the stone lions give us ambiguity without freedom, while the shot-in-depth gives us freedom without ambiguity.[5] If there is only a single, unambiguous way to "read" a shot, I don't see how this process relates to any acceptable definition of freedom.

And how about Woody Allen's parody of the identical lions in *Love and Death?* With one slight difference. Rather than showing us the first lion asleep, the second lion sitting, and the third standing erect (as Eisenstein did), Allen's first lion sits, his second stands erect, and his third lies asleep (dazed, tongue hanging out, pooped). Obviously, Allen's parody-montage (which he flashes during a sexual encounter) implies Boris's sexual arousal and performance, followed by his postcoital collapse from exhaustion. Have we no freedom with Allen's sequence?

First, we have the freedom to make a connection between the previous action (a sexual encounter) and the three positions of the stone lions. The movie's structural succession demands that we make some connection (since the lions appear out of the blue), but we are free to make any connection we want (including the wrong ones), just as we are in *Nashville*, *Potemkin*, and *Citizen Kane*. We are also free to make none at all—and a certain percentage of the audience probably saw the lions as some goofy Woody Allen irrelevancy.

Second, we are free to make a connection between these lions and their progenitors in *Potemkin*—a choice requiring us both to know that Eisenstein used three lions and (if we are to make the fullest connection) to know the order of the three positions, since Eisenstein's sequence of "erection" is converted into Allen's sequence of "exhaustion." Probably, a fair percentage of the audience failed to make the full and complete connection between Woody Allen's lions, their precise order, their sexual imagery, and *Potemkin*'s. So Allen's parody allows the audience the freedom to understand as much of the device as it can, on whatever level it can. So do *Potemkin*, *Nashville*, and *Kane*. To claim that a shot-in-depth gives the audience more interpretive freedom than a metaphoric montage sequence would be parallel to the claim that a painting of a landscape gives us more interpretive freedom (because we must assimilate its elements, which exist simultaneously in space) than a poetic description of that landscape (because the poet breaks the wholeness of nature into bits and pushes the individual words at us, one by one).

There is a similar kind of freedom in one of those concentrated images of a human face in a typical Hollywood talkie. The viewer has the freedom to perceive however much is going on under the placid and mysterious surface of, say, Garbo's face, and the sensitivity of the viewer (and the viewer's sensitivity to Garbo) will determine how much of that freedom he can exercise. The fact that Kenneth Tynan and Roland Barthes can write whole pieces on the semiotic richness of Garbo's face and others can look at that face without seeing anything more than just a pretty face is proof of the kind of freedom we have with one of these concentrated images. There is simply no kind of image that does not allow us to exercise whatever powers of perception or sensitivity we might have—not to mention our freedom to integrate those images with the film's systems of succession. Every cinema shot is a mixture of freedom and control, plan and accident. The artist controls the dominant and primary function, information, and effect of the shot, while we, the viewers, are free to perceive, notice, or find anything else in the shot that we wish or can. Nor does the integration of explicit dialogue limit our freedom, for we are then free to discover or perceive or feel any of the contrapuntal or harmonic complexities in the interplay of image, succession, and sound.

But if the fact is that we are no *less* free to exercise whatever individualities of judgment and perception that we possess, the contrary fact is equally true: we are no *more* free to exercise them. Although the content of one of these scattered images appears to be more random, the director has carefully planned it so that it conveys its primary and essential information while, at the same time, throwing up a smoke screen of apparent artlessness and randomness. The appearance of accident and unselectivity in such a shot is a stylistic and rhetorical choice—like the use of the hand-held camera and lens flare—to convince the viewer (gain his or her conviction) that the event is real and natural rather than artificial and contrived. To produce such an effect is the result of careful integrative decisions in "choreographing" the objects, activity, and composition in the content of the image.

But such an integrative decision is no freer nor more artless than its opposite, concentrated effect—as can be made clear with an analogy to the theater. One way to focus our attention in the theater is to shrink the human action and speech onstage into a tiny spot of light. When Büchner's Woyzeck or Brecht's Baal stands alone to soliloquize, the stage lighting inevitably shrinks so that he fills a single pool of light. But in Chekhov, in which a whole society of human beings express their feelings and fears alternately and consecutively, the lighting generally remains bright and even, so as to include the entire society onstage. Within this evenness, however, both Chekhov and the director of the production orchestrate the confessional moments so that they seem to speak to and intensify one another, and so that we receive the information of each one without divorcing any of them from one another. What the Chekhov method loses in rhapsodic intensity and shattering revelation it gains in irony, subtlety, and breadth.

Similarly, these scattered cinema images are carefully orchestrated to catch the eye, ear, and attention of the viewer at precisely the moment when they should while, at the same time, appearing so random and accidental that the viewer feels he is exercising his own choice. When listening to a symphony, I might feel that I have isolated the unique solo passage of a flute or clarinet for myself, although the composer or conductor has carefully smuggled that solo passage into the orchestral fabric to be noticed at precisely that time. So, too, the viewer of one of these scattered cinema images might operate under the illusion that he has selected the meaning in that image. (And that illusion is an undeniable potential source of our conviction in that moment.)

But the irony of this scattered randomness is that its artlessness is extremely artful; the cinema demonstrates yet again the tension between art and nature that is at its essence and is capable of infinite variations and extensions. With a moviemaker like Miklós Jancsó, his scattered, "artless" images are often so lengthy (perhaps ten minutes), so complex in their patterns of movement, so complicated in their camera activities of tracking, panning, tilting, and zooming, that I am repeatedly amazed that the director can choreograph so much activity within a single shot. But this amazement does not convince me that Jancsó has eliminated artifice from the cinema simply because he does not make a cut; on the contrary, his shots seem magnificent contrivances—at least and as obviously artificial as the entire painted universe of *The Cabinet of Dr. Caligari* or Mickey Mouse.

A second way to challenge the integrative assumption that words and imagistic succession make competitive and mutually exclusive demands on the viewer's attention is to bombard the viewer's senses with these conflicting stimuli in the hope of achieving some other kind of stimulation from the bombardment. This deliberate oversaturation of the senses is the method of many experimental films (say, Bruce Baillie's *Quick Billy,* which combines words, split screens, montage, music, color symbolism, superimpositions, and bizarrely personal images at the same time). It is also the method of several popular movies (most notably the climactic space ride of *2001* or Ken Russell's *Tommy,* which seems a slick, pop, decorative bastardization of the Baillie saturation effect).

One of the clear assumptions of the oversaturated Baillie integration is that the viewer cannot "get" the entire experience of the film in a single viewing. He or she can get an atmosphere, a feel, a texture, an occasional glimmer of meaning perhaps, but not "get" the entire system of the film, which makes its significance and meaning comprehensible and full. To comprehend the experience of the whole film, to "read" everything that has been built into it, requires repeated viewing. It also requires stopping the projector to study individual frames—in effect halting the cinema's succession and converting the individual image into a still-life composition. Descriptions of certain oversaturated films (for example, P. Adams Sitney's careful analyses of the films of Gregory Markopoulos, who strings together perhaps thirty-five successive shots, each only one or two frames long) are impossible without making cinema into not cinema. Although the same principle might underlie the oversaturation and bombardment of *Tommy*, there are those who feel that its blastingly sensual surface is all that there is to the film, and to "get" that at first viewing is to "get" everything the movie has to offer. In this sense, *Tommy*'s integration would be no different from that of *Monterey Pop* (or some other purely musical-performance rock film), in which the sights and sounds *are* the experience.

For the sake of narrative as the dominant principle of structural succession, any number of other affective cinematic elements of succession, image, and sound must be subordinated and sacrificed. In a movie (a filmed narrative) the individual image exists not solely for itself but also to serve the structural succession in which it functions and the "course" of which it somehow advances. The film that defines its structural succession solely in terms of integrating image, imagistic succession, and sound (like Breer, Fischinger, Baillie, and perhaps *Tommy*) need not subordinate the power of any purely kinetic and sensual element for the sake of mimesis. But in making this purely kinetic integration, the cinema almost necessarily makes another sacrifice—it seems to restrict the length of time that this time-art can fully, effectively, and legitimately generate.

Narrative films often have little difficulty filling their two-hour ($\pm$ twenty minutes) boundaries, maintaining intense audience interest throughout (when they are properly built—and often even when they are not). Although non-narrative films occasionally last more than an hour, they much more frequently last less than twenty minutes.* The fascinat-

---

* I must confess to finding the longest non-narrative films extremely trying—whereas I find the shorter ones consistently fascinating, fulfilling, and fulfilled. And I am not alone. The appreciation and enjoyment of the lengthy non-narrative films is a connoisseur's pleasure—and the number of connoisseurs is a very small one.

ing succession of kinesis and perception loses its fascination once we perceive the kinetic design and perceptual point. Narrative structure has been one of the consistent means for the time-arts to extend the duration of their temporal experience. Lyric poems, symphonic music, "pure" dance, expository essays, and "absurd" drama have tended to fulfill much shorter temporal structures than narrative poetry, opera and mass, narrative ballet, narrative fiction, and linear drama. By imprisoning our attention and imagination within the surrogate existence of a mimetic universe of art, narrative is capable of generating the longest, largest works of time-art, which keep our intense interest despite their length and even increase our interest as they progress and extend themselves. But the integration that narrative cinema demands is the sacrifice of the purely kinetic effects of succession, image, and sound for the cumulative mimetic power of structural succession.

The power of narrative over the human imagination becomes clear in that it controls and organizes our attention not just the first time we experience a movie. (Even an unconvincing narrative that we recognize as flaccid and fatuous often succeeds in arresting us with its basic narrative question: What is going to happen next?) But narrative interest also succeeds in exercising an identical control on repeated viewings of the same movie. The customary way to explain the fact that narratives can bear experiencing more than once is to claim that we perpetually discover new interests and pleasures with each viewing—new details of style, new insights into personality, new complexities of structure. Well, we certainly do. But even more interesting to me is that we rediscover the *same* interests and pleasures each time we experience a rich and compelling narrative. Although I know very well that the image of a sled will conclude the quest in *Kane* (or that Nora will slam the door in *A Doll's House*, or that little Miles's heart will unexpectedly cease to beat), I still participate experientially in these processes as if I did not know what I obviously know. This virginal participation in the narrative experience is an essential characteristic of narrative itself, indicating its pervasive structural power. Further, it is a characteristic of narrative in any medium—novel, play, or cinema—all of which are capable of engaging us with an experience that feels fresh and new despite the number of times we have already experienced it.

How is this possible? Obviously, because the way we know what a narrative is about is not the way we know it as we experience it. My knowledge of *Citizen Kane* (I could perhaps discourse for pages on its content—and I have) is very different from my knowledge of it as I "live through" it. The two kinds of knowing (cognitive and experiential) are responsible not only for the perpetual freshness of "old" themes in narratives, but also for the perpetual freshness of repetitive narrative experiences themselves. To take advantage of this general power of narrative, the cinema must subordinate its equally powerful kinetic possibilities to the flow of structural succession.

The integrative principle of most movies, therefore, assumes that the various cinematic elements must be ordered, subordinated, and arranged so that the narrative will be compelling and comprehensible upon first viewing (and upon any subsequent viewings)—without halting the temporal flow that is the essence of narrative. The opposite integrative principle—the oversaturation of kinetic effects, a deliberate refusal to order and integrate—either assumes that the work cannot possibly be comprehended and felt without repeated study (which would then make the film like a painting, in which the study is the experience) or assumes that the kinetic overstimulation and oversaturation *is* the experience of that work and there is nothing further to be comprehended.

The style and vision of a cinema artist can usually be equated with his integrative choice in mixing his particular cinematic compound. Chaplin, for example, eliminates the effects of imagistic succession, prolonging our concentration on the literal succession of frames. Within such a literal succession, the evocative and affective qualities of the individual images necessarily shoulder the heaviest burden of communicative responsibility. Within those images, Chaplin deliberately curtails the purely kinetic, atmospheric, and potentially distracting possibilities in their filming and toning. His lighting is generally bright and functional; his camera position is usually intimate enough so that we can see Charlie well, but distant enough so that we can see all or most of him. However, Chaplin's manipulation of camera perspective is one of his subtlest yet most effective cinematic choices. One of the reasons that his shooting ratios (the amount of footage exposed compared to the amount used in the finished work) were so high (the highest in cinema history, perhaps 100 to 1, as opposed to the 10 to 1 of conventional movie shooting and 5 to 1 of television filming) was that he experimented with the camera's distance and perspective until he was sure that it had found the exactly right place to film and communicate the action.

Chaplin's reducing our attention on the filming and toning of the image places the communicative responsibility on the content of his images. And here, too, Chaplin makes an integrative decision that is consistent with the others: he eliminates the attraction of the peripheral so that the objects, composition, and activity of the image's content draw our attention to the focal figure (Charlie)—what he is doing and with or to what. Chaplin then integrates these concentrated and fully developed images into a pattern of structural succession that is not a linear story—a structure which would not suit the length and fullness of Chaplin's image-vignettes. Chaplin's structural succession is a thematic "journey" (a journey either in space or in the mind or both) which compares and contrasts each of these extended image-vignettes that Chaplin's method allows us (indeed, forces us) to see so fully and so well. And when Chaplin integrated sound into the compound (particularly in *City Lights* and *Modern Times*), he used it to illuminate and comment upon the content and activity in each of his extended images.

Conversely, Keaton's integration of the cinema's elements takes account of the effects of both image and succession—in particular, of the differing probabilities, credibility, and delights of each system. The difference between his movie-montage sequence in *Sherlock Jr.* and the breathlessly exciting surprises of its climactic chase is the difference between two opposite integrative principles. The former sequence—Buster trapped in a universe of movie montage—is a perfect dissertation on the differences between the temporal and spatial continuity of the natural universe and the temporal and spatial successiveness of the cinema universe. While Buster maintains his human singleness and continuity, the movie environment surrounding him changes suddenly and uncontrollably. Although he remains in the same "place" (the same relative compositional space within the frame), the location and the image change relentlessly around him—from garden to mountaintop, to ocean shore, to desert, to snowbank, to lions' lair. Keaton knows that the instantaniety of succeeding images—of switching instantly to a different time or place—is one of the fascinating, unique, and unnatural delights of cinema.

But he also knows (as he reveals in the movie's later chase sequence and in every one of his miraculous stunts in every movie) that a magnificent feat of physical skill, an incredible movie stunt, seems magnificently "incredible but true" only if the cinema suppresses its delights of succession to show the entire, unfaked stunt actually performed in a single continuous shot. Although Keaton used editing to drive the rhythms of *Sherlock Jr.*'s climactic chase (and rhythm is another of the powers of imagistic succession), he performs his amazing stunts in single images without a cut, realizing that the incredible feat of physical skill required the same kind of uninterrupted literal succession of frames as did the supple subtlety of Chaplin's mime.[6]

The variant types of experimental films also owe their variation to differences in integrative choices. Our conviction in the complexity of a "design" film (or "graphic" film) such as Fischinger's, Breer's, Lye's, or Whitney's is generally the product of its integrating interestingly evolving visual patterns with a structural succession that develops and complicates its evolution and with a musical score that supports the rhythms and tones of those evolving shapes and colors. But an interesting difference between Oskar Fischinger's integration and John Whitney's is that whereas Whitney's visual patterns are more precise, mathematical, and symmetrical than Fischinger's (for Whitney generates his patterns and colors by computer rather than by brush), Fischinger's musical scores tend to be more stately, formally structured, and severe. Fischinger uses tightly structured musical compositions—as Bach Brandenburg Concertos, Wagnerian themes, even "The Stars and Stripes Forever"—while Whitney uses much looser, freer music—totally improvisatory jazz, or an impromptu Indian raga. The integration of loose visual forms with tighter music in Fischinger contrasts with Whitney's integration of tight visual forms and loose music.

Len Lye's films feel much freer and looser than both, combining his free-flowing drawn-on-film forms with popular music and jazz. Lye's visual forms are far less austere and formal than those of Fischinger, an animator who painted his patterns in very precise compositions and then photographed them; Lye drew his casual squiggles, lines, and blotches directly on the celluloid itself. Norman McLaren, who also draws directly on celluloid, makes films that are frequently humorous and clever integrations of sights and sounds, for he also has drawn his sound tracks. Since the cinema produces sounds by shining a light beam through visual patterns, it in effect produces sound in the same way it produces an image. So there is no reason why the visual patterns of the sound track cannot be drawn by hand, rather than recorded by machine—just as the visual images can be drawn directly on the celluloid itself. McLaren achieves a delightfully clever and comic counterpoint between the look of the forms he draws for his images and the sounds they produce when drawn on the track—a kind of cinematic onomatopoeia in which abstract forms sound the way they look.

Our conviction in the richness of a perceptual film (Brakhage's, Baillie's, Snow's) does not result from the pure delight in the visual-musical kinesis (as in graphic films), but in the allusive and elusive relationship of the film's kinetic-mimetic elements to human sensation, perception, and experience. Maya Deren's integration in *Meshes of the Afternoon* dissolves objective reality of time and space into a surreal dream world (that either may or may not be a dream), a world that is clearly neither ordinary reality nor purely a dream, but some kind of subjective and imaginative zone between them. It is a world of pure sensation and imagination which invites us to use our own senses and imaginations in experiencing it, our own semiconscious semidreams, rather than depicting either a lucid "imitation of a human action" or a pure series of pleasantly evolving designs.

The effects and resonances of this film are attributable not to Maya Deren's surprising images but to the bizarre surprises of her imagistic and structural succession. To summarize the film briefly, a woman enters a house to examine it and some of its objects (a key, a flower, a knife, a phonograph, a telephone, a bed, a loaf of bread). She then glimpses another woman outdoors who looks exactly like herself (is she dreaming or awake?), and who enters the same house again to examine the same or similar objects in a similar way. And then this second woman sees a third woman (exactly like herself) do the same thing again. The three female selves (all played by Maya Deren) eventually meet one another and share the same frame around a dining-room table. Then a man enters that same house in a similar way to begin a sexual encounter with one of the female selves. Except when he enters the house a second time, he finds the woman (or one of the women) apparently dead, her throat cut, draped with seaweed. The experience of *Meshes of the Afternoon* feels very much like attempting to get at the essence of a clever series of Chinese boxes—ripping off the lid of one box to find another box inside, and then tearing off that cover to find another box, and so on *ad infinitum*.

Now there is nothing about the individual images of the film that produce this experience. Deren uses no distortion lenses (an occasional wide-angle lens or unfamiliar camera angle disorients our eye very slightly and subtly), no superimpositions, no scratches on the emulsion. We can see the photographic objects crisply and well. The bizarre element of Deren's integration is the way the images succeed one another. Why do they do so? What is the coherent "story" in this structure that repeatedly starts to make narrative sense only to dissolve into mystery? What is the significance of the objects that recur as if they had significance without ever explaining their significance?

In one sequence the woman slashes at the man with a knife only to shatter his face as if it were a mirror; it has indeed been his face reflected in a mirror, and, as it shatters, its fragments fall on a desolate beach; the tide of that beach then washes the glass fragments that began as a man's face in a woman's bedroom. In another sequence, a foot takes four continuous and rhythmic steps, except that the physical environment changes (from sand, to grass, to mud, to carpet) during each apparently continu-

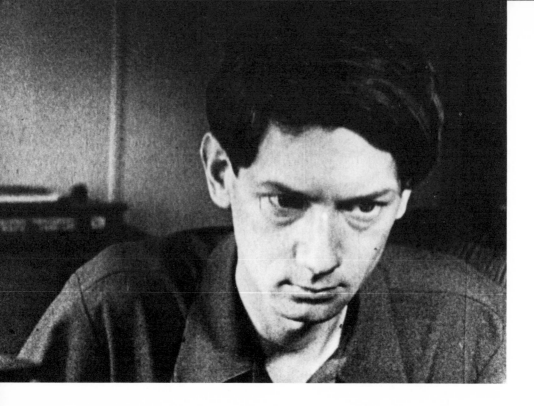

Meshes of the Afternoon: the mysteriousness of its structural succession. Inside a bedroom, the man's face (Alexander Hammid) shatters like a mirror to reveal the ocean through its gaping hole; the tide then washes the shards of his mirrored face.

ous step (as in the montage sequence of *Sherlock Jr.*). Such sequences reveal that Deren's integration makes a successive cinema unity out of individual fragments that make no temporal, spatial, or narrative sense in natural or rational terms. (Precisely the same could be said of the classic Dali-Buñuel collaboration, *Un Chien andalou*, which makes a similar integrative choice.)

On the other hand, Bruce Baillie's *Quick Billy* or Stan Brakhage's *Dog Star Man* oversaturate and overstimulate our senses with their complexities of color, design, superimposition, cutting, and split screen, not simply to delight us with kinesis but to depict their own spiritual autobiographies (the means of making their inner lives manifest and visible to us and to themselves). The visual kinesis alludes to their own feelings and perceptions, and the elusively successive and superimposed images invite us to "tune in" to their inner lives and, in the process, to "tune in" to our own. Our impression of richness about the integrations of such perceptual films depends on whether they seem to extend or expand our perception of inner realities (psychological, emotional, sexual), of outer realities (social, natural), or both.

Dog Star Man produces this experience by its integrating complexities of both succession and image. Like *Meshes of the Afternoon*, Brakhage's imagistic and structural successions do not produce a coherent narrative but present recurring and rhythmic patterns and motifs. A man (the film's title character) climbs a snowy hill with a dog. His ascent is interrupted by an occasional tumble. At the film's conclusion the man chops wood (a metaphor for building, constructing? for splicing images of film?). There are shots of the sun (the star of the title, perhaps?), of trees, of different seasons, of an infant (and the innocent, virginal way it sees the world as sparkling shapes), of sexual organs. Despite these recurring images—and their cosmological implications—the film, like Deren's, makes no narrative sense.

But unlike Deren's teasing suggestions of continuity, Brakhage's film aggressively proclaims it will make none by doing violence both to our expectations about literal succession (not simply to those of imagistic and structural suggestion, as Deren did) and to the filming and toning of the images themselves. Brakhage plays with literal succession by using both accelerated and slow motion, by prolonging the literal succession of some shots of extraordinary lengths, and, conversely, by making other images as brief as a single frame. He does violence to the image by tinting it, by using anamorphic distortion, by deliberately under or overexposing it, by using multiple levels of superimposition, by alternating between positive and negative or monochrome and color, by incorporating lens flare, and even by making individual frames as collages of other bits of cinema images. These integrative decisions produce the oversaturation and sensual bombardment of the Brakhage experience.

Indeed, such differences in integrative principles account not just for differences in style, but even for the ways that two cinema artists view the world and human experience. Many of the differences between the artistic "visions" of Ingmar Bergman and Luis Buñuel, the differing ways they view human and social experience, can be traced to the differing ways they integrate the cinema's elements. Bergman's primary source of information and power is his manipulation of the individual image. The visual qualities of the image—its toning, composition, décor, human faces and figures, color, activity—are his primary tools for illuminating his meaning and gaining our conviction. Bergman served his apprenticeship in the theater, and he has refused to desert the stage for the cinema exclusively. So it is not surprising that to the communicative power of the individual image he adds the specific evocations and meanings of dialogue, which integrate well with the extended image.

Not that Bergman does not occasionally use the effects of cinema succession—for example, the rhythmically terrifying and suspenseful cutting in the attic sequence of *The Magician* or the breakfast-table sequence of *Persona*, in which he visually and aurally "plays back" the identical dialogue scene three times, blending the speaker and listener into a single face. But when Bergman manipulates the surprises of imagistic succession, he does so in a deliberately tricky way that calls attention to the tricks and artifice of his art. Bergman rather consciously transposes the human action out of the ordinary key of objective, material reality and into a special and subjective key of imagination, irrationality, and artifice. And the difference between these two cinematic integrations—the usual reliance on the image as opposed to the occasional tricks of succession—mirrors the difference between the two opposite poles of reality and imagination that Bergman sees in human experience: objective reality as opposed to the subjective perception of it, human reason as opposed to the human imagination which produces works of art. These thematic contrasts dominate each of Bergman's movies, yet the contrast comes to life in the movies not just because of its embodiment in images, dialogue, characters, and structures, but because his integrating the cinema elements of image and succession also conveys the distinction between objective reality and the subjective perceiving and experiencing of it.

Buñuel, however, uses the effects of cinema succession to attack the notion that objective and subjective perception can be differentiated at all. Buñuel movies are often lacking in many of the cinematic virtues: the acting frequently runs from poor to indifferent; the costumes, sets, and décor are frequently careless or undistinguished (especially in the Mexican movies); his composition is often strictly functional rather than striking. All these apparent "deficiencies" are symptomatic of his inattention to the evocative richness of the individual image (precisely the qualities at which Bergman excels).

But Buñuel deliberately subordinates the evocations of the image to the surprises of imagistic and structural succession. Primarily because an implication of the stable, carefully textured and arranged image (coupled with extending its length in the literal succession of frames) is that both space and time are stable. For Buñuel, the stable cinema image responds to the comfortable human assumption that space and time are indeed objective, measurable, and controllable. But he views all human experience as a subjective fantasy—our imposing our views, assumptions, and values on experience, which is essentially neutral or even chaotic.

In Buñuel movies, this subjective fantasy often takes the form of a single character's personal vision of experience: the lecher's paranoia in *El*, Belle's fantasy life in *Belle de Jour*, which may or may not be a fantasy. But even more interesting are the Buñuel movies in which he exposes the communal fantasies that pass for objective reality: that heresy and its opposite ("true" knowledge) exist (in *The Milky Way*); that religion (established or personal) is an ideal or even suitable response to the human condition (in *Viridiana*); that the word "liberty" responds to some actual or possible quality that exists in human society and the human condition (*Le Fantôme de la liberté*).

Like Georges Méliès, Buñuel knows what miraculous things the cinema can achieve by stopping the camera and starting it again. Unlike Méliès, Buñuel passes off these magical, synthetic tricks as ordinary realities. By simply making a cut he brings people into rooms who could not possibly have got there by any physical means (by entering through a door, window, or whatever), but could get there only by means of the cinema's imagistic succession. Buñuel manipulates structural succession not only by yoking together vignettes that make no linear or temporal sense (like Chaplin's vignettes, they make thematic sense), but by composing each of those vignettes as inexplicable jumbles of time, space, and events. The temporal-spatial-logical jumble of the Buñuel movie reflects a reality in which imagination, fantasy, and idea are as solid and ordinary realities as any.

While Bergman's movies show human beings wrestling with problems that seem both serious and solid (like his handling of the image itself), Buñuel sees both seriousness and solidity as human fantasies and fictions. His movies are a bit like W. C. Fields's *Never Give a Sucker an Even Break*—a burlesque on the orderly, "well-made" movie—because Buñuel believes that such a movie answers to a vision of life as orderly and well-made. Of course, there is gleeful, iconoclastic humor in Buñuel's method (as there is in both Fields and the classic surrealists); the act of destruction is an act of joyful liberation. Bergman's humor is a bitterly ironic *leitmotif* in movies that are generally deadly earnest, questing, and serious. Buñuel attaches absolutely no importance to being earnest or serious, for seriousness is another of the communal fantasies that human beings use to impose meaning on life.

In Buñuel's view, his games with imagistic and structural succession, in which nothing follows spatially, temporally, or narratively (despite, like Maya Deren, his teasing promises that something *might* follow and make sense), accurately mirror reality and nature (of which all our views and about which all our values are instilled in us from birth by parents, school, church, culture, and the rest). The "logical," linear successions of images and events that organize most movies are merely the unconscious products of such teaching. For Buñuel to devote more care and attention to the spatial qualities, to the image, in his movies would be a kind of philosophical contradiction—like the contempt for production values in the joyous Marx Brothers movies at Paramount, which turned into reverentially grand production numbers in their MGM movies (and thereupon swallowed the spirit of the helpless Marxes).

Whether you prefer Bergman's movies to Buñuel's (and whether you find them more "cinematic") may well depend on how much importance you attach to the visual texturing and subtlety of the individual image. It may also depend on whether you understand Buñuel's principles (or antiprinciples) of succession and whether you sympathize with that vision of human experience. And the very difference between these two kinds of criteria in the two previous sentences indicates that there is more to cinema's integration than its simply synthesizing the various cinema elements into effective, evocative, illuminating compounds (compounds that are both comprehensible and compelling).

Now, one of the recent trends in cinema theory is to concentrate exclusively on this compounding of elements rather than on what such compounds imply about human experience and whether such implications are interesting or boring, intelligent or stupid, relevant or worthless to our own views of human experience. Both Andrew Tudor and Victor Perkins insist that cinema theory must leave off normative prescriptions to illuminate the "synthetic" blends of various films and filmmakers.[7] Even that metaphor of synthesis echoes my metaphors of elements, compounds, and integrations. Behind the notions of both synthesis and of integration is an analogy to chemistry—that the cinematic work is a complex "universe" composed of many elements that can be mixed and compounded in an infinite number of ways. Just as there are no abstractly better or worse chemical compounds, there are no cinematic compounds that are necessarily better or worse than any others.

Although this view is certainly true in the abstract, there are certain chemical compounds that are better than others at doing certain things (for example, DDT kills insects better than water does) and there are certain chemical compounds that we might find pleasanter than others (for example, gin tastes better than DDT, although for some Scotch tastes better than gin and for others milk tastes better than either). Although the notions of both synthesis and the integration of elements express the idea that the cinema integrates its various elements with one another, it does not convey the fact that the cinema also integrates its elements with us. Any full discussion of the cinema's integration must consider both the internal integration of its elements and the integration of the work with the values and perceptions of its receivers.

THE MOVIE MICROCOSM

In his valuable theoretical study *Film as Film*, Victor Perkins argues against discussing movies except as self-contained universes, as microcosms of "balance, coherence, and complexity."[8] Perkins maintains that if the movie microcosm is to be discussed *as film* (or as movie), it can be only in terms of its own internal integration, in terms of the "meaningful interaction of [its] elements." He defines "the normal function of the director" as

> not to devise stories and not to construct painterly patterns but to realize given material and organize it into significant form. In order to comprehend whole meanings, rather than those parts of the meaning which are present in verbal synopsis or visual code, attention must be paid to the whole content of shot, sequence, and film.[9]

This "attention . . . to the whole" is of course an implication of my own discussion in the past several chapters as well.

Although I strongly support the Perkins view so far as it goes, it really does not go very far. For it leaves something important out of the "meaningful" cinema experience (indeed, of the experiencing of any art). To put Perkins's view in more common terms, he urges us to pay close attention to the particular way each particular cat has been skinned. But his insistence on accepting the "given material" ignores such questions as whether that particular cat was worth the skinning at all, or whether another kind of cat or even a rabbit might have been more worth skinning. To leave these civeted metaphors, Perkins's view excludes two important questions from a consideration of film *as film:* (1) whether the movie has anything to do with matters we consider significant, relevant, or "meaningful" outside the movie; and (2) whether the movie could have been done more "meaningfully" in some other way or in some other art or whether it has already been done more "meaningfully" in another movie or some other art.

Perkins's limited idea of a "meaningful" interaction of artistic elements is especially clear in his longest chapter, "The World and Its Image," in which he specifically examines those movies he considers exemplary and significant syntheses of balance, coherence, and complexity. Just a list of titles might be revealing: *The Courtship of Eddie's Father, Marnie, Johnny Guitar, Carmen Jones, Lord Jim* (the movie—directed by Richard Brooks), *Rebel Without a Cause, Elmer Gantry, The Cardinal, Rope, The River of No Return, Exodus, Psycho*. The list reveals a number of things—a fondness for Hitchcock, Nicholas Ray, Otto Preminger, and

Richard Brooks; a general preference for color, the wide screen, and the mid-fifties to early sixties; a provocative and deliberate attempt to avoid the prewar American masters and the postwar European ones. Although the list smells more than faintly of the *auteur*ist line, it is entirely to Perkins's credit that he discusses these films without the vague cliché and aggressive assertion that often pass for *auteur* "criticism." Perkins's discussion of these movies is extremely detailed and careful, indeed convincing that a very great craft and conception operate in each of the scenes he discusses.

Despite this depth, detail, and insight, however, I come away from this chapter with the same general opinions about the movies that I took into it: one of them (*Psycho*) seems a genuine masterwork;* several others (in particular, Nicholas Ray's) appear to be entertaining, well-crafted works that moved and shook me; but most of the rest seem banal abominations that are, at best, well crafted (and many of them don't even seem to satisfy my understanding of the term "well crafted"). Indeed, if I recognized Perkins's titles as a truly representative sampling of the best that the movie art had attained, I would not spend much time watching or writing about movies. So let me spend a bit more time examining why I cannot see the greatness that Perkins does in these movies. Perhaps it will illuminate the final and ultimate integration of our cinema experiences.

Perkins spends some 1,200 words analyzing a single scene in Otto Preminger's *Carmen Jones*—the interrelation of camera placement, cutting, physical movement, music, and dramatic function as Carmen entices Joe while riding with him in a jeep.[10] Perkins carefully traces the way that a shift in camera position reveals an internal, psychological moment of liberation; he traces the way that the compositions of the individual images reveal the values and attitudes of the two human participants; he traces the way that the resonances of the actors (in particular, Dorothy Dandridge's "abundant sensuality") reveal the tension and conflict between them. Let me accept, for the moment anyway, that Preminger's scene actually contains these revelations and that they are genuinely revealing.

Unfortunately, Perkins does not speak to any of my difficulties with this scene. First, do I find Dorothy Dandridge sensual at all (abundant or otherwise) when I know that she is not singing with her own voice (for I have heard her own "pop" singing voice, and the voice that now

---

* In all fairness to Perkins, let me mention that his longest discussion in the chapter (of some eight pages) is of *Psycho*. This indicates to me that Perkins, like most of us, can discuss something most fully and lengthily when he has something worth discussing.

issues from her lips is not the voice that I know she has)? The Bizet music demanded a dubbed soprano. Second, do I find Harry Belafonte (the Joe in the jeep) anything but a wooden nonpresence? His contemporary popularity as a sexy folk and calypso singer seemed the only excuse for his movie "star"dom. Third, how do I ignore my social discomfort with the racial premise of this movie? It is a typical piece of white stereotyping: the shiftlessness and rampant sexuality of darkies. Fourth, how do I feel about this movie version of a previous Broadway stage version that already seemed to bastardize and vulgarize a very familiar, famous, and colorful opera? What do I think of "La Habañera" as a popular song called "Dat's Love"? Fifth, do I feel any psychological subtlety or texture in the sequence at all? A movie actress seems to do a typical musical number in a typical movie musical, accompanied by a full symphony orchestra. And so, finally, do I have any real *conviction* in the sensuality of the sequence (its raison d'être for Perkins)?

No, I find it an attempt to render sensuality (clearly Preminger's intention) that, for me, lacks all sensuality: the performers are wrong, the music is wrong, the conception is banal (or vulgar). Even the idea of sensuality behind the sequence seems a stock, Hollywoody, "literary" conception of sensuality—like D. W. Griffith's depictions of those Victorian abstractions of Sensuality and Sin. I have no conviction that the scene means what it purports to mean; it merely alludes to attitudes rather than making me feel and experience them.

Perkins's analysis is brilliant at finding what the scene would like to do to an audience. The fact that it fails to do it to me can be traced to a lack of connection between the attitudes and values behind the creation of this scene (in the creator's "mind") and my own attitudes and values toward those same issues. I simply cannot give Preminger an unchallenged and unquestioned right to manipulate this "given material"—especially since that "given" includes racial issues, Bizet, Belafonte, a dubbed Dandridge, the tension between artifice and internal psychology in any filmed musical number, and the problems of adapting stage material into filmed material. When Anna Karina (in *Vivre sa vie*) sings her sensual song in a poolroom, totally unaccompanied (no symphony orchestra behind her), using her own thin, tentative voice, moving sensually, spontaneously, improvisationally, in the process of hypnotizing one of the young players, I feel her hypnotic sensuality completely. I also feel that Godard understands what sensuality is and that he and I and everyone else who "buys" the scene understand it similarly. Preminger's idea of sensuality seems to manipulate the grossest Hollywood cliché, which begins with scarlet lipstick, rouge, and a cigarette—and pretty much ends there.

Immediately following his discussion of *Carmen Jones,* Perkins briefly discusses a single image from Richard Brooks's filmed version of *Lord Jim.*[11] Perkins develops the way that Brooks parallels the attitudes of his movie's protagonist (Jim) and antagonist (Brown)—revealing that they are the light and dark sides of a single coin.

> The hero, a dreamer haunted by his vision of an inhuman grandeur, is standing on a fog-bound raft in the middle of a river. By his side is Gentleman Brown, the cynical chief of a gang of cut-throats. Brown is trying to persuade Jim to arrange his escape from an ambush; his remarks repeatedly hint at bonds, recognized or obscured, that make Jim "one of us." While they talk, Jim, fair-haired and dressed in light colours, faces out across the water, raising his right hand to lean against the raft's guide-rail. Then Brown, a swarthy, black-bearded figure in bowler hat and dark suit, takes up the same position—except that he holds to the rail with his left hand.

Perkins admits that Brooks derives his image from the Conrad novel, from which the movie as a whole derives. But a question that he never asks (and a question which the attention to film *as film* excludes) is whether this movie (or any other movie) has done a "good" job in adapting this novel (or any other novel). Perkins would consider the common question Is the movie as good as the book? an illegitimate question.

Although there is a sense in which it might be illegitimate, the question also seems inevitable. It is impossible for most human beings to look at a movie only *as film*—as if movies were the only artistic experiences in the universe and artistic experiences were the only human activity. On any given evening, a human being can decide to see a movie, read a novel, go to a concert, stay at home to watch television or listen to music, or to do none of these things, but, instead, talk with friends, do chores around the house, go drinking in a bar, dancing in a discotheque, or simply to bed. To talk about film only *as film* would be parallel to talking about war exclusively as a series of strategies and tactical maneuvers—without considering such related phenomena as the fact that wars kill people, that they cost a lot of money in order to produce a lot of waste and destruction, and that they cause personal discomfort and social upheaval. Most people consider the cinema *as human experience,* not simply as cinema (although the consideration of the movie *as movie* is a necessary first step).

This relating of movie experiences to our general views of human experience seems especially appropriate, since, first, movies are very deeply rooted in social, natural, and emotional experience; and, second, movies often adapt works from other forms into cinema. Given the exis-

tence of both Conrad's *Lord Jim* and Brooks's *Lord Jim,* we have the
right to ask which is "better," since we have the choice to spend our time
with either (or both or neither). I found Perkins's reference to *Lord Jim*
especially astonishing since this particular movie seems the quintessential
Hollywood Disaster in adapting a Great Work of Serious Literature into
a movie (although Brooks's other Great Attempt, his adaptation of *The
Brothers Karamazov,* runs it a close race to the disaster line). Since so
many of us do compare our experience of the resulting movie with our
feelings about the richness of the novel (or play) from which it was
adapted, I think it useful to ask what we precisely are comparing—what
our personal evaluations ("as good as," "better than," or "worse than") of
two works really mean.

The usual argument that a movie adaptation is inferior to the book
cites omitted or undeveloped details of style and content: the movie left
out such-and-such characters and such-and-such events; it lacked the
dense or lovely prose style of the novel; it made the characters less subtle
and complex by reducing them to types or by making their feelings so
externally explicit; it lacked the intellectual probing of the book; it lacked
the texture of the novel because it kept the events of the plot without the
emotional and spiritual material that linked them; and so forth. All these
specific objections imply that the artistic microcosm of the movie seemed
less whole and less complex than the artistic microcosm from which the
movie was adapted.

There is obviously a good deal that is complex about the movie of
Lord Jim (and about any movie). The huge number of elements of
succession, image, and sound that any movie must integrate to "make
sense" (even if not good sense) guarantees that any cinematic work, no
matter how apparently simple, is an overwhelmingly complex compound
of both simultaneous and sequential techniques and devices. The budget-
ary immensities and technological difficulties of simply making a more or
less coherent work of cinema guarantee that any movie will be a more
complex integration of technological elements than any novel. Obviously,
then, to find the novel of *Lord Jim* more complex than the movie is not to
find it more complex technologically. Richard Brooks's *Lord Jim* is a vast,
wide-screen, color movie with stars, extras, scenic views, complex camera
strategies, hundreds of shots, mammoth scenes of staged spectacle, and
so forth.

To find this kind of technological dexterity and difficulty in a narrative
work of mimesis less complex than the interrelation of character, events,
prose, and style in Conrad's novel is perhaps a sign of a 2,500-year-old
Aristotelian prejudice—against the purely kinetic elements of spectacle

and melody. However, it might also be a sign of our demand that a mimetic work requiring our complete conviction owes its first obligation to the complexity and richness of its mimesis.* In cinema, if the kinesis does not serve and enrich our conviction in the mimesis of the narrative, it disrupts rather than aids the unity and density of that artistic microcosm.

If the microcosm of Conrad's *Lord Jim* feels more rich, complex, and whole than that of Richard Brooks's *Lord Jim,* it is because its mimesis is more rich, whole, and complex, and because its style enriches that mimesis rather than exists as a pleasant adornment to be admired in itself. In the Conrad novel, Jim is far more than "a dreamer haunted by his vision of inhuman grandeur" and Brown is far more than "the cynical chief of a gang of cut-throats." What is more about them is what is more about Conrad's novel.

If, conversely, the microcosm of Stephen Spielberg's *Jaws* feels richer than that of Peter Benchley's *Jaws* (as is true of so many not-Great, not-Serious, melodramatic novels that are adapted into cinema), it might be because it is more whole (stripping away Benchley's secondary and inessential interests in adulterous love affairs and the pettiness of local officials) and more complex (using the kinesis of cinema to make that melodramatic experience more concretely and more vicariously terrifying). And if Jack Clayton's *The Innocents* and Henry James's *The Turn of the Screw* feel equally rich, whole, and complex, it might be because the mimesis of the two works is equally rich, whole, and complex (their integrating either prose or cinema style with a careful handling of narrative point of view to spin a puzzling story about what might be actual phantoms or mere phantasms). A director's ability to "devise stories" is indeed an artistic virtue of a mimetic form that tells stories, and his ability to "construct painterly patterns" is indeed a virtue of a kinetic art that uses such patterns as one means to convey its stories and their resonances.

But because cinema is capable of an immense range of artistic intentions, from purest mimesis to purest kinesis, quite the opposite microcosmic principle of integration is responsible for the internal complexity and wholeness of cinematic works (like Breer's, Whitney's, or Fischinger's) devoted wholly to kinesis and visual perception. In these works, the ability to "construct painterly patterns" is essential to their power and appeal, for their makers define them as painterly patterns in motion. To

---

* Obviously, Verdi's *Otello* is less complex mimetically than Shakespeare's *Othello.* Why does no one ask if *Otello* is as good as *Othello?* Perhaps because the mimesis of opera requires only a limited conviction, but the mimesis of cinema, fiction, and drama requires our complete conviction to be experienced completely.

clog such a work with narrative structural demands would be as contradictory as to construct a mimetic work of cinema in which the mimesis was clogged rather than aided by kinesis.

Now, how can we differentiate between movies whose mimesis seems equally rich or between lyric films whose kinesis seems equally complex? How can we assess the relative value of *Stagecoach* and *Persona*, or of *Wavelength* and *Dog Star Man*? And how can we distinguish between rich mimetic microcosms and complex kinetic ones? How can we assess the relative value of *Stagecoach* and *Wavelength*? Precisely these questions of artistic value account for the controversies and conflicts in film thinking and film criticism today.

The dominant conflict of values in movies parallels the opposition between the traditional (or classical) novel and the modernist one. Some argue that movies should tell entertaining stories in a transparent style that delights, moves, or amuses its audience (and despite their differences, Andrew Sarris, Pauline Kael, François Truffaut, and Stanley Cavell all belong to this group). For such writers, the ultimate cinema microcosms are the most stylish, most unique, most unified, and most compelling genre movies of Hollywood's Studio Past—and whatever later movies effectively manipulate the same assumptions. Like the novels of Fielding, Dickens, Thackeray, and Trollope, such movies go about their unselfconscious business of engaging us with stories packed with as many touches of wit, charm, beauty, grace, and observant detail as the art of their makers can manage. An essential characteristic of the cinema experience is that it be an enjoyable one. In this view, the movies should accept the task of telling stories without worrying either themselves or us with the problems of how to tell stories or why tell stories.

On the contrary, the modernist movie critic (John Simon, Dwight Macdonald, and Stanley Kauffmann would be among their number) values those movies which parallel modernist fiction and drama, whose central concerns are precisely the problems of how to tell the story and why tell a story. As opposed to traditional drama and fiction, modernist literature is self-conscious both about how to devise works of art in a particular form and why to add one more piece of matter to the universe of art and nature that already exists. The first concern of modernist literature is the self-conscious questioning of accepted social and moral values. The traditional novel, play, or movie either accepts the culture's established values or questions them in a subtle way that notes the inevitable ironies, paradoxes, and contradictions rather than insists that they are intolerable, indefensible, and inhuman. Modernist works tend to be iconoclastic—and so the preference of modernist or traditionalist movies is a political position as well as an aesthetic one.

Second, modernist literature devotes itself to the self-conscious questioning of the means that a mimetic art uses to tell stories. In the same way that *Ulysses* is about how to write a novel (indeed, how to write *this* novel) and *Waiting for Godot* asks what a play is, *Persona, 8½, Last Year at Marienbad,* and *The Discreet Charm of the Bourgeoisie* (to name just a few examples) ask, What is a movie? How do you make a movie? How do you make *this* movie? If such serious investigations produce a cinema experience that can be considered enjoyable, the definition of "enjoyment" would certainly differ from that for traditionalist movie critics.

There is plenty of evidence to support either contention—that movies must or must not be modernist. Those who reject the modernist movie might claim that the special conditions of cinema exclude it from the concerns of modernism: either because film records the world of nature itself in a way that no other art can; or because movies are mass-produced by entertainment factories; or because movies are a popular art intended for the masses, while the aspirations of modernism are both intellectual and elitist; or because movies are big business, not personal expression. Those who claim that movies have the same modernist rights as any other art might argue that the cinema itself is a product of modernist culture and that its past seventy-five-year history recapitulates and telescopes the evolution of literature over the past two centuries—an original commitment to realism, followed by the commitment to modernism. If *Citizen Kane* is, by consensus, America's greatest movie, the consensus results from the irony that traditionalist critics take it as a traditional movie and modernist critics as a modernist one.

Because the cinema combines the appeals of both the literary and the plastic arts, and because modernist evolution in the plastic arts has differed somewhat from its evolution in literature, those critics who most value the lyric (or experimental) cinema are most strongly influenced by modernist trends in painting and sculpture rather than in literature. The modernist play or novel, while questioning its narrative or mimetic tools, still preserves its temporality and its mimesis. For without them, it is not a play or novel. That paradox is at the center of modernist literature and movies—just as Fellini's 8½ questions whether it can possibly be made, but there it is on the screen before us, obviously made.

But a painting or piece of sculpture still remains a painting or piece of sculpture without imitating or referring to anything else in nature. It still remains a three-dimensional object in space or a framed two-dimensional object on which some substance has been applied. The "narrative" of narrative literature and the "narrative" of narrative painting mean two different things—despite the apparently identical term. In painting, narrative is synonymous with representation—one of the spatial *possibilities* of painting. In drama and fiction, however, narrative is synonymous with the temporality of mimesis (whether it be a mimesis of an action, or of consciousness, or of unconsciousness)—without which it is not drama or fiction. "Abstract" plays or novels (say William Burroughs's or Samuel Beckett's) are not abstract in the same sense that abstract paintings refer to nothing in nature except themselves.

The central concern of modernist painting has been to explore the material conditions and processes of painting itself—of applying shapes and/or color to two-dimensional surfaces. Because the cinema is capable of a pure kinesis (and as abstract a one as painting), many cinema critics feel that the noblest thing the cinema can do is to explore itself. For these critics (Annette Michelson, P. Adams Sitney, and Gerald O'Grady among them), the only serious work of cinema is an exploration of the essential cinema condition—of "images coming off a machine."[12] To adulterate such an exploration with the narrative assumptions of literature is either to pander to popular taste, or to try to make money, or to use the cinema as the mere means to an experience rather than as the end of the experience itself. In such a view, the question of enjoyment in the cinema experience might be not only irrelevant but barbarous.

An alternative theoretical position tends to value the same experimental films, but for a different reason. Rather than stressing the parallels with modernist painting's investigation of its own materials and processes, theorists such as Gene Youngblood, William Earle, Stan Brakhage, and, from time to time, P. Adams Sitney, link these lyric films with the Romantic tradition—the artist's refusal to serve any preconceptions of art or to mold his own work according to any preexisting forms; the unswerving commitment to the inner life and the naked imagination.

In rejoinder, the movie critic (traditionalist or modernist) might reply that the cinema work about nothing but itself is narcissistic and masturbatory—much ado about truly nothing. Cinema can be important only by being about important things outside itself; in itself it has no importance whatever. Further, to make an abstract work that is a naked proclamation of self, of the inner life and the imagination, is not in itself of value—if that inner life makes no sense to others when externalized in the form of cinema, or if that naked self had very little of interest to proclaim in the first place.

What significant results could language produce (either artistic or utilitarian) if words did not refer to things outside themselves, but were only about themselves? Although Gertrude Stein and Tristan Tzara reveal the possibility of an abstracted language, of language as sound, must every serious writer use language only as sound? Behind this conflict of cinema values lie those fundamental questions of analogy. Is the cinema more analogous to words, which are necessarily a means to an end—either utilitarian or beautiful? Or is it more analogous to graphic art, which, despite an occasional utilitarian purpose (posters, advertisements, home decorating), has the almost exclusive artistic purpose of being itself, whether it refers to anything outside itself or not? Or is it more like music, whose notes, rhythms, and progressions might be bent to utilitarian ends (advertising jingles, tonal underscoring), but in themselves refer to nothing except themselves? The analogy that the theorist perceives will almost certainly determine the kinds and works of cinema he perceives as most valuable.

Because the cinema has an enormous range of possibilities, it is not surprising that any one of them can be offered as its noblest and most serious sort. The parallel between cinema and music produces the claim that the most unique and important contribution of cinema is its weaving a "musical" spell of mood, resonance, and progression from either its visually evolving shapes (as Fischinger did) or the rhythms of cutting its celluloid pieces (as Eisenstein did). Because film alone can record natural reality, you can argue that cinema must dedicate itself to reality—to bring us closer to the natural world with which we have lost contact, to strip away the romanticizations that produce wars and tyrannies, or to teach us something useful rather than simply to divert us while passing the time. In such a system of values, nonfiction films—and those movies that come closest to embracing the styles and aims of nonfiction filming—would be the most valuable kind. But because cinema can depict absolute unrealities (the spatial and temporal impossibilities first discovered by Méliès and later refined, explored, and exploited by Buñuel, Deren, and Resnais), you can argue that its true business is to reveal this world of impossibility, imagination, and dream, which no other medium can do so concretely and so convincingly.

The fact is that cinema can do any number of things that no other art or system of communication can do so effectively or in precisely the same way. To seize on any one of those as its most valuable and important kind is to respond less to the demands of cinema itself than to your own vision of both art and life. Although taste may not be disputable, it is at least definable.

The ultimate importance that we attach to a work of cinema is whether it seems important, relevant, and true to our view of both human and artistic experience—whether it depicts issues that seem genuine, genuinely important, genuinely convincing, genuinely "true," genuinely moving, and genuinely revealing. The cinema is as adequate, as effective, a means for depicting such issues as any other art. I cannot honestly distinguish between the artistic, intellectual, and experiential value of Renoir's *Rules of the Game* as opposed to Mozart's *The Marriage of Figaro,* or Ford's *The Good Soldier,* or Shakespeare's *Troilus and Cressida;* or Chaplin's *City Lights* as opposed to Shakespeare's *As You Like It;* or Bergman's *Smiles of a Summer Night* as opposed to Shakespeare's *A Midsummer Night's Dream;* or Kurosawa's *Throne of Blood* as opposed to Shakespeare's *Macbeth;* Eisenstein's *Potemkin* as opposed to Prokofiev's Fifth Symphony, Disney's *Skeleton Dance* as opposed to Saint-Saëns's "Danse Macabre," Breer's *Blazes* as compared to Kandinsky's *Loosely Bound,* or Welles's *Citizen Kane* compared to Fitzgerald's *The Great Gatsby* or Conrad's *Heart of Darkness*. They all seem equally whole, complex, and significant universes of art.

The experience of cinema is unique in that the kinesis of sight, sequence, and sound is the source of both its comprehensibility and its power. That kinesis can be either the means of propelling the cinema's mimesis or can be savored and enjoyed for its own sake or can give rise to parallel sensations and thoughts in the viewer's own imagination. By integrating the three systems of succession, image, and sound, kinesis produces our understanding of and conviction in each of the successive moments of the cinema experience; and the uninterrupted accumulation of each of these moments produces our whole experience with that cinema microcosm. Those cinema microcosms that seem most complex and significant to each of us are those in which we personally find the most complex and unified integrations of technical elements, of kinesis and mimesis, and of part and whole. They are also those that seem to bear the closest relationship to realities (both inner and outer) as each of us defines those realities for ourselves, and to shed the most illuminating and revealing light on what are for us the most complex and important realities and human experiences.

Notes

1/What Isn't Cinema

1. Panofsky refers to animation once in a footnote (and not very perceptively). For the others, animation simply does not exist as cinema. In the Mast and Cohen anthology *Film Theory and Criticism,* there are two good theoretical pieces (by Gilbert Seldes and Joe Adamson) on the values and claims of animation. Interestingly, both pieces agree that the basis of animation is a wild and deliberate violation of natural reality.

2. This paraphrase of the final sentences of the Panofsky essay reveals the essential similarities in the realist theorists.

3. From the conclusion of Francis Sparshott's "Basic Film Aesthetics," in the Mast and Cohen anthology.

4. I will dismiss as irrelevant any of those recording materials—particularly Marey's glass plate and paper-roll film—in cinema prehistory. The striking discovery that suddenly led to the invention of the cinema was George Eastman's celluloid, which W. K. L. Dickson ordered from Eastman for Edison's motion picture experiments in 1888.

5. From "Film and Theatre," in Mast and Cohen, p. 253.

6. See *Film as Art,* pp. 199–229.

2/Art and Nature

1. From "Film and Theatre," in Mast and Cohen, pp. 255–6.

2. I discuss the "probabilities" of comedy in detail on pp. 9–13 of *The Comic Mind.*

3. "The Imagination of Disaster," in Mast and Cohen, p. 436.

3/Kinesis and Mimesis

1. Susanne K. Langer, in *Feeling and Form,* made one of the fullest comparisons of film and the "dream mode." Siegfried Kracauer, despite his view of film as reality, also compares the cinema experience to dreaming (in *Theory of Film,* pp. 163–6). And Parker Tyler (in both *The Hollywood Hallucination* and

Magic and Myth of the Movies) expands the notion of individual dreaming to mass, cultural, mythic dreams.

2. Kael, Pauline, "On the Future of the Movies," *The New Yorker,* August 5, 1974, pp. 43–58.

3. Croce, Benedetto, *Theory of Aesthetic,* Chapter I, "Intuition and Expression."

4. Todorov, Tzvetan, "Les Catégories du récit littéraire," *Communications* 8 (1966), pp. 125–151. The word Todorov uses to describe the reader's psychological acceptance of the artistic microcosm as "real" is *vraisemblance,* of which there is no precise English equivalent and for which "verisimilitude" is a weak substitute.

5. Scholes, Robert, "Narration and Narrativity in Film," paper delivered at the International Symposium in Film Theory and Practical Criticism, University of Wisconsin (Milwaukee), November 22, 1975. Recently published in a special edition of the *Quarterly Review of Film Studies,* October, 1976.

6. This Bazin dictum, from his essay "Theater Cinema, Part II" (in *What Is Cinema,* vol. I, pp. 95–124), is as applicable to the problem of filming musical theater as it is to any other kind of filmed play.

4/Kinesis and Conviction

1. See Raymond Durgnat's *The Crazy Mirror,* pp. 233–9, for a sampling of Lewis criticism.

2. Carringer, Robert, "Rosebud, Dead or Alive: Narrative and Symbolic Structure in *Citizen Kane,*" *PMLA,* vol. XCI, no. 2, March 1976, pp. 185–93.

3. I have already compared these two films at length in *The Comic Mind,* pp. 254–6, but the theoretical issues bear repeating here. Despite my own displeasure with *What's Up, Doc?,* I think it worth mentioning that Howard Hawks considers the Bogdanovich comedy as the equal of his own.

4. The observation is originally V. F. Perkins's (first in an issue of *Movie,* then expanded in *Film as Film,* pp. 121–4), but is probably most familiar as quoted in Charles Barr, "CinemaScope: Before and After" (in Mast and Cohen, pp. 120–46).

5/Succession

1. The key Eisenstein passages are in Mast and Cohen, pp. 75–89, and in Eisenstein's collection of essays, edited by Jay Leyda, *Film Form.*

2. Frank Capra assigns this commercial reason for Ford's tight shooting ratios in an interview for the American Film Institute, "One Man—One Film," reprinted in Glatzer and Raeburn, eds., *Frank Capra: The Man and His Films,* pp. 16–23. But in an unpublished interview with F. Anthony Macklin, Howard Hawks claims that Ford filmed in single takes to keep the performances spontaneous.

3. That such punctuation marks are truly effects of cinema succession be-

comes clear when we remember that originally they were not done in the lab by a printer, but in the camera by the photographer. The cameraman would close or open the diaphragm for the fade-out and -in while the film flowed forward; and for the dissolve he would combine adjusting the lens opening with winding the film backward to expose it a second time, producing the impression of overlapping.

6/Projection

1. In that essential essay "Theater and Cinema, Part II." I clearly find Bazin's discussion of the issue the most revealing, useful, and precise one we have.

2. In *Film as Art* (pp. 9–11, 35–38) and Mast and Cohen (pp. 196–7).

7/Classification of the Image

1. Christian Metz, the most distinguished semiologist to tackle the question, agrees (see Mast and Cohen, p. 116). But many experimental filmmakers and theorists do not. Both Gregory Markopoulos ("Toward a New Narrative Film Form," *Film Culture*, 31, Winter 1963–64, pp. 11–12) and Stan Brakhage ("Metaphors on Vision," *Film Culture*, 30, Winter 1963) insist that the frame and not the shot is the essential cinematic unit; the development of a film takes place not between shots but between frames. This view is perfectly true in a sense, and in that sense is consistent with my definition of literal succession.

But if literal succession is to be the only and essential kind of cinematic succession, the choice negates those forms of cinema that require our discerning and recognizing the objects, events, or persons in the extended series of frames that make up a shot. Consistent with their theories, Brakhage's films dispense with this kind of recognition (on which narrative depends) altogether, while Markopoulos develops a "narrative" that makes a kind of inner, psychological, poetic sense, but no sequential narrative sense.

The loss of such sequential sense seems the inevitable consequence of defining the frame and not the shot as the smallest indivisible unit of significant cinema meaning. Indeed, Metz insists on the shot as a unit precisely because he is interested only in narrative cinema and the making of sequential sense. But the Brakhage aesthetic was to produce seeing *without recognizing*—comparable to his own discovery of a new kind of "vision" when he threw away his glasses in order to see. This sort of vision is incompatible with the Aristotelian assumptions about mimesis, in which we must *recognize* the objects of imitation in order to participate in the narrative. This theoretical clash of frame and shot is yet another restatement of the argument about whether cinema images are more like photographs or musical notes.

The world of cinema is broad and complex enough to embrace both poles, and there is nothing in my definitions to prevent the literal succession of frames and the imagistic succession of shots from being identical in certain kinds of films or sequences of films.

2. See Mast and Cohen (pp. 107–9) for Metz's development of this distinction. My difficulty with Metz's separating denotation from connotation in the cinema is that I don't believe they can be separated. Most denotative information is also colored with connotative cues to evoke our emotional responses to it at the same time (i.e., we are asked to know and *know* the information in both senses of knowing at the same time).

3. For a historical and technological summary of color film and processing, see the introductory section of Manvell, Roger, ed., *The International Encyclopedia of Film.*

4. See Pudovkin, V. I., *Film Technique and Film Acting.*

5. Paper delivered by Robert Kolker at the annual meeting of the Society for Cinema Studies, New York University, April 1975.

6. From *The World Viewed*, p. 37. The same implication exists in any of the other realist theorists, such as Bazin and Kracauer.

7. This issue has been discussed by Münsterberg (in *The Film: A Psychological Study*, pp. 76–7), by Cavell (in *The World Viewed*, pp. 25–9), by Panofsky (in Mast and Cohen, pp. 165–6) by Bazin and Sontag (in their essays comparing film and theater), and by Allardyce Nicoll (in his book on the same subject). In his book of film theory, Leo Braudy spends a lot of time and detail on the distinctions between stage and screen "acting."

8. *The World Viewed*, p. 29.

9. *The Photoplay*, p. 76, and in Mast and Cohen, pp. 242–3.

8/(Recorded) Sound

1. See Dickson, W. K. L., *A History of the Kinetograph, Kinetoscope, and Kinetophonograph.*

2. Harry M. Geduld's recent history, *The Birth of the Talkies,* traced the interrelationship of talking pictures and the radio.

3. Panofsky's dictum (in Mast and Cohen, p. 157) is: "the sound, articulate or not, cannot express any more than is expressed, at the same time, by visible movement." Note that Panofsky's principle of "co-expressibility" is not at all that sound and picture should be harmonious. His words "any more" imply that sound cannot even supplement the information of the visuals. Further, that information must come from "visible movement." So how can one explain the power of Ozu's films in which conversation is often juxtaposed with stasis, with no visible movement? How can one understand the power of the child-murder in *M* when the mother calls out her daughter's name, "Elsie!" and the images are deliberately of empty corridors, stairways, and rooms where there is no movement whatsoever (implying death and desolation)?

4. See *Film as Art*, pp. 199–230.

5. Cavell's demonstration of the mysterious differences between bodies and photographs (*The World Viewed*, pp. 16–23) is so complete and precise that I need not repeat it here.

6. Once again the discussion returns us to the Bazin essay on "Theater and Cinema." I think the problem that Bazin was demonstrating was that in the theater the words have a much greater "weight" since they carry the greatest part of the semiotic burden. Although the words on a stage are supplemented by lighting, décor, physical movement, stage groupings, the sounds and volumes of voices (i.e., Aristotle's spectacle and melody), the text remains the dominant communicative system of information in the theater. In the cinema, however, the words share the semiotic responsibility with several other equally compelling, complex, and complete systems of communication—the systems and subsystems of succession and the image. Naturally, the words will have a different "weight," a different semiotic responsibility, in the two different forms.

7. See *The New Yorker*, September 21, 1957, p. 70. At the one New Jersey theater which used the flashing frames, Coca-Cola sales rose 18 percent and popcorn sales rose 57 percent.

8. Cavell also does a careful job distinguishing between recorded sights and sounds, between photographs and phonograph recordings, in *The World Viewed* (pp. 16–23). For the complete argument, rather than my summation, see his discussion.

9. For Kracauer's complete discussion of the filmed musical, see his *Theory of Film*, pp. 145–9.

10. I compare silent comedy with ballet in *The Comic Mind*, p. 202.

11. "Plastic material" was Pudovkin's term for the concrete, physical objects that became communicative in the silent cinema—for example, Chaplin's hat and cane, the religious icons in Pudovkin's *Storm Over Asia*, or the straw hats in Lubitsch's *The Marriage Circle*.

9/Integration

1. The essay is "The Evolution of the Language of Cinema," in *What Is Cinema?*, vol. I, pp. 23–40, and Mast and Cohen, pp. 90–102.

2. I analyze this particular sequence in detail in the second edition of *A Short History of the Movies*, pp. 190–1, 210.

3. In "The Evolution of the Language of Cinema."

4. The Bazin-influenced theorists (Barr and Perkins among them) accept this notion of freedom in realistic cinema without ever asking, first, is freedom truly possible in any traditionally coherent art (neither Barr nor Perkins is a Dadaist; they assume that each element of a work has a single, predetermined intention); and, second, whether the kind of "freedom" we enjoy with a composition in depth (or width) is any different from any other kind of interpretive freedom we have with any work in any style. In sum, they never define freedom, nor do they attempt to relate the concept to the fixed, predetermined patterning which they assume is synonymous with art.

5. In *Film as Film*, pp. 101–3. The other realist theorists find such montage devices either too explicit, too vague, or both. This ironic contradiction illu-

minates the applicability of Münsterberg's statement that the ultimate unity of the cinema is a matter of mind rather than of individual images. Interpretive freedom—as well as our perceiving the unity in a cinema experience—is a product of mental unity, and that unity can result from extended images (in depth, width, or time) or from our synthesizing the montage pieces.

6. Bazin's essay "The Virtues and Limitations of Montage" (*What Is Cinema?*, vol. I, pp. 41–52) effectively reveals the loss of credibility from handling certain kinds of actions (particularly those in which there is some threat to human life) by means of montage. The danger and suspense of seeing the threat and the potential victim together in the same frame (i.e., the lion and the lady) rather than split into two different frames by means of montage cannot be underestimated. We need only see some cheap, B-movie jungle adventure to know how apparent it is that studio action has been juxtaposed with stock footage of dangerous beasts. Keaton manipulates the same string—neither divorcing his body from the dangerous surroundings nor breaking the maneuvers of that body into a series of staged and faked pieces. The Keaton stunts require a unity of both time and space for their breathtaking effectiveness. Chaplin's refusal to edit is similar but softer, producing not taut suspense, but the subtlety of magic without trick.

7. See Perkins's *Film as Film* (pp. 59–70) and Tudor's *Theories of Film* (pp. 161–4).

8. *Film as Film*, p. 189.

9. Ibid., p. 79.

10. Ibid., pp. 79–82.

11. Ibid., p. 82.

12. This phrase, perhaps the essence of modernist cinema thinking, has an interesting history. Its most familiar source is Annette Michelson's classic essay on the aims of modernist, non-narrative cinema, "Film and the Radical Aspiration" (revised version in Mast and Cohen, pp. 469–87). But the phrase derives originally from a 1953 symposium in New York on "Poetry and the Film," at which Parker Tyler, Willard Maas, Dylan Thomas, Arthur Miller, and Maya Deren were panelists. Ironically, this modernist phrase was originally uttered by that archrealist Arthur Miller.

Bibliography

Adamson, Joe. "Suspended Animation," in Mast, Gerald and Cohen, Marshall, eds. *Film Theory and Criticism: Introductory Readings.* New York, London, and Toronto: Oxford University Press, 1974, pp. 391–400.

Andrew, J. Dudley. *The Major Film Theories: An Introduction.* London, Oxford, New York: Oxford University Press, 1976.

Arnheim, Rudolf. *Film as Art.* Berkeley and Los Angeles: University of California Press, 1966.

Balázs, Béla. *Theory of the Film: Character and Growth of a New Art.* New York: Dover Publications, 1970.

Barthes, Roland. *Semiology of the Cinema.* Boston: Beacon Press, n.d.

Barr, Charles. "CinemaScope: Before and After," in Mast, Gerald and Cohen, Marshall, eds. *Film Theory and Criticism: Introductory Readings.* New York, London, and Toronto: Oxford University Press, 1974, pp. 120–46.

Bazin, André. *What Is Cinema?* Volume I. Berkeley and Los Angeles: University of California Press, 1967.

Bluestone, George. *Novels into Film.* Berkeley and Los Angeles: University of California Press, 1966.

Bobker, Lee R. *Elements of Film.* Second edition. New York: Harcourt Brace Jovanovich, 1975.

Brakhage, Stan. "Metaphors on Vision," in *Film Culture,* 30, Winter 1963.

Braudy, Leo. *The World in a Frame: What We See in Films.* Garden City, N.Y.: Doubleday, 1976.

Brownlow, Kevin. *The Parade's Gone By.* New York: Knopf, 1968.

Burch, Noël. *Theory of Film Practice.* Translated by Helen R. Lane and with an introduction by Annette Michelson. New York: Praeger, 1973.

Carringer, Robert. "Rosebud, Dead or Alive: Narrative and Symbolic Structure in *Citizen Kane,*" in *PMLA,* XCI, 2, March 1976, pp. 185–93.

Cavell, Stanley. *The World Viewed: Reflections on the Ontology of Film.* New York: Viking, 1971.

Croce, Benedetto. *Aesthetic.* New York: Noonday, 1959.

Dickson, W. K. L. *A History of the Kinetograph, Kinetoscope, and Kineto-phonograph.* New York: Arno Press, 1970.

Durgnat, Raymond. *Films and Feelings.* Cambridge, Mass.: The M.I.T. Press, 1967.

———. *The Crazy Mirror: Hollywood Comedy and the American Image.* New York: Horizon Press, 1970.

Earle, William. "Revolt Against Realism in the Films," in Mast, Gerald and Cohen, Marshall, eds. *Film Theory and Criticism: Introductory Readings.* New York, London, and Toronto: Oxford University Press, 1974, pp. 32–42.

Eisenstein, Sergei M. *Film Form.* Edited and translated by Jay Leyda. New York: Harcourt Brace Jovanovich, n.d.

———. *The Film Sense.* Edited and translated by Jay Leyda. New York: Harcourt Brace Jovanovich, n.d.

Geduld, Harry M. *The Birth of the Talkies: From Edison to Jolson.* Bloomington, Indiana and London: Indiana University Press, 1975.

Gessner, Robert. *The Moving Image: A Guide to Cinematic Literacy.* New York: Dutton, 1968.

Giannetti, Louis D. *Understanding Movies.* Second edition. Englewood Cliffs, N.J.: Prentice Hall, 1976.

Harrington, John. *The Rhetoric of Film.* New York: Holt, Rinehart and Winston, 1973.

Huss, Roy, and Silverstein, Norman. *The Film Experience: Elements of Motion Picture Art.* New York: Harper & Row, 1968.

Kael, Pauline. *I Lost It at the Movies.* Boston: Little Brown, 1965.

———. "Raising Kane," in *The Citizen Kane Book.* Boston: Little Brown, 1971.

———. "On the Future of the Movies," in *The New Yorker,* August 5, 1974.

Kracauer, Siegfried. *From Caligari to Hitler.* New York: Noonday, 1959.

———. *Theory of Film: The Redemption of Physical Reality.* London, Oxford, New York: Oxford University Press, 1960.

Langer, Susanne K. *Feeling and Form.* New York: Scribner's, 1953.

Lessing, Gotthold Ephraim. *Laocoon: An Essay Upon the Limits of Painting and Poetry.* New York: Noonday, n.d.

Lindgren, Ernest. *The Art of the Film.* London: Allen and Unwin, 1963.

Lindsay, Vachel. *The Art of the Moving Picture.* Revised edition. New York: Macmillan, 1922.

Manvell, Roger, ed. *The International Encyclopedia of Film.* New York: Crown, 1972.

Markopoulos, Gregory. "Toward a New Narrative Film Form," in *Film Culture,* 31, Winter 1963–4.

Mast, Gerald. *A Short History of the Movies.* Second edition. Indianapolis: Bobbs-Merrill, 1976.

———. *The Comic Mind: Comedy and the Movies.* New York: Bobbs-Merrill, 1973.

Merleau-Ponty, Maurice. "The Film and the New Psychology," in *Sense and Non-sense*. Translated by Hubert L. and Patricia A. Dreyfus. Evanston, Ill.: Northwestern University Press, 1964.

Metz, Christian. *Film Language: A Semiotics of the Cinema*. Translated by Michael Taylor. New York: Oxford University Press, 1974.

Michelson, Annette. "Film and the Radical Aspiration," in Mast, Gerald and Cohen, Marshall, eds. *Film Theory and Criticism: Introductory Readings*. New York, London, and Toronto; Oxford University Press, 1974, pp. 469–88.

Mitry, Jean. *Esthétique et psychologie du cinéma*. Two volumes. Paris: Editions Universitaires, 1963–65.

Münsterberg, Hugo. *The Film: A Psychological Study*. New York: Dover, 1969.

Nicoll, Allardyce. *Film and Theatre*. New York: Thomas Y. Crowell, 1937.

Panofsky, Erwin. "Style and Medium in the Motion Pictures," in Mast, Gerald and Cohen, Marshall, eds. *Film Theory and Criticism: Introductory Readings*. New York, London, and Toronto: Oxford University Press, 1974, pp. 151–69.

Perkins, V. F. *Film as Film: Understanding and Judging Movies*. Harmondsworth, Middlesex, England: Penguin Books, 1972.

Pudovkin, V. I. *Film Technique and Film Acting*. Edited and translated by Ivor Montagu. New York: Grove Press, 1960.

Richter, Hans. "The Film as an Original Art Form," in *Film Culture*, I, 1 January 1955.

Sarris, Andrew. *The American Cinema: Directors and Directions 1929–1968*. New York: Dutton, 1969.

———. "Notes on the *Auteur* Theory in 1962," in Mast, Gerald and Cohen, Marshall, eds. *Film Theory and Criticism: Introductory Readings*. New York, London, and Toronto: Oxford University Press, 1974, pp. 500–15.

Seldes, Gilbert. "The Lovely Art: Magic," in Mast, Gerald and Cohen, Marshall, eds. *Film Theory and Criticism: Introductory Readings*. New York, London, and Toronto: Oxford University Press, 1974, pp. 379–90.

Simon, John. *Movies into Films*. New York: Dial, 1971.

Sitney, P. Adams. *Visionary Film: The American Avant-Garde*. New York: Oxford University Press, 1974.

———, ed. *Film Culture Reader*. New York: Praeger, 1970.

Sontag, Susan. "Film and Theater" and "The Imagination of Disaster," in Mast, Gerald and Cohen, Marshall, eds. *Film Theory and Criticism: Introductory Readings*. New York, London, and Toronto: Oxford University Press, 1974, pp. 249–267, 422–437.

Sparshott, F. E. "Basic Film Aesthetics," in Mast, Gerald, and Cohen, Marshall, eds. *Film Theory and Criticism: Introductory Readings*. New York, London, and Toronto: Oxford University Press, 1974, pp. 209–232.

Spottiswode, Raymond. *A Grammar of the Film*. Berkeley and Los Angeles: University of California Press, 1950.

Stephenson, Ralph and Debrix, J. R. *The Cinema as Art*. Baltimore: Penguin, 1965.

Tudor, Andrew. *Theories of Film*. New York: Viking, 1973.

Tyler, Parker. *The Hollywood Hallucination*. New York: Simon and Schuster, 1970.

————. *Magic and Myth of the Movies*. New York: Simon and Schuster, 1970.

————. *The Shadow of an Airplane Climbs the Empire State Building: A World Theory of Film*. Garden City, N.Y.: Doubleday, 1972.

Wollen, Peter. *Signs and Meaning in the Cinema*. Third edition. Bloomington, Ind. and London: Indiana University Press, 1974.

Youngblood, Gene. *Expanded Cinema*. New York: Dutton, 1970.

Index

Numbers in **boldface** denote extended discussions. Numbers in *italic* refer to illustrations.